跨文化沟通与商务礼仪

综合教程

主　编◎郑春萍
副主编◎王　霞
编　者◎陶　晶　郝劲梅

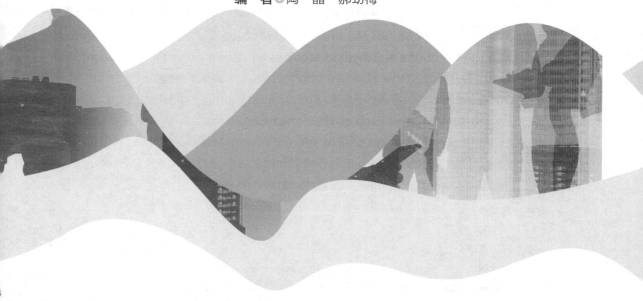

Intercultural Communication
and Business Etiquette

清华大学出版社
北京

内容简介

本书以跨文化交际学理论为指导，结合区域国别研究的相关成果，围绕亚洲、北美洲、欧洲、大洋洲、南美洲和非洲的 15 个国家和地区，概要地介绍了各地的文化习俗、商业惯例和沟通礼仪。教材价值引领与知识传授并重，通过解析国际商务语境中的跨文化差异，介绍各地的商务礼仪常识，提升学习者的语言综合应用能力与跨文化商务沟通技能；教材实用性与可操作性兼顾，各单元配有听力练习、正误判断、单项选择、案例分析及微型调研等学习任务，在夯实学习者英语语言基本功的基础上，增强其跨文化实操与创新能力。教材还配有丰富的线上教学资源，包括各单元的微课视频及访谈讲座视频，充分拓展学生的自主学习和教师的混合式教学实践。

本教材适用于普通高校修读相关课程的本科生、研究生，以及致力于提升英语语言能力和跨文化商务沟通能力的商务人士等。

图书在版编目（CIP）数据

跨文化沟通与商务礼仪综合教程 / 郑春萍主编. —北京：清华大学出版社，2023.12
ISBN 978-7-302-63052-4

Ⅰ.①跨…　Ⅱ.①郑…　Ⅲ.①文化交流—高等学校—教材②商务—礼仪—高等学校—教材
Ⅳ.①G115 ②F718

中国国家版本馆CIP数据核字（2023）第043955号

责任编辑：曹诗悦　许玲玉
封面设计：李伯骥
责任校对：王凤芝
责任印制：丛怀宇

出版发行：清华大学出版社
　　　　　网　　址：https://www.tup.com.cn, https://www.wqxuetang.com
　　　　　地　　址：北京清华大学学研大厦 A 座　　　　　邮　编：100084
　　　　　社 总 机：010-83470000　　　　　　　　　　　邮　购：010-62786544
　　　　　投稿与读者服务：010-62776969，c-service@tup.tsinghua.edu.cn
　　　　　质量反馈：010-62772015，zhiliang@tup.tsinghua.edu.cn
印 装 者：三河市铭诚印务有限公司
经　　销：全国新华书店
开　　本：185mm×260mm　　　印　张：18　　　字　数：373 千字
版　　次：2023 年 12 月第 1 版　　　印　次：2023 年 12 月第 1 次印刷
定　　价：78.00 元

产品编号：092106-01

序　言

这是一个全球互联互通、人类命运与共的新时代。对我国高等教育而言，这也是一个需要大力培养和努力塑造具有家国情怀、国际视野、全球意识、融通中外的创新型人才的新时代。这个时代要求我们的课程和教材致力于培养一大批具有中国深度、全球广度、人文高度的跨文化交流引领者和人类命运共同体建设者。我们的学生不仅应该具有知周中外、道济天下的人文情怀，也应该具有文化交流、文明互鉴的胜任能力。

学习外语不仅仅在于学什么，更在于学后能做什么。我们所处的世界是一个各国、各民族、各种文化相互关联的整体，这个互联的世界应该是一个互助和共享的世界，我们需要秉持"永恒之道""共存之道"和"共为之道"，不仅要关注当地问题，也要关注全球问题。我们的外语课程和外语教材应该帮助学生了解不同地区人民的生活方式、思维方式和文化传统，在领悟世界文化的多样性和丰富性的同时，客观、理性、辩证地看待世界，形成正确的价值观念、健康的审美情趣、积极的道德情感、有效的成事能力。

在此背景下，北京邮电大学郑春萍教授主编的《跨文化沟通与商务礼仪综合教程》应运而生。我应邀有幸审读了春萍及其团队基于教学需求和教学实践而编写的教材全稿。该教材名副其实，旨在系统地传授跨文化沟通与商务礼仪知识和规范，发展学生在真实世界中的跨文化沟通能力和商务合作能力。教材突出了三个方面的教与学：一是基于跨文化与国别区域研究的相关成果，介绍各国的基本概况、文化取向与跨文化差异；二是讲解各国商务人士在仪容仪表、言谈举止等方面约定俗成的礼仪规范与跨文化沟通策略；三是配套设计了类型丰富、难度渐进的课后习题，增强教材的实用性与可操作性。

该教材特色鲜明、结构严谨、内容充实、习题丰富，兼具理论性与实践性。全书概览部分从学理层面探讨了理解跨文化差异的理论模型与分析框架；单元教学部分选取了六大洲 15 个国家和地区，概要地介绍了各地的文化习俗、商业惯例和沟通礼仪。教材扎根中国、放眼世界，对于读者理解各地概况、文化价值与商务礼仪等提供了有益的参考。教材内容与课程教学有效融合，有望为学习者开展开放、恰当、有效的跨文化商务沟通奠定基础，为高校培养具有全球胜任力，具有全球视野、融通中外的跨文化创新人才提供了丰富的教学素材。

积极有效的跨文化沟通和商务活动在很大程度上取决于交际各方的礼仪规范和行为。礼仪是衡量一个民族文化底蕴的重要标准。中国素有"礼仪之邦"之称，其礼仪文化源自商周。"礼"字最早出现于商代甲骨文，本意指祭神、敬神，逐步引申指"礼节""礼仪"。西周之初，周公制礼作乐，开创了礼乐文化。《礼记·乐记》对礼乐及其作用作了明确的阐释："乐者，天地之和也；礼者，天地之序也。和故百物皆化，序故群物皆别。"春秋时期，君子富好行其德，"仓廪实而知礼节，衣食足而知荣辱"出自管仲之口。

《跨文化沟通与商务礼仪综合教程》在落实中华优秀传统文化进课程、进教材、进课堂的方面迈出了坚实步伐，意义重大。党的二十大报告提炼了中华优秀传统文化的精髓："中华优秀传统文化源远流长、博大精深，是中华文明的智慧结晶，其中蕴含的天下为公、民为邦本、为政以德、革故鼎新、任人唯贤、天人合一、自强不息、厚德载物、讲信修睦、亲仁善邻等，是中国人民在长期生产生活中积累的宇宙观、天下观、社会观、道德观的重要体现。"因此，外语教材在讲述大千世界故事的同时，应该积极融入中华民族的"宇宙观、天下观、社会观、道德观"。

当下我们的教育应该立足中华民族伟大复兴的战略全局和世界百年未有之大变局。教材不是我们学生的全部世界，世界应该成为我们学生的全部教材。我们的高等教育应该以多元世界为校园，我们的学生应该以多元世界为课堂，站稳中国立场，站在全球角度，将中国故事跟世界故事联系在一起，谱写旨在弘扬全人类共同价值、创造全人类美好未来的新篇章。我们所编写的跨文化交流与商务礼仪的教材，应该帮助学生理解和跨越文化差异、观点差异、价值差异，尊重世界文化和商务礼仪的多样性，理解中外文化的基本特点和异同，了解跨文化商务活动的礼仪规范，学习如何与不同语言文化背景的人士进行有效的跨文化沟通，发展跨文化全球胜任力。

近年来，跨文化全球胜任力得到各国的普遍重视。经济合作与发展组织在 2022 年全球胜任力论坛上发布了基于最新研究的报告《大局思维：为互联的世界培养"全人"的原则与实践》（"Big picture thinking: How to educate the whole person for an interconnected world—Principles and practices"）。全球胜任力是一种涉及认知、社会情感和公民发展等方面的多维能力，包括审视问题的能力、理解观点的能力、跨文化互动的能力和采取行动的能力。培养学生的全球胜任力旨在帮助走向世界、走向未来的学生学会如何有效运用知识、技能、态度和价值观，与来自不同文化背景的人交流与合作，为世界繁荣和可持续发展作出积极贡献。因此，全球胜任力所倡导的学习不再只是知识的积累，而是在复杂多变的真实的社会环境中思考和应用知识，在真实情景中体验并付诸行动。

培养全球胜任力应注重社会化学习，倡导学生融入社会和文化群体，发展沟通与合作能力，在沟通交流中更好地学习，尤其是强调在真实世界和解决问题中学习。我们应该基于学科，并从跨学科乃至超学科的视角思考当下的教育和教学，不囿于单一学科领域，而是通过跨学科主题学习、项目化研究和社会实践，认识世界、反思自我、体验社会、丰富人生，形成开放的态度、辩证的思维、高阶的认知以及为集体福祉和可持续发展采取行动的能力。

中国日益融入世界，世界各国文化、风俗等的不同带来国际商务沟通礼节和礼仪上的差异。在当下共建人类命运共同体的征程中，熟谙各国文化与礼仪规范将成为"促进各国人民相知相亲，尊重世界文明多样性，共同应对各种全球性挑战"的重要基础。外语教育的重要使命之一在于引导学生有效面对日益复杂的世界，使学生自信地参与跨文化沟通与合作，不断提升国家的文化软实力和中华文化的影响力。

《跨文化沟通与商务礼仪综合教程》的推出恰逢其时，是为序！

梅德明

2023 年 2 月 15 日

于上海外国语大学

前　言

在全球互联互通、人类命运与共的新时代，中国迫切需要了解本国国情、熟谙沟通话语、具有国际视野、通晓国际规则的复合型人才。国际商务的从业者唯有熟悉各国文化传统与发展历史，坚持求同存异，才能实现高效的沟通与合作。对于即将融入全球商务环境的广大中国学子，了解各国概况、知晓商务文化、掌握习俗礼仪尤为重要。丰富的跨文化知识和良好的商务礼仪与沟通技能不仅能够开拓学习者视野，也将成为开启其职业生涯大门的金钥匙。

本教材以跨文化交际学理论为指导，选取了亚洲、北美洲、欧洲、大洋洲、南美洲和非洲的 15 个国家和地区，概要地介绍了各地的文化习俗、商业惯例和沟通礼仪。教材旨在帮助学习者掌握国际商务礼仪常识，在国际交往中树立良好的个人形象，为实现有效、高效的跨文化沟通奠定基础。

教材的编写思路与特色主要体现在以下几个方面：

1. 概述各地的社会文化与商务礼仪：教材围绕六大洲 15 个国家和地区的概况、社会文化、商业惯例和沟通礼仪，力求做到取材面广，教学内容少而精，引导学习者初步掌握各地的社会文化概况与商务礼仪常识。

2. 解析国际商务礼仪的跨文化差异：教材以跨文化交际学为理论基础，结合霍夫斯泰德文化维度理论，剖析商务沟通行为与礼仪规范的跨文化差异。通过国际商务沟通案例，引导学生分析论证，提升思辨能力。

3. 创新教学案例的设计与综合操练：教材聚焦于提升学习者的英语综合应用能力与跨文化沟通技能，设计了多种形式的教学案例与综合练习。注重开拓学习者视野，巩固课堂所学，提升解决实际问题的能力。

4. 指导任务型与项目式的个性化学习：教材结合任务型与项目式学习，引导学习者开展调研分析与展示。重视提升学习者调查研究与实践创新的能力，体现"品格塑造、知识掌握、能力培养"的育人格局。

5. 搭配丰富的线上资源：教材除教学课件之外，还配有线上微课视频 16 集、访谈与讲座视频 20 集，突破了纸质书的边界，能够进一步开拓学习者视野，赋能教师的混合式教学实践。

教材除全书概览（Introduction）外共 15 个单元，每单元均由以下 6 个部分组成：

1. 各地概况（Overview）：概述选定国家和地区的地理、人口、历史、经济、世界影响与重要节日，介绍各地概况与发展现状，开拓学习者的国际视野。

2. 文化维度（Cultural Orientations）：采用霍夫斯泰德文化维度理论，分析各地的文化特征，提升学习者的跨文化素养。

3. 商务礼仪（Business Practices and Etiquette）：概述各地商务会面、商务谈判、商务接待、沟通习俗、商务馈赠与商务着装等礼仪规范，指导学习者了解各地的商务礼仪与禁忌。

4. 沟通技巧（Tips）：针对多元的国际商务沟通情景，解析商务沟通技巧，为学习者开展国际商务沟通提供实战指导。

5. 综合练习（Exercises）：设计了事实填空、听力填空、正误判断、单项选择与案例分析五类学习任务，在夯实学习者英语语言基本功的同时，提升其跨文化思辨能力。

6. 微型调研（A Mini Business Project）：设置真实情景下的跨文化沟通或国际商务项目，搭建可行脚手架，引导学习者自主探索，将所学知识内化并有效应用至实践。

郑春萍负责全书的框架设计、初稿撰写与统稿，王霞负责综合练习的审定，陶晶负责沟通技巧与案例分析的初稿撰写，郝劲梅负责各单元内容的审校。外籍专家Catherine Harrington（新西兰）、Ruth Dunstan（澳大利亚）、Lalhlpuii Sailo（印度）、Joe Davies（英国）对全书的文稿进行了多轮修改与润色。15 个国家和地区的学者为本教材录制了 20 集访谈与讲座视频。教材编写过程中得到了北京邮电大学的相关领导和同事的大力支持，近 20 位本科生和研究生参与了素材收集、整理，以及教学课件制作，在此表示衷心感谢。

本教材内容素材源自郑春萍主讲的全校公选课"跨文化沟通与商务礼仪"（原名"国际商务礼仪"）。该课程自 2007 年开设至今，已建设成为一门特色鲜明的通识类公共基础课（英文授课）。2020—2022 年，课程入选北京邮电大学"高新课程"建设项目，配套教材获校级教材建设专项资助，课程及主讲教师获校级本科课程思政示范课程与教学名师等奖项。主编团队从最初的教学实践，到 2009 年的选题策划，再到 2023 年教材的付梓出版，历经十五年的课程建设。十年磨一剑，希望这本教材在实际应用过程中能够获得广大师生的认可。由于编者水平有限，疏漏在所难免，不当之处恳请同行批评指正。

编者

2022 年 12 月

Contents

Unit 10

Unit 11

Unit 12

Unit 13

Unit 14

Brazilian Culture, Customs, and Business Etiquette 241

Unit 15

South African Culture, Customs, and Business Etiquette 259

Introduction

Understanding Culture and Cultural Differences

Defining "Culture"

The Chinese word "wenhua" (Chinese: 文化) is the translation for the English word "culture", which appeared in the *Book of Changes* (one of the oldest Chinese classics) in China or earlier. It "took on the main meaning of cultivation or tending… though with subsidiary medieval meanings of honor and worship" (Williams, 2015: 49). In 1926 and 1927, Liang Qichao expressed his view of "wenhua" in the *Research Method on Chinese History*. He pointed out that "wenhua" had two meanings: In the broad sense it included politics and economy, while in the narrow sense it referred only to the important factors in human activities, such as language, words, religion, literature, fine arts, science, history, and philosophy (as cited in Huang, 2006). According to Huang (2006), this definition is a mark of the formation of the modern concept of "wenhua" in China.

The English word "culture", derived from the Latin root *colere* (to inhabit, nurture, or respect) and the Latin word "cultūra" (cultivating or agriculture), carries various meanings in different contexts. Gustav F. Klemm, an influential German ethnographer and the founder of anthropology, proposed that culture consists of customs, information, skills, family and public life in peace and war, religions, sciences, and arts. He was considered the first scholar to endow culture with an anthropological and ethnographical meaning (as cited in Xiao, 2012). English anthropologist Edward B. Tylor also used the term "culture" in his book, *Primitive Culture*, published in 1871. Tylor noted that "culture" is "that complex whole which includes knowledge, belief, art, law, morals, custom, and any other capabilities and habits acquired by man as a member of society" (Tylor, 1987: 1). In 1952, two famous American anthropologists, Alred L. Kroeber and Clyde Kluckhohn, compiled a list of 164 different definitions in their book named *Culture: A Critical Review of Concepts and Definitions*.

Different definitions of "culture" reflect different perspectives of or theoretical approaches to understanding human activities, or criteria for evaluating human activities. Apte (Asher, 1994: 2001), writing in the ten-volume set *Encyclopedia of Language and Linguistics*, summarized the problem as follows: "Despite a century of efforts to define culture adequately, there was in the early 1990s no agreement among anthropologists regarding its nature." If we try to list different elements that are true of culture, there may be an endless list of aspects including the following:

- Culture has to do with values and beliefs.

- Culture involves customs and traditions.

- Culture is collective, and shared by a group.

- Culture is learned.

- Culture influences and shapes behavior.

- Culture is transmitted from generation to generation.

- Culture is often unconscious; people are sometimes not aware of how their behaviors and attitudes have been shaped by their culture.

- People in all cultures have common needs.

  …

In this textbook, we regard culture as a system of beliefs, values, and assumptions about life that guide behavior and are shared by a group of people. If we compare culture to an iceberg, it includes both visible and invisible parts. The tip of the iceberg includes visible behaviors and artifacts which can be easily observed in our social life. The remaining huge chunk of the iceberg hidden below the surface includes the invisible aspects of a culture, such as one's fundamental beliefs, values, ways of thinking, and worldview. While the visible tip may change—as an iceberg will melt with sun and rain, the culture's invisible and fundamental aspects change very slowly (Weaver, 2006). Both visible and invisible aspects are transmitted from generation to generation, rarely with explicit instructions.

"Cultural Orientations" and Three Influential Analytical Models

Cultural orientations or dimensions refer to generalizations or archetypes that allow us to study the general tendencies of a cultural group and how most people in a cultural group tend to think, feel, or act. It is not about identifying what is the right or wrong way of behaving, but about understanding how and why we are different. By describing and explaining cultural differences through the lens of cultural orientations, we can understand each other across cultures and avoid creating stereotypes.

Several approaches have been taken to quantify cultural orientations or cultural value dimensions. As summarized by Samovar and Richard E. Porter (2004), there are three paradigms at the core of these studies, namely, the cultural value dimensions of Hofstede (1997), the cultural value dimensions of Kluckhohn and Strodtbeck (2012) and the high-context and low-context culture pattern of Edward Hall (1970).

2.1 Hofstede's Analytical Model

Geert Hofstede (1928–2020), a Dutch social psychologist, defined culture as "the collective programming of the mind distinguishing the members of one group or category of people from others". He conducted a comprehensive study of how values in the workplace are influenced by culture, and observed patterns of thinking, feeling, and behaving of people across different cultures. He and his colleagues then put forward six fundamental issues that social organization itself needs to address, and proposed a six-dimensional model (6-D Model) for analyzing and understanding cultural orientations (Hofstede, 1997). The six dimensions are power distance, individualism vs. collectivism, masculinity vs. femininity, uncertainty avoidance, long-term vs. short-term orientation, and indulgence vs. restraint. Each dimension is roughly measured on a scale from 0 to 100 points.

2.2 Fons Trompenaars and Charles Hampden-Turner's Analytical Model

Trompenaars (1953–), a Dutch organizational theorist and management consultant, cooperating with a British academician, Hampden-Turner (1934–), did meticulous research on cross-cultural dimensions of business executives. Their collaborative work *Riding the Waves of Culture* was first published in 1993. In this book, they postulated several cultural value orientations. Some of these value orientations can be regarded as nearly identical to Hofstede's dimensions while others offer a somewhat different perspective. In the 2012's version of *Riding the Waves of Culture*, Trompenaars and Hampden-Turner identified five cultural value dimensions of how people relate to others and further summarized the differences between the two extremes of these dimensions. Later, they further added two dimensions to the model and proposed another two dimensions concerning people's attitudes toward time and environment. The seven dimensions are universalism vs. particularism, communitarianism vs. individualism, neutral vs. affective, diffuse vs. specific, achievement vs. ascription, sequential time vs. synchronous time, and internal direction vs. outer direction.

2.3   Edward Hall's Analytical Model

Edward Twitchell Hall, Jr. (1914–2009), an American anthropologist and cross-cultural researcher, introduced differing context cultures in his book *The Silent Language,* namely high- and low-context culture. High-context culture refers to societies or groups where people have close connections over a long period of time. Many aspects of cultural behavior are not made explicit because most members know what to do and what to think from years of interaction with each other. On the contrary, low-context refers to societies where people tend to have many connections but of shorter duration or for some specific reason. In these societies, cultural behavior and beliefs may need to be spelled out explicitly so that those coming into the cultural environment know how to behave. People's communication style also varies due to the differences in high- and low-context cultures.

The Six-Dimensional Model (6-D Model)

In this textbook, we mainly employed the 6-D Model to analyze the cultural orientations of 15 different cultures. If we examine a nation's culture from the perspective of the 6-D Model, we can obtain an overview of its culture in terms of the following six dimensions. Although it may not be precise enough to present the complexity and diversity of a culture, it does provide us with a possible approach to reflect on our own cultural orientation and show us a rough picture of the nation.

3.1 Power Distance

Power distance is defined as the extent to which the less powerful members of institutions and organizations within a country expect and accept that power is distributed unequally. This dimension deals with the fact that all individuals in societies are not equal, and it expresses the attitude of the culture toward these inequalities among us.

With a high score on this dimension, a culture accepts that power is distributed unequally. People in this society believe that it is acceptable to have a certain degree of inequality among people. On the contrary, with a low score on this dimension, a culture prefers a relatively equal distribution of power, and people in this society believe that it is not that acceptable to have inequality among people.

3.2 Individualism vs. Collectivism

The fundamental issue addressed by this dimension is the degree of interdependence a society maintains among its members. It has to do with whether people's self-image is defined in terms of "I" or "We". Individualism refers to the societies or cultures in which the interests of individuals prevail over the interests of the group.

With a high score (individualism) on this dimension, or in individualist societies, people are expected to look after themselves and their direct family only. Individualism emphasizes individual goals, individual rights, autonomy, self-reliance, achievement orientation, and competitiveness. On the other hand, with a low score (collectivism), or in collectivist societies, people belong to "in-groups" that take care of themselves in exchange for loyalty. Collectivism emphasizes collective goals, collective rights, interdependence, and affiliation.

3.3 Masculinity vs. Femininity

The fundamental issue in this dimension is what motivates people in a culture, wanting to be the best (masculine) or liking what you do (feminine). A high score (masculine) on this dimension indicates that society will be driven by competition, achievement, and success, with success being defined by "the winner" or "the best in the field" —a value system that starts in school and continues throughout organizational life. A low score (feminine) on the dimension means that the dominant values in society are caring for others and quality of life. A feminine society is one where quality of life is the sign of success and standing out from the crowd is not admirable.

3.4   Uncertainty Avoidance

The dimension of uncertainty avoidance has to do with the way that a society deals with the fact that the future can never be known. Should people try to control the future or just let it happen? This ambiguity brings with it anxiety, which different cultures have learned to deal with in different ways. Uncertainty avoidance reflects the extent to which the members of a culture feel threatened by ambiguous or unknown situations and have created beliefs and institutions that try to avoid these.

A high score on this dimension indicates that the members of a culture may feel threatened by ambiguous or unknown situations and would exert every effort to create beliefs or institutions to avoid these ambiguities. On the contrary, a low score on this dimension indicates that the members of a culture feel relatively at ease when they are threatened by ambiguous or unknown situations and may be more tolerant of these ambiguities.

3.5   Long-term vs. Short-term Orientation

This dimension describes how every society must maintain some links with its own past while dealing with the challenges of the present and future. Different societies prioritize these two existential goals differently. Normative (short-term) societies, which score low on this dimension, for example, prefer to maintain time-honored traditions and norms while viewing societal change with suspicion. In contrast, those with a culture that scores highly on this dimension take a more pragmatic (long-term) approach. People with long-term orientation encourage thrift and efforts in modern education to prepare for the future.

3.6　Indulgence vs. Restraint

One challenge that confronts humanity, now and in the past, is the degree to which small children are socialized. Without socialization, we do not become "human". This dimension is defined as the extent to which people try to control their desires and impulses, based on the way they were raised. Relatively weak control is called "indulgence" and relatively strong control is called "restraint".

4 Understanding Culture and Cultural Orientations Critically

Cultural orientations refer to the inclination to think, feel, or act in a way that is culturally determined. Cultural orientations define the basis of differences among cultures such as self-identity, interpersonal relationships, communication, and ways of resolving conflicts. The concept of cultural orientation offers a framework for describing and explaining cultural differences. When we explore cultural orientations with the 6-D Model, we shall keep the following in mind:

- There will always be exceptions because each individual culture features its own history, complexity, and diversity, and our complete outlook is shaped by our background, experiences, and interactions.

- There is no right or wrong for each orientation style or one superior orientation over another. Cultural orientations are indicators of a culture's preference in thinking, feeling, or acting. The six dimensions are about understanding the ways people move along different value spectrums.

- Understanding culture and cultural orientations critically enables us to expand our knowledge and improve our awareness of how other people may think and their potential reasons for acting in a certain way. Cultural orientations only explain cultural tendencies and are not inflexible descriptions or overgeneralizations (stereotypes). No one totally belongs to only one cultural orientation but could lie somewhere on a continuum bounded by the extreme on both end. The analytical frameworks of cultural orientations provide us with possible approaches to better understanding and resolving intercultural and organizational culture challenges.

References

Apte, M. 1994. Language in sociocultural context. In R. E. Asher (Ed.), *The Encyclopedia of Language and Linguistics. Vol. 4*. Oxford: Pergamon Press, 2000–2010.

Hall, E. T. 1970. *The Silent Language*. New York: Anchor Press.

Hofstede, G. H. 1997. *Cultures and Organizations: Software of the Mind*. New York: McGraw Hill.

Huang, X. 2006. The formation of modern concepts of "civilization" and "culture" and their historical practice in late Qing and early Republican China. *Modern Chinese History Studies,* (6), 1–34 (in Chinese).

Kluckholn, F. R. & Strodtbeck, F. L. 1961. *Variations in Dimensions*. New York: Harper & Row.

Samovar, L. A. & Porter, R. E. 2004. *Communication Between Cultures* (5th ed.). Belmont: Wadsworth.

Trompenaars, F. & Hampden-Turner, C. 1998. *Riding the Waves of Culture: Understanding Cultural Diversity in Global Business*. New York: McGraw Hill.

Weaver, G. 2006. The American cultural tapestry. *Society & Values of E-Journal USA*. Washington: Bureau of International Information Programs of the U.S. Department of State.

Williams, R. 2015. *Keywords: A Vocabulary of Culture and Society*. New York: Oxford University Press.

Xiao, J. 2012. Misunderstanding of culture: Re-interpretation of Tyler's concept of culture and science of culture. *Social Sciences Abroad,* (3): 33–46 (in Chinese).

Unit 1

Chinese Culture, Customs, and Business Etiquette

China: Overview

1.1 Geography and Demographics

Geography

The People's Republic of China is located in the eastern part of the Asian continent, on the western Pacific rim. It is a vast land, covering about 9.6 million square kilometers. Additional offshore territory, including territorial waters and the continental shelf, totals over three million square kilometers, bringing China's overall territory to almost 13 million square kilometers, according to the statistics released by the official website of Chinese government in 2020.

The vast land expanses of China include plateaus, plains, basins, foothills, and mountains. China has numerous rivers and lakes. More than 50,000 rivers have drainage areas that exceed 100 square kilometers with over 1,500 rivers exceeding 1,000 square kilometers. The Yangtze River, the longest in China and even in Asia, is the third-longest in the world. The Yellow River, "Mother River of the Chinese People", is just behind the Yangtze, both flowing into the Pacific Ocean. China also has large areas of mountainous land, about two-thirds of the country. The ranges mainly run from east to west and from northeast to southwest. Among these mountains, some reach to the sky, and others are lower with charming scenery. Due to the geographical differences, residents of various regions are featured by distinctive lifestyles and customs.

Population and People

With a population of over 1.4 billion (in 2022, according to the World Bank data), China is a unified nation composed of 56 different ethnic groups, forming a big family of the Chinese nation. The Han nationality accounts for over 91% of China's population, and the other 55 groups are generally referred to as "ethnic minorities". According to the seventh census of China in 2021, the Zhuang, Uygur, Hui, Miao, and Man are the most populous ethnic groups after the Han, each with a population of more than 10 million. As part of the population, they spread over a wide area and live all over China. The Chinese government respects the unique culture of all ethnic groups and spares no effort to protect, study, and excavate their cultural treasures.

Language

The official national language of China is *Putonghua*, the contemporary standard Chinese. In 2020, 80.72% of China's population spoke *Putonghua*. In addition, there are mainly ten groups of Chinese regional dialects, including Mandarin, Jin, Wu, Min, Hakka, Yue (Cantonese), Xiang, Gan, Hui, and Pinghua dialects. In each dialect area, there are also several sub-dialects and a variety of "local languages". The Chinese language has been widely used around the world, and a growing number of people are learning it. Chinese, together with Arabic, English, French, Russian, and Spanish is the current official and working languag of the United Nations (UN). The UN and its affiliates observe the UN Chinese Language Day every year on or around April 20. On Chinese Language Day, events are held to showcase the beauty and rich history of the Chinese language and culture. Moreover, seminars featuring prominent Chinese authors, poets, and calligraphers, concerts featuring Chinese music, martial arts performances, and calligraphy exhibitions are held around the world.

1.2   History, Economy, and World Influence

History in Brief

The origin of Chinese civilization dates back to the Paleolithic Age (Old Stone Age) when Homo erectus lived in the area more than a million years ago. There is considerable evidence of Homo erectus at sites such as Lantian of Shaanxi, Hexian of Anhui, Yuanmou of Yunnan and, the most famous, that of Peking man at Zhoukoudian, Beijing municipality in China. One archaeological site in Shanxi Province dates back to some 1.27 million years ago. Then around 10,000 BCE, came the Neolithic Age (New Stone Age), which carries evidence of proto-Chinese millet agriculture. The settlement along the famous Yangtze River is said to be around 8,000 years old. In the latter half of the Neolithic Age, the establishment of the Yellow River civilization led to the Yangshao culture, which is known to have yielded the most significant sites from the era.

China is one of the world's oldest continuous civilizations. The early Chinese civilization included the Xia Dynasty which remained from around 2100 BCE until 1600 BCE, and is described in the ancient *Records of the Grand Historians (Shiji* in its

Chinese name, the history of China written in a biographic-thematic style from 109 to 91 BCE by Sima Qian). Pottery and shells belonging to this period have been excavated. Following the Xia Dynasty is the Shang Dynasty which existed from 1600–1046 BCE. The oracle bones from this period were found with divination records inscribed on them. China was ruled by powerful dynasties for thousands of years. The last dynasty, the Qing Dynasty, ended in 1911 and the People's Republic of China was established in 1949.

Before the foundation of the People's Republic of China, China suffered over 35 million casualties in the Chinese People's War of Resistance Against Japanese Aggression (1931–1945). As claimed by President Xi Jinping at the commemoration of WWⅡ victory on September 3, 2015, "The victory of the Chinese People's War of Resistance Against Japanese Aggression is the first complete victory won by China in its resistance against foreign aggression in modern times. This great triumph crushed the plot of the Japanese militarists to colonize and enslave China and put an end to China's national humiliation of suffering successive defeats at the hands of foreign aggressors in modern times. This great triumph re-established China as a major country in the world and won the Chinese people respect of all peace-loving people around the world. This great triumph opened up bright prospects for the great renewal of the Chinese nation and set our ancient country on a new journey after gaining rebirth."

After the founding of the People's Republic of China, especially after the reform and opening-up, the Chinese people have found a unique path of socialist modernization. On this path, China has made remarkable achievements, completing a development process in a generation (about 30 years). In terms of the Gross Domestic Product (GDP) and the overall state of the economy, the development path that the Chinese people have found is more meaningful, and different from that of any Western country.

The year 2021 witnessed the 100th anniversary of the founding of the Communist Party of China. In 2022, the 20th National Congress of the Communist Party of China was held in Beijing. President Xi Jinping summarized the great achievement in the past decade, which is marked by three major events of great immediate importance and profound historical significance for the cause of the Party and the people: "We embraced the centenary of the Communist Party of China; we ushered in a new era of socialism with Chinese characteristics; and we eradicated absolute poverty and finished building a moderately prosperous society in all respects, thus completing the First Centenary Goal." With the leadership of the

Communist Party, Chinese people have gained historic victories in revolution and socialist construction, and today we are forging confidently ahead toward the great goal of socialist modernization.

Economy in Brief

Since China began its reform and opening-up in 1978, its GDP has grown for many years by nearly 10% annually. According to the World Bank, China today is an upper-middle-income country and the second-largest economy in the world when measured by nominal GDP. A forecast cited by *The Guardian* states that China may become the world's largest economy in nominal GDP by 2028.

China has a developing market-oriented economy that is incorporated into its economic planning through industrial policy and its strategic five-year plan. The economy includes state-owned enterprises and mixed-ownership enterprises, as well as a large domestic private sector, and is open to foreign businesses in a system known as China's market economy.

According to reported statistics by *Global Times*, the total assets held by Chinese state-owned enterprises, excluding those operating in the financial sector, hit 268.5 trillion yuan (about $41.96 trillion) in 2020, indicating a steady rise over the prior year despite the effect of COVID-19 on the economy. Ninety-one of these enterprises entered the 2020 *Fortune* Global 500 companies. It is for the first time that the number of *Fortune* Global 500 companies based in China (including the Taiwan region) exceeded that of the US (133 vs. 121).

China is also the world's largest manufacturer and exporter. It has always focused on providing stable market expectations and a clear and fair business environment. It is also committed to strengthening the regulatory system and the rule of law to further support the market system. China has become a major trading partner for more than 140 countries and regions. It leads the world in the total volume of trade in goods, and it is a major destination for global investment and a leading country in outbound investment. Through these efforts, we have advanced a broader agenda of opening up across more areas and in greater depth.

World Influence

With its vast territory, China is central to important regional and global development issues. Its economic growth at reasonable levels has an important positive effect on the growth of the rest of the world's economies.

China is a permanent member of the United Nations Security Council and a founding member of several multilateral and regional cooperation organizations such as the Asian Infrastructure Investment Bank, the New Development Bank, the Shanghai Cooperation Organization (SCO), and the Regional Comprehensive Economic Partnership (RCEP). It is also a member of the BRICS, the Group of Twenty (G20), the Asia-Pacific Economic Cooperation (APEC), and the East Asia Summit (EAS). China has worked hard to build a globally-oriented network of high-standard free trade areas and accelerated the development of pilot free trade zones and the Hainan Free Trade Port. As a collaborative endeavor, the Belt and Road Initiative has been welcomed by the international community both as a public good and a cooperation platform.

According to Premier Li Keqiang's Government Work Report on March 5, 2022, "China will continue to pursue an independent foreign policy of peace, stay on the path of peaceful development, work for a new type of international relations, and endeavor to build a human community with a shared future. We will pursue the Global Development Initiative and promote the shared values of all humanity. China will always work to safeguard world peace, contribute to global development, and preserve international order. We stand ready to work with all others in the international community to make new and greater contributions to promoting world peace, stability, development, and prosperity."

President Xi Jinping stated in the Report to the 20th National Congress of the Communist Party of China on October 16, 2022: "Building a human community with a shared future is the way forward for all the world's peoples." China promotes the development of a human community with a shared future and stands firm in protecting international fairness and justice. China also advocates and practices true multilateralism through taking a clear-cut stance against hegemonism and power politics in all their forms and opposing unilateralism, protectionism, and bullying of any kind.

1.3 China's Holidays

According to the official website of the Chinese government, there are currently seven statutory or public holidays in China, including New Year's Day, the Spring

Festival, the Qingming Festival, Labor Day, the Dragon Boat Festival, the Mid-Autumn Festival, and National Day. Their respective holiday schedules are shown in Table 1–1.

Table 1–1   A List of Main Holidays in China[1]

Day	Date	Holiday Name
Saturday	Jan. 1	New Year's Day
Sunday to Monday	Jan. 2–3	New Year's Day Holiday
Monday to Friday	Jan. 31–Feb. 4	Spring Festival Holiday
Tuesday	Feb. 1	Spring Festival
Sunday	Apr. 3	Qingming Festival
Monday to Tuesday	Apr. 4–5	Qingming Festival Holiday
Sunday	May 1	Labor Day
Monday to Wednesday	May 2–4	Labor Day Holiday
Friday	June 3	Dragon Boat Festival
Saturday	Sep. 10	Mid-Autumn Festival
Monday	Sep. 12	Mid-Autumn Festival Holiday
Saturday	Oct. 1	Chinese National Day
Sunday to Friday	Oct. 2–7	Chinese National Day Holiday

The National Day of the country is celebrated every year on October 1 for the founding of the People's Republic of China on October 1, 1949, and is usually a seven-day holiday (including weekends). Public places are decorated with a festive theme for this holiday.

The Spring Festival or the Chinese New Year is the most distinctive traditional festival in China. It falls on the first day of the first lunar month of the year. Various activities are held all over the country for its celebration. This festival is also the most important occasion for family reunions, for which some people may need to travel long distances. Airports, railway stations, and long-distance bus stations can be very crowded at this time, which is known as the Spring Festival rush. Strictly

---

1   This table only takes the year 2022 as an example since the specific date for some holidays may change according to the annual calendar.

speaking, the Spring Festival starts from the beginning of the twelfth lunar month and lasts until the middle of the first lunar month next year. During this period, the most important days are Spring Festival Eve and the first three days of the Lunar New Year. The Chinese government now stipulates that the Chinese Lunar New Year is a seven-day holiday.

China is famous for its cultural diversity. Besides the public holidays at the national level, there are a number of ethnic minority festivals celebrated across China. Well-known ones include the Tibetan New Year, Corban Festival, Mongolian Nadam Fair, Shoton Festival, Water Splashing Festival, Sisters Meals Festival, March Fair, Drying Clothes Festival, Torch Festival, and Knife-Pole Festival. Moreover, several holidays are established for a designated group of people, such as Women's Day (March 8), Youth Day (May 4), Children's Day (June 1), Teachers' Day (September 10), and Double Ninth Festival (also known as Chongyang Festival, or the Senior Citizens' Festival, held on the ninth day of the ninth lunar month).

Special celebrations are also organized on the anniversaries of the founding of the Communist Party of China (July 1) and the People's Liberation Army (August 1), the launch of reform and opening-up (December 18), the victory in the Chinese People's War of Resistance against Japanese Aggression and the World Anti-Fascist War (September 3), and the victory of Chinese People's Volunteers entering the Democratic People's Republic of Korea to fight the War to Resist US Aggression and Aid Korea (October 25).

Chinese Cultural Orientations

The culture of China, based on the Chinese civilization, fully integrates the cultural elements of all regions and ethnic groups. The Eastern civilization system deeply influenced by Chinese civilization is called the "Han cultural circle". Chinese culture has not only exerted an important influence on Japan and the Korean Peninsula, but also had a far-reaching impact on Southeast Asian and South Asian countries such as Vietnam and Singapore, as well as the Americas. China's growing national strength and considerable rise in international status have made its culture a greater influence around the globe. It is noteworthy that Confucius' teachings and philosophy underpin Chinese culture and society. They have played a vital role in shaping the character, behavior, and way of life of the Chinese people and remain influential across China today.

If we examine Chinese culture from the perspective of the six-dimensional model (6-D Model) of culture orientations (please refer to the Introduction of the textbook), we can obtain an overview of Chinese cultural orientations in terms of the following six dimensions. Although it may not be precise enough to present the long history, complexity, and diversity of Chinese culture, it does provide us with a possible approach to reflect on our own cultural orientations and show us a rough picture of the nation. In the following section, we will try to apply the 6-D Model as a reference to further analyze Chinese cultural orientations.

• Power Distance

China scores relatively high on this dimension, which indicates that people in Chinese society believe that it is acceptable to have a certain degree of inequality among people. For instance, in a business setting, the relationship between subordinates and superiors, or between junior and senior employees, tends to be hierarchical. Generally speaking, individuals are susceptible to authority, and they are optimistic about people's leadership and initiative. In the workplace, Chinese people are accustomed to "shouhao benfen" (Chinese: 守好本分) and "buyao yuewei" (Chinese: 不要越位), which suggests that people should fulfill their own duties so that the whole society can develop harmoniously and healthily.

• Individualism vs. Collectivism

China scores relatively low in terms of individualism, which means that China is a relatively more collectivist culture, where people usually start with the interests of the group, not necessarily their own. "Zhong" (Chinese: 忠) or loyalty is a virtue that defines a person's moral commitments to the surrounding social, cultural, and historical community. This community, according to the Confucian ideal, is not just a collection of atomic individuals, but an organic unit with which each person forms a unique identity, of which each individual is an irreplaceable member.

• Masculinity vs. Femininity

China scores relatively high on the masculinity dimension, which implies that it is a more success-oriented or success-driven culture. Many Chinese employees tend to sacrifice family and leisure for work. Another example is that Chinese students, or rather their parents, are very concerned about their test scores and rankings, as this is the main criterion for school success, although things are changing in China today.

• Uncertainty Avoidance

China appears to have a low score on uncertainty avoidance, which suggests that Chinese people may be comfortable with ambiguity in some cases. Therefore, it is best for Western business partners to simply ask when in doubt to avoid misunderstandings or false assumptions. By doing so, you are showing interest and seriousness, which is an act of respect, something a Chinese business partner understands well and is therefore more than happy to explain whatever the situation is.

• Long-term vs. Short-term Orientation

China scores relatively high on long-term orientation, which means it is a relatively pragmatic culture. The frugality and perseverance of the Chinese people are a good example. A popular four-character Chinese idiom "weiyu-choumou" (Chinese: 未雨绸缪), which literally means to repair one's house before it rains, also indicates that Chinese people believe that it is crucial to plan ahead. However, the market economy and globalization have exerted great influence on the modern life of the Chinese people, and the score on this dimension is very likely to change over the next decade.

• Indulgence vs. Restraint

China scores low on the indulgence dimension, indicating that it is a relatively conservative culture. In a restrained society, people place less value on leisure time, usually suppress the satisfaction of their own desires, believe their actions will be constrained by social norms, and feel guilty about their indulgence. This orientation may be partly due to the teachings of Confucius. The following passage (translated by KU Hung-ming) from *Analects of Confucius* (Chinese: 《论语》), embodies Confucius' vocal emphasis on self-restraint.

Confucius's most beloved disciple, Yen Hui once enquired what constituted a moral life. Confucius answered, "Renounce yourself and conform to the ideal of decency and good sense." "If one could only", Confucius went on to say, "live a moral life, renouncing himself and conforming to the ideal of decency and good sense for one single day, the world would become moral. To be moral, a man depends on entirely upon himself and not upon others." The disciple then asked for practical rules to be observed in living a moral life. Confucius answered, "Whatever things are contrary to the ideal of decency and good sense, do not look upon them. Whatever things are contrary to the ideal of decency and good sense, do not listen to them. Whatever things are contrary to the ideal of decency and good sense, do not utter them with your mouth. Lastly, let nothing in whatever things you do, act or move, be contrary to the ideal decency and good sense." (*Analects* ⅩⅡ, 1) (Chinese: 颜渊问仁。子曰：" 克己复礼为仁。一日克己复礼，天下归仁焉。为仁由己，而由人乎哉？ "颜渊曰：" 请问其目。"子曰：" 非礼勿视，非礼勿听，非礼勿言，非礼勿动。") The core of Confucius' thought is "benevolence" and "propriety", and "etiquette" is the essence of Chinese culture (for example, we often say that China is a country of etiquette). Despite the fact that "Li"(Chinese: 礼) can be understood differently as "etiquette", "rites", "ritual practices", or "the ideal of decency and good sense", there is no doubt that Confucius considered self-restraint and compliance with social norms as essential for living a moral life. As Chinese culture has long been influenced by Confucius' thought, the control of emotions, restraint, obedience, and "face" are highly valued in Chinese culture.

Chinese Business Practices and Etiquette

3.1 Business Appointments

- In the Chinese business context, it is essential to establish business contacts with business partners. Try to find the right contacts to help you arrange appointments with local businesses and government officials. Those established organizations can also help you identify importers, buyers, agents, distributors, and joint venture partners.

- In China, both business and government hours are generally from 8:00 a.m. to 5:00 p.m., Monday through Friday. Employees usually have breaks between

noon and 1:30 p.m. Make an appointment before visiting a business partner.

- Do not arrange business appointments or trips during the Spring Festival (the Chinese New Year). Many businesses are closed for a week around the holiday. The date of the new year varies according to the lunar calendar.

3.2 Business Negotiations

- During business negotiations, be fully prepared to introduce your products or services. It is recommended to send electronic files to your business partners in advance. You can also prepare the necessary copies of your proposal for distribution.

- Chinese businesspeople are cautious about business affairs, and usually expect to establish long-term relationships with business partners. Never exaggerate a product or service, because Chinese people believe that humility is a virtue, and also because they will investigate your claims.

- Carry business cards with a Chinese translation printed on the back. Take business cards seriously and do not keep them too casually in your back pocket or elsewhere.

3.3 Business Entertaining

- Chinese people are famous for their hospitality. In Chinese business settings, business lunches are popular. Chinese businesspeople would like to treat their business partners to formal dinners. Most dinners start between 6:30 p.m. and 7:00 p.m. and last about two hours. If you are the host, you should arrive 30 minutes before the guest. If you are a guest, be sure to arrive promptly or even a little earlier. Banquet tables are usually round and dishes are placed on a large Lazy Susan (revolving plate). Never begin to eat or drink before the host does.

- Chinese people eat with chopsticks and drink soup with spoons. When you finish eating, put your chopsticks on the table or chopstick rest. It is impolite to stick chopsticks directly into your rice bowl. As a guest, if you are not used to using chopsticks, ask the host to prepare a knife and fork. You can also tell the host about your dietary preferences or food allergies in advance.

- At a meal, eat lightly at the beginning, since there may be a number of courses later. Don't be offended if your host keeps filling your bowl with food or encouraging you to drink. They do not intend to ask you to eat or drink more than enough, but just to show their hospitality.

- Toasting is popular in China. At the banquet, the host starts off with a toast, which continues throughout the evening. It is acceptable to toast with a soft drink, but wine and beer are also available. If you don't want to drink any more, you can politely tell the host directly.

3.4　Business Protocol

Greetings

- Most people you meet should be addressed with a title and their name. If a person does not have a professional title (President, Engineer, Doctor), simply use Mr. or Madam, Mrs., Miss, or Ms., plus the name. Chinese names are arranged in a different order in English, and the family name usually comes before the given name.
- Chinese people are sensitive to status and titles, so you should use official titles as much as possible, such as General Manager, Committee Member, or Bureau Chief whenever possible. Introductions of business partners tend to be formal, with courtesy rather than familiarity preferred.

Gestures

- Chinese people do not use gestures very often when speaking. Excessive use of gestures can be considered a distraction. They do not touch each other frequently, especially among strangers. Avoid making exaggerated gestures or using dramatic facial expressions.
- Handshaking is a common way of socializing in Chinese business settings. When you visit a company, factory, or school, you may be greeted with applause. The usual response is to applaud back.

3.5　Business Gift-Giving

- When giving a gift, make it clear that the gift is on behalf of the whole company and is aimed at the entire team on the receiving end. Be sure to give the gift to a recognized leader among your trading partners. Gifts of this sort might include items from your region, such as local handicrafts, historical memorabilia, or illustrated books. However, when giving gifts, you need to be careful and make sure not to give overly lavish gifts in business settings, as it could be seen as a bribe. Gifts should be given and received with both hands. In China, gifts are usually not opened in the presence of the giver.

- In China, recipients tend to politely excuse themselves for not accepting a gift, or "wanyan-xiejue" (Chinese: 婉言谢绝). Furthermore, the recipient usually claims that he or she is not entitled or worthy of the gift, or "wugong bushoulu" (Chinese: 无功不受禄). These reflect a key concept in Chinese culture, "keqi" (Chinese: 客气). "Keqi" not only means considerate, polite, and well-mannered, but also represents Chinese people's humility. Joyce Millet (a cross-cultural training professional) once claimed, "Chinese etiquette requires a person to decline two or three times before accepting a gift, invitation, or other offerings, especially when the relationship is not very close." In this case, it is expected that gift-givers will stick to their views.

- The gift of a clock may offend the Chinese recipient, as clocks are often associated with funerals. "Sending clocks" sounds like "songzhong" (Chinese: 送终) which means to attend a funeral in Chinese. Since red represents joy in Chinese culture and is a lucky color, if possible, you can choose to wrap gifts in red. Pink and yellow are happy and prosperous colors, and they are also good choices. Do not use white or black, which are the colors usually used for funerals. Ask for appropriate paper at your hotel or gift shop when wrapping gifts.

- During Chinese New Year, the elders in the family are accustomed to putting money in red envelopes as gifts to children. This gift is called "hongbao" (Chinese: 红包). In some companies, employers may also give each employee a "hongbao" in recognition of their contribution to the company throughout the year. People also send digital "hongbao" through WeChat, especially during important festivals.

3.6 Business Outfit

- Dressing appropriately is essential for ensuring success in business. When you are invited to a business event in China, dress conservatively. Men usually wear suits, shirts, and ties. Women should also wear conservative suits, blouses, and low heels. Appropriate colors include black, gray, and sometimes light blue. Bright colors are inappropriate.

- If it is a very formal reception, for instance, organized by a government agency or a foreign diplomat, ladies may prepare evening gowns and high heels. Gentlemen may wear suits and ties.

- When you are invited to attend an event, you can wear jeans or sneakers if the dress code is smart and casual. Sportswear is acceptable for both men and women. Shorts are also appropriate when exercising.

Tips: Preparing for the First Business Trip Abroad

Planning your first business trip abroad can be exciting, and daunting, but it can also be stressful. If you want everything to go as smoothly and stress-free as possible, you can refer to the handy tips below.

- **Get a passport.**
  A passport is a travel document issued by a country's government to its citizens. It certifies the identity and nationality of its holder primarily for the purpose of international travel. Before you prepare for your first business trip abroad, you must have a valid passport that is within its expiration date. The time to obtain a passport varies from country to country, and in China, it usually takes less than 15 days for getting your first passport ready after your submission of the application.

- **Get your visa after having your passport.**
  A visa is a conditional authorization granted to a foreigner by a territory, allowing him or her to enter, remain within, or leave that territory. Not all countries offer visas on arrival. Depending on your nationality, each country has different arrangements, and requirements can change. Waiting for a visa can vary depending on the time of year and the specific consulate or embassy, so

submit your visa application early and ensure it will be valid for your entire stay.

- **Check with your insurance carrier and your medications.**

  Ask your medical and homeowner's insurance providers whether your policy applies overseas for emergencies. If you use medication, ensure you have enough to last the entire trip period. Carry a copy of your prescription or medical records for added security. Some countries won't let you enter without proof that you've been immunized against certain diseases, such as yellow fever or malaria. All immunizations must be recorded and presented on an official International Certificate of Vaccination.

- **Ensure your credit card and phone will work in the country you're visiting.**

  Most foreign banks have switched to chip-and-PIN technology, and fewer businesses abroad accept the outdated magnetic strip cards. Activate the global roaming capabilities of your cell phone in case you need to make a call.

- **Check multiple hotel sites before you book.**

  A number of popular booking sites are now available for hotel investigation and reservation. Those sites may provide substantial information about the location, service, and expenses of hotels around the world. Download apps and maps beforehand. Many apps are available that will help you plan your trip and navigate while being there.

- **Keep copies of documents on hand.**

  If something happens to your passport or wallet, you'll need all of your identifying information. Use your phone's camera to take a photo of the important passport pages (personal information and visas, taking a good care of your cellphone, of course) and photo ID to take with you in an emergency. You can also send electronic copies of important documents to your personal e-mail in case printed versions are not available. You may also ask your family to keep an extra copy of the documents.

- **Consider hiring a local guide.**

  Whether you're on a private walking tour or a multi-day group tour, local guides are more qualified to keep you safe. It is worth having a tour guide who speaks the local language and knows more about the local area.

Enjoying your first international business trip really matters. The more experience you gain, the better you will be able to handle different situations in an international exchange or business trip.

Exercises

5.1   Fact Files

Directions: Complete the following table and find the key facts about China.

Official Name	
Capital City	
Official Language(s)	
Currency	
Population (Year 2022)	
The National Flower	
Current President	

5.2   Compound Dictation

Directions: Listen to the passage and fill in the blanks with the words or expressions that you hear.

China is located in eastern Asia and on the western coast of the Pacific Ocean. The land area is about 9.6 million square kilometers, the eastern and southern continental (1)_____ are more than 18,000 kilometers, and the water area of the inland and border seas is about 4.7 million square kilometers.

China shares (2)_____ with 14 countries and is (3)_____ to eight countries on the sea. Beijing is the capital city of China. China's (4)_____ is high in the west and low in the east, with mountains, plateaus, and hills covering about 67%, and basins and (5)_____ accounting for about 33% of the land area. The mountain (6)_____ mostly run east-west and northeast-southwest.

China is a (7)_____ emerging economy in the world. It is a (8)_____ multi-ethnic country, with the Han nationality having the largest population and the other 55 ethnic groups having relatively small populations.

Major Chinese traditional festivals include the Spring Festival, (9)_____ Festival, Qingming Festival, Dragon Boat Festival, Mid-Autumn Festival, etc. In addition, all ethnic (10)_____ retain their own traditional festivals.

5.3   True or False: Chinese Customs and Etiquette

Directions: Put T for true or F for false for each of the following statements.

(   ) 1. Chinese people view punctuality as a virtue. Therefore, you should arrive at meetings on time or slightly early.

(   ) 2. You should never criticize a Chinese colleague in front of someone else or do anything else that will cause them to lose face or "mianzi".

(   ) 3. In China, you should begin to eat or drink before your host does.

(   ) 4. Cheek kissing between business associates is common in China.

(   ) 5. If a Chinese person declines a gift from one to whom he is not very close, he really means it. You should not insist at all.

5.4   Multiple Choice: To Know More About China

Directions: Mark the correct answer to each question. Look up the following facts on the Internet or in some reference books and try to get more background information.

1. How many major cuisines are there in China?

   A. Six.   B. Seven.   C. Eight.   D. Nine

2. Which of the following cities served as the capital of the Six Dynasties in ancient China?

   A. Nanjing.   B. Beijing.   C. Shenyang.   D. Xi'an.

3. What's the name of China's national anthem?

   A. Ode to the Yellow River.

   B. My People, My Country.

   C. March of the Volunteers.

   D. Five-star Red Flag Fluttering in the Wind.

4. Which Chinese beverage was brought back to Europe in 1610 by the Dutch and was loved by Europeans?

   A. Tea.   B. Wine.   C. Beer.   D. Alcohol.

5. When did China implement the policy of reform and opening-up?

   A. 1977.   B. 1978.   C. 1979.   D. 1980.

5.5   Case Study

Directions: Read the following case and answer the questions.

> Xiao Lin, a secretary at a Chinese company, was asked to pick up Peter Green, a 65-year-old senior consultant at an American company. When they met at the airport, Xiao Lin found Mr. Green carrying a heavy piece of luggage. The following is a conversation between Xiao Lin and Mr. Green.
>
> Xiao Lin: Hello, Mr. Green. Welcome to Beijing. You must be very tired. Let me help you with your luggage...
>
> Mr. Green: Oh, it's fine. I can manage myself.
>
> Xiao Lin: Okay. But considering your age, I think it would be better that I...

1. What went wrong in this case and why?

2. Conduct further research and make a comparison between Chinese and American people's attitudes toward aging.

6 A Mini Business Project

Directions: Suppose that you will have a one-week business trip to a famous city abroad, for example, Paris, the capital city of France. Please explain your plan based on the following outline.

- getting prepared to go abroad;
- choosing appropriate ways of transportation;
- booking a suitable hotel;
- visiting must-see scenic spots;
- calculating the cost and preparing the budget;
- working out a one-week itinerary.

Note: You or your team is asked to prepare a presentation using PowerPoint slides, and write an executive summary using Microsoft Word. You may use appropriate visual aids (e.g., video clips) to support your presentation, and you may also refer to the sample project files online for reference.

Words and Expressions

affiliate	/əˈfɪlieɪt/	n.	附属机构，分支机构
allergy	/ˈælədʒi/	n.	过敏，过敏症
bully	/ˈbʊli/	v.	恃强凌弱
centenary	/senˈtiːnəri/	n.	一百周年（纪念）
divination	/ˌdɪvɪˈneɪʃn/	n.	预测；占卜
eradicate	/ɪˈrædɪkeɪt/	v.	根除，消灭
excavate	/ˈekskəveɪt/	v.	发掘，挖掘（古物）
frugality	/fruːˈgæləti/	n.	俭省，节俭
hegemonism	/hɪˈgemənɪzəm/	n.	霸权主义
hierarchical	/ˌhaɪəˈrɑːkɪkl/	adj.	分等级的
humility	/hjuːˈmɪləti/	n.	谦逊，谦恭
lavish	/ˈlævɪʃ/	adj.	奢侈的
memorabilia	/ˌmemərəˈbɪliə/	n.	纪念品
neolithic	/ˌniːəˈlɪθɪk/	adj.	新石器时代的
nominal	/ˈnɒmɪnl/	adj.	名义上的；（数量或价值）票面的
oracle bones		n.	甲骨
overly	/ˈəʊvəli/	adv.	过度地；极度地
paleolithic	/ˌpæliəˈlɪθɪk/	adj.	旧石器时代的
peninsula	/pəˈnɪnsjələ/	n.	半岛
porcelain	/ˈpɔːsəlɪn/	adj.	瓷制的
pragmatic	/prægˈmætɪk/	adj.	讲求实际的，务实的；实用主义的

prioritize	/praɪˈɒrətaɪz/	v.	按优先顺序列出；优先考虑（处理）
renounce	/rɪˈnaʊns/	v.	声明放弃，抛弃
sneaker	/ˈsniːkə(r)/	n.	<美>球鞋；运动鞋
statutory	/ˈstætʃətri/	adj.	依照法令的，法定的
susceptible	/səˈseptəbl/	adj.	易受影响的
unilateralism	/ˌjuːnɪˈlætərəlɪzəm/	n.	单边主义
vocal	/ˈvəʊk(ə)l/	adj.	直言不讳的，大声表达的

Notes

Scan the QR code for more information about Chinese culture.

Unit 2

Indian Culture, Customs, and Business Etiquette

India: Overview

1.1 Geography and Demographics

Geography

India (the official name is the Republic of India) is known as a subcontinent or a peninsula as it is surrounded by water, namely the Arabian Sea to the west, the Lakshadweep Sea to the southwest, the Bay of Bengal to the east, and the Indian Ocean proper to the south. It is bounded to the northwest by Pakistan, to the north by China, Nepal, and to the northeast by Bhutan, Bangladesh, and Myanmar (Burma).

Population and People

According to the World Bank, Indian population was estimated at around 1.4 billion in 2022. Growing urbanization, rising education levels, specifically among women, and increasing alleviation of poverty have led the growth rate in India to decline significantly over the past decades.

Language

There is no national language in India. Hindi in Devanagari script is the official language of the government with English as a provisional official sub-language. Each individual state legislature has the right to adopt any regional language as an official language. The Indian Constitution lists 22 languages as official languages and awards six languages as classical languages due to their rich and independent nature.

1.2 History, Economy, and World Influence

History in Brief

India owes its name to the mighty river Sindhu (the Indus) in Pakistan. Amazed by its enormous size, the early Aryan settlers called the river Sindhu, which means a huge sheet of water, also used as a synonym for ocean.

The Persian Emperor Darius, in 518 BCE, conquered the area around the river Sindhu and made it a satrapy of his empire. The Persians pronounced "S" as "H", hence Sindhu became Hindu. Later, the Greek invaders changed "Hindu" to "India", subsequently referring to the entire country as India.

The East India Company entered India in 1600, during the reign of the Mughals (1526–1707), creating a platform for the British Crown to slowly gain control of power. In 1858, British Crown rule was finally established, ending the control of the East India Company. The British Crown reigned in India till 1947, when the British Raj partitioned India into two sovereign states, India, and Pakistan. Pakistan was later divided into Bangladesh on the east and Pakistan on the west.

The Indian National Congress, founded in 1885, was instrumental in fighting for independence from the British Raj. In 1930, the Indian National Congress, led by Jawaharlal Nehru and Mahatma Gandhi, adopted a policy of civil disobedience, a movement that showed their defiance against the British monopoly on salt. It was a long struggle that led to India's independence in 1947 on the condition that predominantly Muslim areas in the north would form a separate country, Pakistan. Mohammed Ali Jinnah began to serve as the first governor-general of the Dominion of Pakistan on August 14, 1947, while Jawaharlal Nehru became the first prime minister of the Republic of India on August 15, 1947.

The departure of the colonial rule has left a huge dent in the history of India, inciting bloodshed and communal sentiments in the hearts of the people and entangling the country into a complex dispute to the present day.

Economy in Brief

India has emerged as one of the fastest growing major economies in the world since India's independence from the British Raj in 1947. It is currently classified as a developing market economy. It has become the sixth largest economy by nominal GDP and the third largest by purchasing power parity (PPP) in 2022, according to the World Bank.

India is an agriculture-based country that ranks second globally in food and agricultural production. Although agriculture contributes only about 14% of India's total GDP, it provides employment to nearly 50% of the total population.

Traditionally, India has six major industries, namely iron and steel, textiles, jute, sugar, cement, and paper. Recently, the petrochemical, automobile, information technology (IT), banking, and insurance industries have joined the bandwagon.

Construction and the real estate sector come after agriculture in employment creation and are vital sectors in determining economic activity. Textile, information technology, telecommunication, oil, and automobile industries are among the most important contributors to India's economic growth. The service sector remains the fastest growing sector and accounts for 50% of GDP.

India has the world's fourth-largest natural resources, and its mining sector contributes 11% of the industrial GDP and 2.5% of the total GDP. It is the second largest in coal, cement, and steel production and the third largest in electricity in 2016.

In 2019, the Indian labor force was the second highest in the world, with 520 million workers. India has one of the highest numbers of billionaires and there is extreme inequality in income due to various socio-economic factors such as the practice of caste system, bureaucracy in the government, and other social issues.

World Influence

India has been a member of the World Trade Organization (WTO) from January 1, 1995. India is also a member of the G20, the BRICS, the South Asian Association for Regional Cooperation (SAARC), and the Shanghai Cooperation Organization. It has witnessed phenomenal growth in its economy since the start of the 21st century, with an annual average GDP growth at 6% to 7% and became the world's fastest growing economy from 2014 to 2018.

In recent years, India has become more open to global trade, particularly in the service sector. The United States, China, the United Arab Emirates, Saudi Arabia, Iraq, Singapore, Germany, South Korea, and Switzerland were India's largest trading partners in 2019. In comparison to many countries, its tariffs are high, and investment norms are still restrictive. It is also the world's largest manufacturer of generic drugs, and its pharmaceutical sector fulfills over 50% of the global demand for vaccines.

1.3 India's Holidays

India has three national holidays: Republic Day (January 26), Independence Day (August 15), and Gandhi Jayanti or Mahatma Gandhi's Birthday (October 2). Gandhi Jayanti is celebrated on October 2 to mark the birth anniversary of Mohandas Karamchand Gandhi, who was born on October 2, 1869 in Porbandar, Gujarat. In 1930, he led the Dandi Salt March, a non-violent civil disobedience movement against the British salt monopoly. He deeply influenced personalities from other parts of the world such as Martin Luther King Jr. and Nelson Mandela. Many government offices close on government and public holidays, and some private businesses may close as well.

India has holidays ranging from religious festivals to the birthdays of individuals with historical significance to the foundation days in different states. Furthermore, each of the states has its own holidays besides the national holidays. Table 2-1 is a list of main holidays in India.

Table 2-1 A List of Main Holidays in India in 2022

Day	Date	Holiday Name
Saturday	Jan. 1	New Year's Day
Wednesday	Jan. 26	Republic Day
Monday	Aug. 15	Independence Day
Sunday	Oct. 2	Mahatma Gandhi's Birthday
Wednesday	Oct. 5	Dussehra

Indian Cultural Orientations

The Indian culture has never been rigid and that's why it is surviving with pride in the modern era. It integrates the qualities of various other cultures and comes out as a contemporary and acceptable tradition. That is what is unique about the Indian culture, and it moves on with the time. In the following section, we shall explore the six central dimensions of cultural orientations that define Indian culture.

- **Power Distance**

    India's high power distance value indicates a high level of inequality of power, wealth, and a top-down structure of hierarchy in society and organizations. This means that decision-making in India is concentrated in the hands of the people who are in the higher level of the social ladder or organizations. Individual employees or subordinates have little or no decision-making power and are often obligated to agree with their superiors. Subordinates often expect their superiors to be compassionate toward them, which in turn is reciprocated with their loyalty to them.

• Individualism vs. Collectivism

India, with an intermediate score on individualism, is both a collectivistic and individualistic culture (Hofstede, 2010). The collectivistic orientation indicates a high preference for belonging to a larger social framework where individuals are expected to act in accordance with the greater good of their defined in-groups. This can explain why one's family, extended family, neighbors, work group, and other social networks could influence the actions and choices of an individual in India. Moreover, loyalty by the employee and almost familial protection by the employer are common expectations in its business culture. Hiring and promotion decisions are often made based on relationships, which are the key to almost everything in a collectivist society.

• Masculinity vs. Femininity

India achieves a mediate score on masculinity. It is true that India is very masculine in terms of visual display of success and power, with an ostentatious lifestyle exhibited by its people. However, India also appreciates the value of humility and abstinence and therefore it is not uncommon for Indians to refrain from indulging in masculine displays.

• Uncertainty Avoidance

India has a medium-low preference for avoiding uncertainties. In India, imperfection is well accepted, as is unpunctuality. People do not like to take initiative and prefer to just follow routines. They also get used to bypassing the rules. For Indians, nothing is impossible, and they are very capable of adjusting because they think there is always a better solution beyond the regulations.

• Long-term vs. Short-term Orientation

With an intermediate score on long-term orientation, a dominant preference in Indian culture cannot be determined. In India, the concept of "karma" dominates philosophical thought. It means that a person's actions in this and previous states of existence may decide his or her fate in future existence. Therefore, time is not linear in Indian culture, and is thus not as important as it is to many Western societies, which typically score low on this dimension.

• Indulgence vs. Restraint

India's low score on indulgence indicates that it is a culture of restraint and may tend toward cynicism and pessimism. People in such cultures often believe that their actions are constrained by social norms, and that indulging themselves is somehow wrong.

Indian Business Practices and Etiquette

3.1   Business Appointments

- Be on time to maintain a positive image and introduce yourself to members you do not know. If you would like to contact your Indian counterpart through a phone call, it is usually best to call from 10:00 a.m. onward but no later than 9:00 p.m. Avoid business meetings close to India's major holidays, which your counterpart may observe.

- When you are presenting a business card, use both hands (or the right hand only), making sure that the writing is facing the other person. If you have a university degree, include that information on the card.

- When you are receiving a business card, use both hands (or the right hand only). Do not put the card away immediately, but instead take a moment to examine it carefully, and then place it before you on the table when you are seated. Do not put it in the back pocket of your pants, as this could be taken as you sitting on the other person's face. Similarly, do not write on someone's card unless directed to do so.

3.2   Business Negotiations

- Indian culture is relationship-based. Most Indians do not feel comfortable speaking in a direct and frank manner to those with whom they do not have a strong relationship, so it is important to develop a positive relationship with your Indian counterpart before any negotiations.

- Business negotiations can be a slow process. When proposing negotiations of a deal, Indians will often remain polite throughout, and then enthusiastically repackage the deal to reach an agreement. Make sure you are patient, respectful and friendly without compromising your positions.

- Bargaining is the lifeline of business negotiations in India, so be prepared to adjust your conditions according to the circumstances. After elaborating all the benefits of the deal, Indians often indirectly try to reach a price or figure.

- Workplaces in India are hierarchical, based on age and position. Indian partners may be more flexible in negotiating and compromising between meetings when they are in a position to check with their superiors.

- Indians often tend to be very indirect to avoid losing face through direct refusals. In India, the polite way to say no is to say, "I'll see what I can do" or something to that effect, no matter how impossible the task may be. After they have been queried several times concerning their success, an answer of "I'm still checking" or something similar means "No". Such an indirect response also means, "I'm still your friend or ally; I tried." Therefore, be as transparent as possible with the questions in order to receive a clear yes or no answer (but be cautious in doing this, or you will harm the relationship).

- Everything is subject to change in India, so Indians regard contracts more than agreements of willingness to do business. The specifics of a deal's restrictions and provisions are negotiable depending on the business relationship.

3.3   Business Entertaining

- Business entertaining is a vital aspect of the commercial process in India. Make the most of opportunities to dine with your Indian colleagues and clients, preferably during lunch or dinner engagements.

- Indian cuisine is known for its spiciness, though milder alternatives like omelet can be sought if needed. Vegetarian and non-vegetarian options are available, with a greater emphasis on vegetarian dishes.

- It's worth noting that Hindus avoid beef, while Muslims abstain from pork and alcohol. Dining in India often has an informal feel, with eating by hand being acceptable, although utensils are usually provided. It is considered more polite to eat with the right hand. Tipping around 10% is customary when settling the bill.

3.4   Business Protocol

Greetings

- Greeting with "namaste" (na-mas-tay) by placing both hands together in front of your heart with a slight bow shows respect for Indian custom and is appreciated. When meeting or leaving, men shake hands with men and do not touch women, unless offered by them. Women traditionally do not shake hands with men, but may shake hands with foreign women.

- Titles are highly valued by Indians. Indian surnames usually indicate the part of the country where they are from. Do not address someone by his or her first name unless you are asked to do so, or you are close friends. It is advisable to use titles, including professional titles such as doctor or professor, etc., wherever possible. Courtesy titles such as "Mr.", "Mrs.", or "Miss" are used for those without professional titles. Use "Sir" or "Ma'am" for strangers, and "Uncle" or "Aunty" for a person older than you.

Gestures

- Indians are usually very expressive in their facial expressions and hand gestures. Nodding the head up and down is usually considered positive, however, they have a unique nod that could be very confusing to a foreigner. The Indian nod or "Indian head wobble" can have varied meanings. It can express something like yes, no, maybe, sarcasm, appreciation, teasing someone, or just a dance move, etc., depending on the situation. The use of a head nod can also depend on the relationship between the people talking to each other.

- Keep in mind a few tips for understanding "Indian head wobble". A fast and continuous head wobble means that the person really understands. The more vigorous the wobbling, the more understanding there is. A quick wobble from side to side means "yes" or "alright". A slow soft wobble, sometimes accompanied by a smile, is a sign of friendship and respect.

- As in much of the world, to beckon someone, you hold your hand out, palm downward, and make a scooping motion with the fingers. Beckoning someone with the palm up and wagging one finger can be construed as an insult.

- The comfortable standing distance between two people in India varies with the culture. In general, Indians tend to stand about 3 to 3.5 feet apart. Whistling is considered impolite under any circumstances.

- The head is considered the seat of the soul by many Indians. Never touch someone else's head, not even a pat on the head of a child. Ears are considered sacred appendages, and to pull or box someone's ears is a great insult. Always use your right hand to eat. Avoid using your left hand to offer or accept a handshake, drink, food, money, gift, or card, as it is considered unclean. Therefore, left-handed people in India are still fighting prejudices and pushing for recognition.

- Pointing with a finger is rude. Indians point with the chin. Never point your feet at a person, as feet are considered unclean. If your shoes or feet touch another person, apologize.

3.5　Business Gift-Giving

- Giving gifts at a first business meeting is unusual because it is not customary. Gifts are usually not encouraged by organizations and governments to avoid any legal implications, and if given, they should not be too expensive to be taken as a bribe or too inexpensive to be considered an insult. Gifts can be given and reciprocated when the relationship has flourished.

- Sweets, bouquets, jewelry, perfumes, and scarves are quite neutral items to give. If money is given as a gift, make sure that it is in odd numbers, for example, 21 or 31 Indian rupees. Yellow, green, and red are considered to be lucky colors and are often used to wrap gifts. Gifts are not opened when received; instead, the recipient will put them aside and open them after the giver has left.

3.6　Business Outfit

- For business, it is normal for men to wear a button-down shirt, a suit, and a tie, depending on the formality of the meeting and the industry. However, a full-sleeved shirt with a tie is often acceptable in the warm summer climate. In the IT sector, the dress code is more casual, and you often find employees wearing casual T-shirts and jeans with sneakers. It is also quite acceptable for men to wear long cotton pajama bottoms and kurtas.

- Traditionally, women wear Indian clothes such as salwar kameez (long tunic and loose pants) or saris. Women are increasingly wearing pantsuits or blouses and shirts.

- When invited to social gatherings, it is acceptable to dress casually. If a foreigner wears traditional Indian clothes or costumes, it is appreciated and seen as an expression of friendship and keenness toward Indian culture. In informal situations, it is acceptable to wear jeans with a short-sleeved shirt or T-shirt as casual wear.

4 Tips: Making a Good First Impression

There is an old saying that goes, "You never have a second chance to make a first impression," and research finds that it usually only takes about three seconds to form a first impression of someone. Once people have formed an opinion of someone, it is difficult to change it. Whether you are networking with prospective investors or hosting an event for potential customers, knowing how to make a great first impression can mean the difference between failure and success. Here are some useful tips to help you make a good first impression.

- **Be on time.**
  Arriving early is the first step toward creating a great first impression. When you are going to meet someone for the first time, make sure you are on time. Plan to arrive a few minutes early and allow flexibility for possible delays in traffic or taking a wrong turn. This shows respect for the other person, which gets the relationship started on the right foot.

- **Present yourself appropriately.**

  Physical appearance matters. The person you are meeting for the first time does not know you, so your appearance is usually the first clue he or she has about you. For business and social meetings, dress appropriately. However, appropriate dress varies between countries and cultures, so it is something that you should pay particular attention to when in an unfamiliar setting or country.

- **Do your cross-cultural homework.**

  Before your first contact with your prospective clients, find out more about their country and culture—not just areas such as history or traditions, but also their likely values, behaviors, and expectations of you. However, always bear in mind the dangers of cultural stereotyping. Remember that doing cross-cultural homework also includes knowing your own culture. You need to think about how you might be perceived by clients from other cultures.

- **Pay attention to your posture.**

  Good posture not only makes you look great, but also makes you feel more confident. Stand up straight and lift your head up. Project a positive attitude even in the face of criticism or in the case of nervousness.

- **Be open and confident.**

  Greet with a firm handshake (in cultures where this is acceptable), which can show that you are confident or make the other person feel like you are truly interested in meeting them. Smile so you can put both yourself and the other person at ease. Make eye contact.

- **Use small talk.**

  Conversations are based on verbal give and take. It may be helpful to prepare some questions for the person you are meeting beforehand, or take a few minutes to learn something about him or her. This can be a great way to open the conversation and keep it flowing.

First impressions are a part of our everyday lives, both in and outside the realm of business. Making a great first impression can help you share your ideas or vision with a more receptive, open, and willing audience, and it will also help you establish your credibility, especially if you are new to a specific market or niche in business. When an investor, prospective customer, or business associate views you in a positive and professional light, it is much easier to move forward toward the goals and milestones you have set in place.

Exercises

5.1   Fact Files

Directions: Complete the following table and find the key facts about India.

Official Name	
Capital City	
Official Language(s)	
Currency	
Population (Year 2022)	
The National Flower	
Current President	

5.2   Compound Dictation

Directions: Listen to the passage and fill in the blanks with the words or expressions that you hear.

India occupies the greater part of South Asia. Its government is a constitutional (1)_____ that represents a highly (2)_____ population consisting of thousands of (3)_____ groups and likely hundreds of languages.

Due to the British rule of the subcontinent from 1858 to 1947, many British (4)_____ stayed in places, such as the (5)_____ system of government. India remains within the Commonwealth, and English continues to be a widely-used lingua franca, although Hindi is its official language.

Despite continued domestic challenges and economic (6)_____, contemporary India witnesses increasing physical (7)_____ and cultural dynamism. All the achievements can be seen in its well-developed (8)_____ and highly-diversified industrial base, in its (9)_____ of scientific and engineering personnel (one of the largest in the world), in the pace of its agricultural expansion, and in its rich and (10)_____ cultural exports of music, literature, and cinema.

5.3 True or False: Indian Customs and Etiquette

Directions: Put T for true or F for false for each of the following statements.

(   ) 1. Shaking your head from side to side is a non-verbal signal for "no" in India.

(   ) 2. In India, the caste system has been outlawed by the government.

(   ) 3. During a group meeting, it is customary to greet the youngest member first.

(   ) 4. Feet are considered unclean in India and you should never point your feet at a person.

(   ) 5. Indians appreciate punctuality, which they always put into practice.

5.4 Multiple Choice: To Know More About India

Directions: Mark the correct answer to each question. Look up the following facts on the Internet or in some reference books and try to get more background information.

1. The Council of States in India has a maximum of _____ seats.

   A. 250   B. 545   C. 275   D. 345

2. Indian executives prefer appointments between _____.

   A. 11:00 a.m. and 5:00 p.m.   B. 3:00 p.m. and 4:00 p.m.

   C. 9:00 a.m. and 12 a.m.   D. 8:00 a.m. and 9:00 p.m.

3. Which Mughal Emperor was deported to Rangoon by the British?

   A. Bahadur Shah Zafar.   B. Bahadur Shah II.

   C. Akbar Shah I.   D. Bahadur Shah I.

4. Hindus do not eat _____ and Muslims do not eat _____.

   A. beef; pork   B. pork; mutton

   C. mutton; beef   D. fish; beef

5. The _____ is considered as the seat of the soul by many Indians.

   A. heart   B. head   C. waist   D. stomach

5.5   Case Study

Directions: Read the following case and answer the questions.

> Li Ming is a toy manufacturer in China. One day, he attended a business banquet hosted by his new Indian business associate. To show his love for dosa, a typical South Indian staple, Li Ming picked it up with both hands and gulped it down. He seemed to enjoy the food a lot, but he found that the Indian associate looked a bit awkward.

1. Did Li Ming do something wrong when he enjoyed the meal? Why or why not?
2. Conduct further research and share your understanding of the dining etiquette in India.

6 A Mini Business Project

Directions: Suppose that you have been shortlisted for an interview with Huawei, a leading global ICT and network energy solutions provider in China. How can you make a good first impression at the interview? Please explain how you are going to prepare based on the following outline.

- researching the company and the position offered before the interview;
- making a list of common interview questions and preparing your answers;
- preparing appropriate attire;
- minimizing your stress during the interview.

Note: You or your team is asked to prepare a presentation using PowerPoint slides, and write an executive summary using Microsoft Word. You may use appropriate visual aids (e.g., video clips) to support your presentation, and you may also refer to the sample project files online for reference.

Words and Expressions

abstinence	/'æbstɪnəns/	n.	节制
affiliation	/əˌfɪliːˌeɪʃən/	n.	从属关系；隶属
alleviation	/əˌliːviˈeɪʃn/	n.	减轻，缓和；镇痛物
appendage	/əˈpendɪdʒ/	n.	附加物；附属物
Aryan	/'eəriən/	n.	雅利安人
assertive	/əˈsɜːtɪv/	adj.	坚定自信的；果断的
Bangladesh	/ˌbæŋɡləˈdeʃ/	n.	孟加拉国（南亚国家）
Bhutan	/buːˈtɑːn/	n.	不丹（印度东北部一个国家）
bureaucracy	/bjʊəˈrɒkrəsi/	n.	官僚制度；官僚主义；官僚作风
Burma	/'bɜːmə/	n.	缅甸（东南亚国家，也称 Myanmar）
caste	/kɑːst/	n.	（印度社会中的）种姓
communal	/kəˈmjuːnl/	adj.	公共的；群体的，团体的
construe	/kənˈstruː/	v.	诠释，理解
credibility	/ˌkredəˈbɪləti/	n.	可靠性；可信度
dent	/dent/	n.	凹痕
Devanagari	/ˌdeɪvəˈnɑːɡəri/	n.	梵文
entangle	/ɪnˈtæŋɡl/	v.	使纠缠；卷入；使混乱
gratification	/ˌɡrætɪfɪˈkeɪʃn/	n.	满足；令人喜悦的事物
Hindi	/'hɪndi/	n.	印地语（印度官方语言之一，尤通用于印度北部）
instrumental	/ˌɪnstrəˈmentl/	adj.	起作用的
kurta	/'kɜːtə/	n.	（印度）宽松无领长衬衫
monopoly	/məˈnɒpəli/	n.	垄断，垄断权
Mughal	/'muːɡɑːl/	n.	莫卧儿人
obligate	/'ɒblɪɡeɪt/	v.	（使）负有法律（或道义）责任；使……有义务（做某事）
ostentatious	/ˌɒstenˈteɪʃəs/	adj.	招摇的；卖弄的；夸耀的；铺张的；惹人注目的
partition	/pɑːˈtɪʃn/	v.	分割；使分裂
Persian	/'pɜːʃn/	n.	波斯人
pharmaceutical	/ˌfɑːməˈsuːtɪkl/	adj.	制药的
phenomenal	/fəˈnɒmɪnl/	adj.	非凡的；杰出的
provisional	/prəˈvɪʒənl/	adj.	临时的；暂时的
reciprocate	/rɪˈsɪprəkeɪt/	v.	报答，回报；（感情上）回应

sari	/'sɑːrɪ/	n.	莎丽（南亚妇女裹在身上的长巾）
satrapy	/'seɪtrəpi/	n.	总督辖地
simplistic	/sɪm'plɪstɪk/	adj.	过分简单化的；过分单纯化的
subcontinent	/ˌsʌb'kɒntɪnənt/	n.	次大陆
subordinate	/sə'bɔːdɪnət/	n.	部属，下级；从属，次要
subsequently	/'sʌbsɪkwəntli/	adv.	后来；随后
surpass	/sə'pɑːs/	v.	超过
tariff	/'tærɪf/	n.	（政府对进出口货物征收的）关税；关税表
be bounded by			与……接壤
generic drug			仿制药
Salwar Kameez			莎尔瓦卡米兹女装（印巴妇女穿的一种长开襟衬衣）

Notes

Scan the QR code for more information about Indian culture.

Unit 3

Japanese Culture, Customs, and Business Etiquette

Japan: Overview

1.1　Geography and Demographics

Geography

Japan is an island country located in the Pacific Ocean, east of China, Korea and Russia. Its four main islands constitute at least 97% of the total land area. Situated in the area known as the "Ring of Fire" at the meeting place of several tectonic plates, Japan has many volcanoes and suffers frequent earthquakes. Sometimes these earthquakes result in huge and fatal tsunamis that cause severe damage and casualties. Japan's highest mountain peak, known as Mount Fuji, is actually a volcano, the last eruption of which took place in the year 1707.

Population and People

Japan had a population of 125.1 million in 2022. The population is very dense, mostly in the metropolitan areas such as Tokyo, Yokohama, Osaka, Kyoto, Kobe, and Kawasaki. Tokyo, the capital of Japan, is the largest metropolitan city in Japan with the highest concentration of population.

Language

Japanese is the official language of Japan. It is a complex and subtle language, which is spoken nowhere else in the world as a primary language. There are at least four different levels for expressing politeness in Japanese, of which Japanese women always use one of the more deferential forms. Communication in Japan is often marked by great subtlety. Information is left unspoken and yet can be perfectly understood.

1.2　History, Economy, and World Influence

History in Brief

The land of Japan has been occupied for thousands of years, and the current emperor's dynasty is said to have been founded in 660 BCE. Historically, Japan resisted outside influences, and it often closed itself off from foreigners. However, the United States forcibly opened Japan to foreign markets in 1853 when Commodore Perry sailed his fleet into Tokyo Bay.

What Westerners consider as World War II (1931–1945) was only part of a long-running Asian war in which Japan invaded neighboring nations. Korea was annexed by Japan in 1910, and China was invaded in 1931. The local Chinese troops fought heroically back and thus started Japan's all-out aggression against China and China's War of Resistance against Japanese Aggression. The Japanese aggression caused 35 million deaths and casualties of Chinese people and US$600 billion of economic losses in China. China won the war and Japan surrendered to the Allies in 1945 (14 years later), after which it was occupied by the United States until 1952.

With the aim of demilitarizing and democratizing Japan during its occupation after World War II, the United States instituted many reforms including a decrease in the power of the emperor and decentralization of the government. However, the Japanese have recentralized their government in the past 40 years.

Economy in Brief

Japan is one of the most developed, free-market economies in the world. It is the third largest economy by nominal GDP and the fourth largest by purchasing power parity in 2022, according to the World Bank. It has a well-educated, industrious workforce and its large, affluent population makes it one of the world's biggest consumer markets.

Manufacturing has been the most remarkable and internationally renowned feature of Japan's economic growth. Advanced manufacturing and services now account for the majority of Japan's GDP and employment while primary industries, including agriculture, account for just one percent of GDP. Japan is the world leader in the manufacture of electrical appliances, electronics, automobiles, ships, machine tools, optical and precision equipment, machinery, and chemicals.

Japan's service sector, including financial services, plays a far more prominent role in the economy, accounting for about 75% of GDP. In 2021, Japan Exchange Group was the world's fifth largest stock exchange by market capitalization.

The animation industry is one of Japan's most visually distinctive media industries. In 2019, the combined revenue of the domestic market and the overseas market of the animation industry reached a record of about 2.51 trillion Japanese yen. Overseas revenue in particular, showed a strong growth trajectory in recent years and overtook domestic revenues for the first time in 2020. By 2025, the animation industry is expected to reach a value of $30 billion with over 60% of that revenue to come from overseas.

International trade contributes significantly to Japanese economy, with exports equivalent to approximately 16% of GDP. Japan has few natural resources and its agricultural sector is heavily protected. Japan's main imports include mineral fuels, raw materials, and food.

When Shino Abe was in power as the Prime Minister of Japan, his government implemented a comprehensive policy package known as Abenomics, aimed at reviving the Japanese economy after two decades of deflation, while still maintaining fiscal discipline. This strategy has helped to revitalize the Japanese economy.

World Influence

Japan's economy was the world's second largest from 1968 to 2010, when it was overtaken by China. In 2018, Japan was the world's fourth largest importer and the fourth largest exporter. It has the world's second largest foreign-exchange reserves, worth close to $1.4 trillion. Japan is a member of both the Group of Seven (G7) and the G20.

Japan's competitive edge is now based on its technology to innovation. Innovative technologies and ideas developed in Japan are changing the way people live, not just in Japan but possibly, all around the world. Based on its belief that it is innovation that will resolve the issues they face in the future, the Japanese government is committed to making Japan the first country to prove that it is possible to grow through innovation, even as its population declines. As such, the Japanese government is encouraging various players, including start-ups and "hidden gems" among small- and medium-sized enterprises, to come up with brand-new and innovative ideas to provide the world with solutions to the problems it is facing.

Society 5.0 is Japan's vision for the next step in human evolution after the hunter-gatherer, agrarian, industrial and information society stages. It aims to enhance industrial competitiveness and help establish a society that is more attuned to individual needs. Attention is being focused on the vast potential of accumulating data, and on new technologies of the Fourth Industrial Revolution, which can be harnessed to find solutions to social issues such as the declining birth rate, aging population, and environmental and energy issues.

1.3　Japan's Holidays

There are 16 national holidays in Japan. The National Foundation Day (Kenkokukinen-no-Hi) of Japan is celebrated on February 11th to remind Japanese people of the nation's founding and to foster their love for the nation. The Japanese New Year's Day (Ganjitsu, 元日) is an annual festival with its own custom. Since 1873, the official Japanese New Year has been celebrated on January 1 of each year.

Table 3–1　A List of Some Main Holidays in Japan in 2022

Day	Date	Holiday Name
Saturday	Jan. 1	New Year's Day
Monday	Jan.10	Coming-of-Age Day
Friday	Feb. 11	National Foundation Day
Wednesday	Feb. 23	The Emperor's Birthday
Monday	Mar. 21	Vernal Equinox Day
Tuesday	May 3	Constitution Memorial Day
Wednesday	May 4	Greenery Day
Thursday	May 5	Children's Day
Monday	July 18	Marine Day
Thursday	Aug.11	Mountain Day
Monday	Sep. 19	Respect for the Aged Day
Friday	Sep. 23	Autumnal Equinox Day
Monday	Oct. 10	Health-Sports Day
Thursday	Nov. 3	Culture Day
Wednesday	Nov. 23	Labor Thanksgiving Day

2 Japanese Cultural Orientations

Japanese culture is a blend of ancient traditions and modern innovations that have been shaped by the country's history, geography, and social norms. Key aspects of Japanese culture include a strong emphasis on respect, harmony, and community, as well as a deep appreciation for beauty and nature. The following section provides an overview of six major cultural orientations that are fundamental to Japanese culture.

• Power Distance

With an intermediate score on this dimension, Japan is a borderline hierarchical society. Although it is safe to say that Japanese are always conscious of their hierarchical position in any social setting and act accordingly, Japanese culture is not as hierarchical as some other Asian cultures. This may seem surprising to some foreigners who experience Japan as extremely hierarchical due to their business experience of the painstakingly slow decision-making process. It is true that all the decisions must be confirmed by each hierarchical layer and finally by the top management. However, paradoxically, this shows that in Japanese society there is no single individual who can make autocratic decisions as there are in more hierarchical societies. Another example of not-so-great power distance is that Japan has always been a meritocratic society. There is a strong belief in the Japanese education system that everybody is born equal and that anyone can get ahead and become anything if he or she works hard enough.

• Individualism vs. Collectivism

With an above-intermediate score on individualism, Japanese society still shows many of the characteristics of a collectivistic society, including placing the harmony of the group above the expression of individual opinions, and a strong sense of shame about losing face. Nevertheless, Japanese society is not as collectivist as many other Asian countries. One explanation for this is that Japanese society does not have an extended family system that forms the basis of the more collectivist societies of China and the Republic of Korea. Japan has always been a paternalistic society where the family name and assets were passed down from the father to the eldest son and therefore the younger siblings had to leave home and make their own living with their own core families. One seemingly paradoxical example is that Japanese people are famous for their loyalty to their companies. However, company loyalty is something that people have chosen for themselves. It is thus an individualist choice. The Japanese in-group could therefore be described as situational, while in more collectivist cultures, people are loyal to their inner group by birth, such as their extended family and their local community. So it's not surprising that Japanese people may be considered as collectivist by Western standards but as individualist by Asian standards. They also seem to be more private and reserved than many other Asians.

• Masculinity vs. Femininity

Japan has a very high score on the masculinity dimension. Japanese society is one of the most masculine in the world. However, combined with its mild degree of collectivism, the assertive and competitive individual behaviors which we often associate with masculine cultures, are not so often seen in Japan. What is more common is extreme competition among groups. From a very young age, even as young as at kindergarten, children learn to compete for their groups on sports days (traditionally red teams against white teams).

This group competition is also obvious in corporate Japan, where employees are most motivated when they are fighting in a winning team against their competitors. The pursuit of excellence and perfection in every aspect of life, including in their material production (monodukuri), in material services (e.g., in hotels and restaurants) and in presentation (e.g., gift wrapping and food presentation) is an expression of masculinity in Japan, as is the notorious Japanese workaholism.

• Uncertainty Avoidance

Japan scores very high on this dimension, making it one of the most uncertainty avoiding countries on earth. This is often attributed to the fact that Japan is constantly threatened by natural disasters including earthquakes, tsunamis, typhoons, and volcanic eruptions. Living with the threat of such natural disasters, the Japanese have learned to prepare themselves for any situation. This is true not only for emergency plans and precautions for sudden natural disasters, but also for every other aspect of society. For example, more time and effort is put into feasibility studies, and all of the possible risk factors must be worked out well in advance of any project beginning. Managers ask for all the detailed facts and figures before making decisions. It is safe to say that in Japan, everything is prescribed for maximum predictability. This high need for uncertainty avoidance is one of the reasons why it is so difficult to introduce changes in Japan.

• Long-term vs. Short-term Orientation

Japan scores as one of the most typical long-term oriented societies. Japanese people see their lives as a very short moment in the long history of mankind. According to Japanese culture, you are supposed to do your best in your lifetime and that is all you can do. In Japanese corporations, the value of long-term orientation is constantly reflected in the high rate of investment in research and development (R&D), even in difficult economic times, and in priority to steady growth of market share rather than to a quarterly profit. They all serve to ensure the longevity of the companies. The idea behind it is that the companies are not here to make money every quarter for the shareholders, but to serve the stakeholders and society at large for many generations to come.

• Indulgence vs. Restraint

Japan has a low score on indulgence, indicating a culture of restraint. Restraint societies have a tendency to cynicism and pessimism. Also, in contrast to indulgent societies, restrained societies do not put much emphasis on leisure time, and they control the gratification of their desires. Japanese people with this orientation have the perception that their actions are restrained by social norms and they feel that indulging themselves may be frowned upon.

Japanese Business Practices and Etiquette

3.1 Business Appointments

- The workweek in Japan is generally 48 hours, over a period of 5.5 working days, with no overtime pay. Recently, however, large firms have begun to introduce a five-day week. Few executives take their work home with them.

- Office hours are 9:00 a.m. to 5:00 p.m. or 5:30 p.m. Many people go out for dinner and then return to the office where they work until 9:00 p.m. or 10:00 p.m.

- During holidays, banks and offices are closed, while stores remain open. During three weeks of the year (New Year's holidays, December 28 to January 3; Golden

Week, April 29 to May 5; and Obon, in mid-August), many people visit the graves of their ancestors. Conducting business and traveling are difficult during these periods.

3.2   Business Negotiations

- Be sure to incorporate the word sumimasen すみません (Sorry...) into your conversations when in Japan. Instead of a literal translation of "sorry", sumimasen means "I'm sorry to have troubled you, but thank you." Don't be ingratiating for fear of offending. Just be polite.

- Since age equals rank, show the greatest respect to the oldest members of the Japanese group with whom you are in contact. Negotiations begin at the executive level and continue at the middle level (working level).

- "Connections" are very helpful in Japan. Therefore, choose your intermediaries carefully. Intermediaries should not be part of either company involved in the deal. If you don't have a connection, a personal phone call is better than an e-mail or a letter, as e-mails or letters may not even be answered.

- Don't make accusations or reject anything directly. Be indirect. A Japanese response "I'll consider it" may actually mean "No".

3.3   Business Entertaining

- Business entertaining usually occurs after business hours, and very rarely in your host's home. You will be entertained often, sometimes at short notice. While the first evenings will probably be spent going from bar to restaurant, you may suggest alternatives later. These may include Sumo wrestling or karaoke bars, where you sing along with a video.

- When you are taken out, your host will treat you. Allow your host to order for you (this will be easier, too, since menus are generally in Japanese). Be enthusiastic during the meal and show great appreciation afterward. While business entertaining is primarily for building friendships rather than for doing business, you may not discuss business while eating.

- If you are invited to a Japanese home, be aware that this is a great honor, and you should show great appreciation. When entering a Japanese home, take off your shoes at the door. You will wear one pair of slippers from the door to the living room, where you will remove them. Inside a room, you will sit cross-legged, or with your legs to the side, around a low table with the family. You may be offered a backrest.

- Meals are long, but the evening usually ends at about 11 p.m. Never point your chopsticks at another person. When you are not using them, you should line them up on the chopstick rest. Use both hands to hold a bowl or a cup that you wish to be refilled.

3.4 Business Protocol

- In Japan, the bow is their traditional greeting. If someone bows to greet you, observe carefully. Bow to the same depth as you have been bowed to, because the depth of the bow indicates the status relationship between two people. As you bow, lower your eyes. Keep your palms flat against your thighs. Japanese handshakes will often be weak. Do not interpret this as a lack of assertiveness.

- Use last names plus "san", meaning Mr. or Ms. Do not suggest that a Japanese call you by your first name.

- Japan is a high-context culture and even the smallest gesture carries great meaning. Therefore, avoid expressive arm and hand movements, unusual facial expressions, or dramatic gestures of any kind.

- Pointing is considered impolite. Instead, wave your hand, palm up, toward the object being indicated, as the Japanese do.

- Keep a smile, even when you are upset. A smile can mean pleasure, but it can also be a means of self-control, as it is used to hide displeasure. Laughter can mean embarrassment, confusion, or shock, rather than mirth.

- Silence is not as uncomfortable for the Japanese as it is for North Americans. Rather, it is considered useful. Direct eye contact is not the norm.

3.5 Business Gift-Giving

- Gift-giving is common practice in Japan. Gifts are often given at first business meetings. For the Japanese, the ceremony of gift-giving is more important than the objects exchanged. Don't be surprised by either modest or extravagant gifts.

- Take your clues from the Japanese with whom you work with. Allow them to present gifts first and make your gift of the same quality as theirs.

- The Japanese do not usually open gifts directly upon receiving them. If they do, they will be restrained in their appreciation. This does not mean that they do not like what you have given them.

- Good gifts are imported Scotch, cognac, electronic toys for children of associates or items made by well-known manufacturers. Foreign brands are always the best.

- Always wrap your gifts or have them wrapped by hotel or store services. It is best to buy the paper there, so as not to choose paper colors that are inappropriate in Japan (for example, black and white paper is unacceptable).

- If you are invited to a Japanese home, bring flowers, cakes, or candy. The flowers should not be white, as the color white is associated with death.

- Avoid giving gifts with even numbers of components, such as an even number of flowers in a bouquet. Four is an especially inauspicious number, so never give four of anything.

3.6   Business Outfit

- Men should wear conservative suits, and never appear casual.
- Slip-on shoes are the best, as they need to be removed frequently.
- Women should dress conservatively, keeping jewelry, perfume, and makeup to a minimum. Pants are not appropriate for women.
- Avoid wearing high heels as you will run the risk of towering over your Japanese counterparts.
- In summer, it is very hot in Japan, so bring cotton clothes. Be sure to have enough changes of clothes as the Japanese are very concerned with neatness.
- If you wear a kimono, wrap it left over right. Only corpses wear it wrapped right over left.

Tips: Writing an Effective Resumé

A resumé (sometimes spelled resume or CV) is a document created and used by a person to present his or her background, skills, and accomplishments. Employers use resumés throughout the hiring process to learn about the applicants and decide whether they are a good fit. Therefore, your resumé should be easy to read, summarize your accomplishments and skills, and highlight relevant experience. It's vital that you know how to market yourself and stand out from the pile.

While there are a few commonly used resumés styles, your resumés should reflect your unique education, experience, and relevant skills. You might consider having multiple versions of your resumés tailored to the jobs you're applying for. Here are the steps that will help you organize and design your resumés: (1) Pick the right resumé format and layout; (2) Mention your personal details and contact information; (3) List your work experience and achievements; (4) Mention your top soft and hard skills; (5) Tailor your information for the job advertisement; (6) Proofread your resumés.

When composing the resumé, consider the following key tips.

- **State big achievements first and don't be generic.**
  Include specific details about what you achieved in previous roles using power words like "launched", "influenced", "increased", or "decreased". Avoid overused words like "hardworking", while "team player" and "ambitious" are better expressions to make a hiring manager's eyes glaze over.

- **Keep it short and remove irrelevant or outdated experience.**
  Most people lose interest after two pages. Since the average hiring manager spends only a few seconds on each resumé they review, the resumé needs to be as concise as possible. Avoid including anything that occurred over 15 years ago, if it is not that important.

- **Tailor it to the job and be honest.**
  Match your skills to what your potential employer is looking for. Check and double-check the information included in the resumé, and never lie about yourself. It will come back to bite you. Just don't do it. Remember, being honest is always the best policy.

- **Make it readable and printable.**
  Use Times New Roman or Arial font, no smaller than 11 points. Set your margins no less than 0.5 inches all around. Save it as a PDF version and proofread all the words and expressions.

A solid resumé in hand will greatly increase your opportunities of earning a closer look and getting that interview.

Exercises

5.1   Fact Files

Directions: Complete the following table and find the key facts about Japan.

Official Name	
Capital City	
Official Language(s)	
Currency	
Population (Year 2022)	
The National Flower	
Current Prime Minister	

5.2   Compound Dictation

Directions: Listen to the passage and fill in the blanks with the words or expressions that you hear.

Japan is located in eastern Asia in the Pacific Ocean to the east of China, Russia, North Korea, and South Korea. It continues to evolve in a positive unification of (1)_____. Before conducting business with your Japanese counterpart, you need to do some homework on Japanese business culture and rules.

First is about the etiquette of exchanging business cards. For a Japanese businessman, business begins with the exchange of business cards. Following (2)_____, the card should be presented with both hands to show respect and politeness. It is best to have your information in English on the front of the card and in Japanese on the back. Also, don't put the card in your (3)_____. Put it in a case or a card holder if possible.

Second is about the (4)_____in Japanese corporations. This system is of great importance in Japanese business. In business meetings, the Japanese would (5)_____

_____ in order of (6)_____, with the most senior person at the short side of the conference table far from the door and the youngest one nearest to the door. Since an older age usually (7)_____ a higher rank, you should show the greatest respect to the oldest members of the Japanese group.

Third is about achieving (8)_____ in business. The Japanese are known for their (9)"_____". In a Japanese company, a business proposal should be made in the name of the group. And a success or an honor gained is usually attributed to the (10)_____ of the entire group rather than an individual. Accordingly, the reward also goes to the group.

5.3 True or False: Japanese Customs and Etiquette

Directions: Put T for true or F for false for each of the following statements.

(   ) 1. Exchanging business cards is a serious issue in Japan and you should handle a Japanese associate's business card with care.

(   ) 2. It is important to bear in mind that you should show greater respect to the senior in a Japanese company.

(   ) 3. It is customary for the Japanese to make a noise when eating noodles.

(   ) 4. In Japanese culture, as in many Western cultures, silence is seen as uncomfortable and thus should be avoided whenever possible.

(   ) 5. In Japanese culture, laughter is often used to hide feelings such as nervousness, shock, embarrassment, confusion, and disapproval.

5.4 Multiple Choice: To Know More About Japan

Directions: Mark the correct answer to each question. Look up the following facts on the Internet or in some reference books and try to get more background information.

1. When is the National Foundation Day in Japan?

   A. January 22.   B. February 11.   C. August 12.   D. March 20.

2. What is the meaning of "Kao" in Japanese?

   A. Face.   B. Harmony.   C. Loyalty.   D. Perfection.

3. In the negotiation process, a Japanese response "I'll consider it." may actually mean _____

   A. "I'll think about the proposal carefully."

B. "I agree with your proposal."

C. "No."

D. "It's none of your business."

4. Which one is not the national symbol of Japan?

   A. Sun.　　　　　B. Sakura.　　　　　C. Sake.　　　　　D. Sword.

5. When invited to a Japanese home for business entertaining, you are not supposed to _____.

   A. wear your shoes in the room

   B. sit cross-legged

   C. line up the chopsticks on the chopstick rest

   D. bring candy as a gift

5.5　Case Study

Directions: Read the following case and answer the questions.

In 1974, when US President Gerald Ford visited Japan, the CBS (an abbreviation of its former legal name Columbia Broadcasting System) Broadcasting Inc. was assigned to broadcast all of Ford's activities in the country.

Two weeks before President Ford's visit, CBS assigned a negotiator to Japan to discuss the details. The American representative of CBS, a young ambitious man, made a lot of demands and spoke his mind directly, but his Japanese counterpart only made some polite responses to him and no agreement was reached after the first round of talks.

Two days later, an important official of CBS flew to Japan, apologizing personally for the behavior of the young representative, and then asked what she could do to help with President Ford's visit. This time, the Japanese representative's attitude was different and soon an agreement was concluded.

1. Why did the Japanese representative change his attitude?

2. Conduct further research to find out how both sides finally reached an agreement in this case.

6 A Mini Business Project

Directions: Suppose that you will graduate in one year and plan to find a job after graduation. How can you stand out from the crowd and successfully get the opportunity for an interview? Please explain how to compose your resumé based on the following outline.

- find an appropriate position offered;
- present your contact information and academic background effectively;
- list your work experience and achievements;
- highlight your specific skills for the position;
- format your resumé effectively.

Note: You or your team is asked to prepare a presentation using PowerPoint slides, and write a resumé using Microsoft Word. You may use appropriate visual aids (e.g., video clips) to support your presentation, and you may also refer to the sample project files online for reference.

Words and Expressions

affluent	/ˈæfluənt/	*adj.*	富裕的
agrarian	/əˈgreəriən/	*adj.*	农业的；土地的；耕地的
annex	/əˈneks/	*v.*	并吞，强占
autocratic	/ˌɔːtəˈkrætɪk/	*adj.*	独裁的
cognac	/ˈkɒnjæk/	*n.*	（法国）科尼亚克白兰地，（法国）干邑白兰地
commodore	/ˈkɒmədɔː(r)/	*n.*	海军准将
corpse	/kɔːps/	*n.*	尸体
cynicism	/ˈsɪnɪsɪzəm/	*n.*	愤世嫉俗；犬儒主义
font	/fɒnt/	*n.*	字体；字型
gratification	/ˌgrætɪfɪˈkeɪʃn/	*n.*	满足；满意；快感；令人喜悦的事物

inauspicious	/ˌɪnɔːˈspɪʃəs/	*adj.*	不祥的；不吉的
industrious	/ɪnˈdʌstriəs/	*adj.*	勤奋的
ingratiating	/ɪnˈɡreɪʃieɪtɪŋ/	*adj.*	逢迎的；讨好的
kimono	/kɪˈməʊnəʊ/	*n.*	和服
meritocratic	/ˌmerɪtəˈkrætɪk/	*adj.*	精英管理的；任人唯才的
metropolitan	/ˌmetrəˈpɒlɪtən/	*adj.*	大都市的
mirth	/mɜːθ/	*n.*	欢笑；欢乐
notorious	/nəʊˈtɔːriəs/	*adj.*	声名狼藉的，臭名昭著的
optical	/ˈɒptɪkl/	*adj.*	光学的
paternalistic	/pəˌtɜːnəˈlɪstɪk/	*adj.*	家长式的；专断的
prescribe	/prɪˈskraɪb/	*v.*	规定；命令；指示
revitalize	/ˌriːˈvaɪtəlaɪz/	*v.*	使恢复生机；使复兴
Scotch	/skɒtʃ/	*n.*	苏格兰威士忌酒
sumo	/ˈsuːməʊ/	*n.*	（日本）相扑
tectonic	/tekˈtɒnɪk/	*adj.*	地壳构造的
thigh	/θaɪ/	*n.*	大腿；股
trajectory	/trəˈdʒektəri/	*n.*	轨道；轨迹
tsunami	/tsʊˈnæmɪ/	*n.*	海啸
attuned to			与……协调，一致
extended family			大家庭（几代同堂的家庭）

Notes

Scan the QR code for more information about Japanese culture.

Unit 4

Filipino Culture, Customs, and Business Etiquette

The Philippines: Overview

1.1　Geography and Demographics

Geography

The Republic of the Philippines is located in Southeast Asia and surrounded by seas. Most of the mountainous islands are covered by tropical rainforest and are volcanic in origin. Cagayan River is the longest river in the country. Manila Bay, on the shore where the capital city of Manila lies, is connected to Laguna de Bay, the largest lake in the Philippines, by the Pasig River.

Due to its location on the western fringes of the Pacific Ring of Fire, the Philippines experiences frequent seismic and volcanic activities. Around 20 earthquakes are registered daily, although most of them are so weak that they cannot be felt. The last major earthquake in the Philippines was the Luzon earthquake in 1990. Some famous active volcanoes include the Mayon Volcano, Mount Pinatubo, and Taal Volcano. The eruption of Mount Pinatubo in June 1991 produced the second largest terrestrial eruption of the 20th century.

However, not all notable geographical features are so violent or destructive. The Puerto Princesa Subterranean River is a more serene legacy of the geological disturbances, and provides a suitable habitat for biodiversity conservation. It is home to some of Asia's most important forests.

Population and People

The population of the Philippines in 2022 was estimated to be 115.6 million. There was an increase in population from 2000 to 2019 of approximately 30 million, a 38.5% growth in that time frame, with an average annual growth rate of 1.7% in 2000–2018. Metro Manila, which is the most populous of the three defined metropolitan areas in the Philippines and the fifth most populous in the world, had a population of about 13 million in 2015, comprising almost 13% of the national population. The Philippines is a highly urbanized country, with a total urbanization rate across the country of 51.2%. Manila is one of the top ten richest cities in the

Philippines and also one of the wealthiest urban areas in the world based on its total assets.

Language

The Republic of the Philippines has two official languages: Tagalog (Pilipino or Filipino) and English, with eight major dialects: Tagalog, Cebuano, Ilocano, Hiligaynon or Ilonggo, Bicol, Waray, Pampango, and Pangasinense, and a total of 172 recognized languages, of which three are now extinct. The literacy rate is close to 90%.

1.2   History, Economy, and World Influence

History in Brief

The Philippine Islands have long been inhabited by humans, dating back far before the recorded history of mankind. While many Filipinos live in modern, bustling cities, there are others who live in isolated tropical jungles. The cultural diversity of the country began in the tenth century when Chinese people began to trade with the Filipinos.

The Portuguese navigator Magellan led a Spanish fleet to the Philippines in 1521 and named the islands after King Philip II of Spain. For 350 years, the country was under Spanish rule. In 1898, the United States took control of the Philippines after the Spanish-American War, but the Filipinos had no desire to be ruled by another colonial power and rose up against American rule. The insurrection against the United States lasted for more than 12 years, with hundreds of thousands of Filipinos losing their lives. The nation became the Commonwealth of the Philippines in 1935.

Early in World War Ⅱ, the Japanese conquered the Philippines. In 1945, the Philippines was liberated by Allied troops, made up of both Americans and Filipinos. The Philippines gained full independence on July 4, 1946.

Economy in Brief

The economy of the Philippines was the world's 32nd largest economy by nominal GDP according to the International Monetary Fund in 2021 and the 12th largest economy in Asia, and the third largest economy in the Association of Southeast Asian Nations (ASEAN) after Indonesia and Thailand.

The Philippines is primarily considered a newly industrialized country, with an economy in transition from one based on agriculture to one based more on services and manufacturing. Now it is one of the most dynamic economies in the East Asia Pacific region. With its increasing urbanization, its growing middle class and its large and young population, the country's strong consumer demand supported by a vibrant labor market and robust remittances is the root of the Philippines' economic dynamism. Business activities are buoyant and there have been notable performances in the service sector, including business process outsourcing (BPO), real estate, and the finance and insurance industries.

The momentum of economic growth in the Philippines has been reinforced by a sound economic foundation and a competitive workforce. The average annual growth rate increased to 6.4% between 2010 and 2019, taking the country to an upper middle-income country with a projected per capita income range of US$3,956–$12,235 in the coming years. Although the economic growth of the Philippines slowed in 2019, it was still strong at 6.0% year-on-year.

In recent decades, the Philippines has been investing in technology, buying its first satellite in 1996, and 20 years later, in 2016, launching its first micro-satellite, Diwata-1 on board the US Cygnus spacecraft. With a high concentration of cellphone users, the country has a high level of mobile financial services usage. Filipinos are also considered as the world's top Internet users.

World Influence

The Philippines is a founding member of the UN, the WTO, the ASEAN, the APEC forum, and the EAS. It has an open economy, trading freely with other economies, of which Japan, the United States, China, South Korea, and Germany are considered its top export markets. The Philippines's major exports include electronics, semiconductors, transport equipment, construction materials, and minerals.

Service industries such as tourism and business process outsourcing are considered as having some of the best opportunities for economic growth of the country. The BPO industry is made up of eight sub-sectors: knowledge process outsourcing and back offices, animation, call centers, software development, game development, engineering design, and medical transcription. The IT-BPO industry is playing an important role in the economic growth and development of the Philippines. In 2008, the Philippines actually surpassed India as the main center of BPO services in the world.

1.3   Philippines's Holidays

In the Philippines, the Labor Code specifies two types of holidays: the "regular holiday" and the "special non-working day". There is a difference in the amount of pay that employers are required to pay between the two types of leave.

The Philippines celebrated its independence from Spanish rule more than 120 years ago on the Independence Day. The Philippines flag was unfurled for the first time on June 12, 1898 at an inspiring celebration, which also featured the first public playing of the Philippines national anthem. General Emilio Aguinaldo was responsible for the declaration of independence, but it wasn't until 1962 that then-President Diosdado Macapagal made June 12 a public holiday through a presidential proclamation. Table 4−1 shows a list of main holidays in the Philippines.

Table 4−1   A List of Main Holidays in the Philippines in 2022

Day	Date	Holiday Name
Saturday	Jan. 1	New Year's Day
Tuesday	Feb. 1	Chinese New Year
Friday	Feb. 25	People Power Revolution
Saturday	Apr. 9	The Day of Valor
Thursday	Apr. 14	Maundy Thursday
Friday	Apr. 15	Good Friday
Saturday	Apr. 16	Black Saturday
Sunday	May 1	Labor Day
Tuesday	May 3	Eid'l Fitr
Sunday	June 12	Independence Day
Sunday	July 10	Eidul Adha
Sunday	Aug. 21	Ninoy Aquino Day
Monday	Aug. 29	National Heroes' Day
Tuesday	Nov. 1	All Saints' Day
Wednesday	Nov. 30	Bonifacio Day
Thursday	Dec. 8	Immaculate Conception Day
Sunday	Dec. 25	Christmas Day
Friday	Dec. 30	Rizal Day

2 Filipino Cultural Orientations

Filipino culture is heavily influenced by its history of colonization by Spain, the United States, and Japan, as well as its pre-colonial indigenous roots. With its rich and diverse history, the culture has evolved to incorporate a unique blend of Eastern and Western elements, resulting in a vibrant and dynamic expression. The cultural orientations of the Philippines are explored in greater detail below using the 6-D Model.

• Power Distance

The Philippines has an extremely high score on this dimension. This indicates that the Philippines is definitely a hierarchical society. People accept a hierarchical order in which everybody has their place and for which no further justification is needed. More specifically speaking, hierarchy in an organization is seen as reflecting inherent inequalities. In those organizations, centralization is popular, subordinates expect to be told what to do, and the ideal boss is a benevolent "autocrat".

• Individualism vs. Collectivism

With a relatively low score on the dimension of individualism, the Philippines is considered a collectivistic society. This can be easily seen in the close long-term commitment to the member "group", whether it is the family, the extended family, or extended relationships. Loyalty in a collectivist culture is the top priority, overriding nearly every other societal rule and regulation. Strong relationships are fostered, where each person takes responsibility for members of their own group. In collectivist societies, offense results in shame and loss of face. Employer and employee relationships are perceived in moral terms (just like a family relationship). Moreover, the employee's in-group is taken into consideration when hiring and promoting, and management refers to the management of groups.

• Masculinity vs. Femininity

The Philippines is a masculine society. This means that people live in order to work. Managers are expected to be decisive and assertive, and there is an emphasis on equity, competition, and performance. Conflicts are usually resolved by fighting them out.

• Uncertainty Avoidance

The Philippines has a low preference for avoiding uncertainty. Filipino people have a more relaxed attitude, believing that there should be no more rules than are necessary. Deviance from the norm can thus be tolerated, and if the rules are unclear or ineffective, they should be abandoned or changed. Consequently, in this country, schedules tend to be flexible, hard work is undertaken when necessary but not for its own sake, and innovation is not seen as threatening.

• Long-term vs. Short-term Orientation

The Philippines has a very low score on the long-term orientation, indicating that the Philippines is more a normative than a pragmatic society. People in such societies are normative in their thinking, exhibit great respect for traditions, do not have a strong tendency to save for the future, and have a focus on achieving quick results.

• Indulgence vs. Restraint

The Philippines has a relatively low score on indulgence, which indicates that the Philippines is a culture of restraint, suggesting a tendency to be cynical and pessimistic. Also, in contrast with indulgent societies, restrained societies do not put so much emphasis on leisure time and try to control the gratification of their desires. For instance, family is the basic and most important aspect of Filipino culture. Divorce is normally prohibited by law in the Philippines and marriage annulments are rare.

Filipino Business Practices and Etiquette

3.1 Business Appointments

• When doing business in the Philippines, you will be expected to be on time for meetings, and your Filipino business associates are likely to be reasonably punctual. It is acceptable to schedule your appointments far in advance of your arrival in the country. Appointments are best scheduled for mid-morning, mid-afternoon, or late afternoon.

- However, for social events, everyone is expected to be late, with the highest-ranking person arriving last. So as not to offend, it is suggested to ask your host (in private) what time you should actually arrive.

- It is very difficult to meet decision-makers without an introduction. It is usual to have many appointments with subordinates, and you will not only have to progress through levels of influence, but also have to progress through levels of formality, moving from introductions at social events, to semiofficial luncheons, and to scheduled business meetings. However, you can hire a skilled representative to help cut through some of the levels of management in order to get to the final decision-maker.

3.2 Business Negotiations

- The pace of business negotiations in the Philippines is quite slow, so don't expect to complete a complex transaction in one trip. In this country, social contacts are more important than business contacts. To do business with you, a Filipino must like you and feel comfortable dealing with you. Once they have accepted you, Filipinos are very sociable and love to talk. Be sure to speak in quiet, gentle tones as Filipinos revere harmony.

- It is usual for negotiations to be carried out in a formal and precise manner. You need to pay careful attention to the hierarchy of the negotiators, and always maintain a respectful and professional demeanor. The higher the negotiator's position, the more formal your interactions should be.

- The best way to ensure that a Filipino really means yes, is to get it in writing. If you can, it is advisable to get a written agreement at each stage of your negotiations as Filipinos feel honor-bound to fulfill written commitments.

- Never decline an invitation to a social event. Social interaction, most of which takes place outside of the office, is the foundation of doing business in the Philippines.

3.3 Business Entertaining

- Food is an integral part of Filipino culture, and social occasions always involve food. The standard Filipino greeting "Kumain ka na ba?" actually means "Have you eaten?". A great way to celebrate the conclusion of a business deal is by inviting your Filipino partners to a restaurant for a meal. The person who issues the invitation always pays, unless it is a woman. In this case, most Filipino businessmen will insist on paying the bill.

- You should invite the wives of your business partners to dinner, but not to a luncheon. You can expect to be invited to dinners and parties at the home of Filipino business partners. These parties will traditionally have numerous guests, including many relatives. You may or may not be individually introduced to everyone present. You should show respect to elders.

- Most households in the Philippines have servants, including a cook, so while you can compliment the hostess on the decor, you should be aware that she probably didn't prepare the food herself. Desserts are very popular in the Philippines, at both lunch and dinner, so if you are hosting a meal, don't forget to offer your guests dessert.

- Social events often end with dancing and singing. Don't be surprised if you are invited to sing. Although Filipino men tend to enjoy boisterous partying and hard drinking, public drunkenness is considered shameful, so be sure not to get out of control.

3.4 Business Protocol

Greetings

- Traditionally, in the Philippines, men and women have no physical contact in public. Men should not initiate a handshake with a Filipino woman, but instead wait for her to offer her hand. It is acceptable for foreign businesswomen to initiate a handshake with both Filipino men and women.

- When in the Philippines on business, men should shake hands firmly with Filipino men when introduced and later at subsequent meetings. It is usual for close female friends in the Philippines to hug and kiss when they meet. Close male friends may also exhibit extended physical contact, such as holding hands or leaving an arm around a friend's shoulder.

- The exchange of business cards may be more casual than in other Asian countries. If you give a Filipino businessperson your card, he or she may or may not reciprocate. It is the visiting businessperson who should be the first to offer their business card. Sometimes a Filipino business associate may give you a business card with their home phone handwritten upon it. This can be considered as an invitation to call them.

Titles/Forms of Address

- When addressing Filipinos, it is recommended to use their title followed by their surname. You will find that many professionals have titles because companies in the Philippines tend to reward their employees with titles rather than extra pay or responsibilities. Those without a professional title should be addressed, in English, as Mr., Mrs., or Miss, followed by their surname. Wives of men with important titles are sometimes addressed as "Mrs." followed by their husband's title, for example, Mrs. Senator or Mrs. Mayor.

- It is common in the Philippines to have a nickname. If a Filipino invites you to address them by their nickname, you are expected to do so. After such an invitation, you should reciprocate by inviting them to address you by your nickname. If you don't have one, it might be a good idea to make one up.

Gestures

- Filipinos use eye contact and eyebrow movement as a way to communicate a great deal of information. For example, they may greet each other by making eye contact and then raise and lower their eyebrows. Staring generally has a negative meaning in the Philippines. You should avoid staring at Filipinos, as they may interpret it as belligerence, and if you are stared at, you should look away.

- A traditional Filipino greeting of respect for elders is to place the elder's hand or knuckles on one's own forehead. To indicate an object or a direction, Filipinos often use a glance or purse their lips rather than pointing with their fingers, which could be mistaken as an insult.

- To beckon someone, you can hold your hand out, palm downward, and make a scooping motion with your fingers. If you have the palm up and wag one finger, it may be taken as an insult. Standing tall with your hands on your hips is always interpreted as an aggressive posture, and even as an aggressive challenge. In the Philippines, such belligerence is often met with belligerence.

3.5   Business Gift-Giving

- Gift-giving is an important aspect of Filipino society. The most common gifts are flowers and food, although in some situations it is the tradition to give a handful of small coins.

- If you are invited to a Filipino home, bring (or send in advance) flowers or a delicacy to your hostess. Don't take alcohol or a substantial amount of food, as this may suggest that your host cannot serve enough to satisfy the guests. Exceptions are made for specialty dishes or food from your home country. Sending a thank-you note afterward is appropriate, as is sending a small gift. After a dinner party, guests are often given extra food to take home with them.

- At Christmas, you will be expected to give a small gift, for example, a company calendar, to everyone you know or do business with. This includes all those who work for you, all of the service personnel you deal with on a regular basis (such as postal clerks and security guards), and anyone else who cooperates with you or helps you, such as the secretary of an important client.

- Following common Asian practice, Filipinos tend not to open gifts in the presence of the giver so as to avoid embarrassment if they don't like the gift. Filipinos also hate to appear greedy, and opening a gift immediately would give this impression, so don't be offended if your gift is set aside and ignored. The recipient will thank you for it at a later date.

3.6   Business Outfit

- Due to the climate, business dress is often casual, with men wearing dark trousers and a white, short-sleeved shirt without a tie, while women generally wear white long-sleeved blouses and skirts or pantsuits. Clothes should be neat, clean, and fashionable as Filipinos are particularly style conscious.

- As a visitor to the country, it is best to dress more conservatively until you are certain of the required degree of formality. Men should wear a suit and a

tie, while businesswomen are advised to wear white blouses and dark suits, pantsuits, or skirts.

- For formal occasions, such as going to the theater or to a formal dinner party, men may wear a business suit, but women should wear a cocktail dress. Women are only expected to wear long evening gowns on rare occasions, such as diplomatic functions.

- Nobody should wear shorts or sandals in public, unless they are at the beach. Because Filipinos tend to be competitively fashionable, some offices require their workers to wear uniforms.

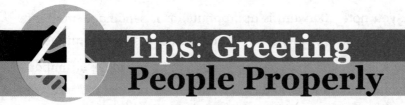

4 Tips: Greeting People Properly

Good greeting etiquette encourages trust from employees, customers and partners and sets the tone for your business dealings.

- **Greet over the phone.**
  When making a phone call to a customer, partner, or colleague, identify yourself by your name and company affiliation. Don't assume that the person on the other end recognizes your voice. Speak clearly and be polite. The same rules apply to receiving phone calls at your business. Have employees identify themselves by name along with the name of the business. Work with your employees to put this phone etiquette into practice and lead by example.

- **Greet through the e-mail.**
  E-mail has become an indispensable part of business communication. It tends to be less formal than traditional business letters. It is still smart to make a good impression when greeting customers, employees, and colleagues through e-mail. Take the time to include a proper greeting at the start. Begin with "Dear..." for more formal correspondence. When dealing with people you are more familiar

with, consider using "Hello (their name)". Taking the time to include a proper greeting in your e-mails shows that you respect the person you are e-mailing.

- **Use names and titles properly.**

In some countries, people prefer to be addressed with his or her last name preceded by the title while in other cultures, people insist on being greeted by their first names immediately after your first meeting. For instance, in Germany, titles such as "Herr Direktor" are sometimes used to indicate a person's prestige, status, and rank. First names are seldom used by those doing business in Germany. In Thailand, however, people address one another by first names and reserve last names for very formal occasions and written communications.

- **Show respect to the rules of physical distance.**

The physical distance between people greeting each other may vary as well. In Western countries, people stand about one and a half meters apart, so they can shake hands without taking a step forward, while in many Arab countries, the distance tends to be shorter—it's about the distance that allows the breath of someone to be felt on the other's face. In those countries and cultures, you could offend your business prospect by stepping back because you think he or she stands too close.

- **Be aware of the cross-cultural differences in greeting.**

Traditional greetings include shaking hands, hugging, kissing, and placing the hands in praying position. A handshake is widely accepted as the norm for greetings in international business settings. However, you'll need to vary the firmness of the handshake depending on the location. Western culture typically perceives a strong handshake as authoritative and confident, whereas many parts of the East perceive a strong handshake as aggressive, and may bow instead. The "wrong" greeting can lead to an awkward encounter.

In international business context, what is considered a proper greeting varies with the culture you are visiting. As a prospective businessperson who may do business abroad someday, you need to be aware of the cultural backgrounds and customs. Take the time to research the culture you are visiting and be prepared to practice proper etiquette.

5 Exercises

5.1 Fact Files

Directions: Complete the following table and find the key facts about the Philippines.

Official Name	
Capital City	
Official Language(s)	
Currency	
Population (Year 2022)	
The National Flower	
Current President	

5.2 Compound Dictation

Directions: Listen to the passage and fill in the blanks with the words or expressions that you hear.

The Republic of the Philippines is surrounded by sea. It is a (1)_____ state in archipelagic (群岛的) Southeast Asia. The Philippines was named after Prince Philip (later King Philip II) of Spain by the Spanish (2)_____ Ruy Lopez de Villalobos during his (3)_____ to the islands from 1542 to 1546.

The Philippines is a (4)_____ presidential constitutional republic, with the President of the Philippines acting as both the head of state and the head of government. It (5)_____ its independence from the Spanish Empire on June 12, 1898, following the (6)_____ of the Philippine Revolution.

It is a founding member of the United Nations and the Association of Southeast Asian Nations. It maintains 63 (7)_____ abroad as well as 180 consulates and three other representations in 2022.

The Philippines has been named as one of the Tiger Cub Economies,

(8)_____ Indonesia, Malaysia, Vietnam, and Thailand. It is (9)_____ one of Asia's fastest-growing economies. By 2035, the Filipino economy is (10)_____ to be the 25th largest in the world.

5.3   True or False: Filipino Customs and Etiquette

Directions: Put T for true or F for false for each of the following statements.

(   ) 1. Doing business in the Philippines is not a highly personalized affair, hence there is no requirement for a personal introduction by a mutual friend or business associate in order to carry out initial negotiations.

(   ) 2. When meeting your Filipino business associates for the first time, it is appropriate to address them with their title and family name.

(   ) 3. You should make continuous eye contact during the negotiation with a Filipino, but avoid staring at your partner.

(   ) 4. The pace of doing business in the Philippines is fast and the decision-making process tends to be highly efficient.

(   ) 5. A vital part of Philippine culture is the concept of "hiya" or "shame". To be shamed is the greatest form of disgrace to a Filipino.

5.4   Multiple Choice: To Know More About the Philippines

Directions: Mark the correct answer to each question. Look up the following facts on the Internet or in some reference books and try to get more background information.

1. Which country has a long relationship with the Philippines, in terms of economy, security, and people-to-people relations?

   A. Canada.   B. The United States.

   C. Australia.   D. Singapore.

2. _____ is a popular and iconic public utility vehicle, which has become a symbol of Philippine culture.

   A. Jeepney   B. Shinkansen   C. Wheelbarrow   D. Tram

3. Which language is not a major foreign language in the Philippines?

   A. Spanish.   B. Arabic.   C. French.   D. Chinese.

4. Who is dubbed as the "Father of Philippine Cinema"?

    A. Antonio Ramos.   B. Lino Brocka.

    C. José Nepomuceno.   D. Joyce Bernal.

5. Which is the main pairing of utensils seen at Filipino dining tables?

    A. Spoon and fork.   B. Spoon and chopsticks.

    C. Knife and fork.   D. Knife and spoon.

5.5   Case Study

Directions: Read the following case and answer the questions.

>   Mr. Tanaca is a Japanese businessman and had never worked overseas before he was sent to the Philippines last year to be the country manager for the company. In the first few weeks after he arrived in the country, he met some company executives who were hospitable and cheerful but did not give him their business cards or even did not carry cards with them. Later, Mr. Tanaca also found that the Filipino employees were not punctual and changed jobs every two to three years. It took him some time to get used to the differences.

1. What differences can you identify between Japanese and Filipino business practices based on Mr. Tanaca's case?

2. Conduct further research and try to elaborate the pros and cons of job-hopping in different cultures.

A Mini Business Project

Directions: Suppose that you are at a product launch, and there are several business partners from different countries, such as Germany, England, the US, and Thailand. Please explain how you would greet them and introduce them to your boss based on the following outline.

- using proper titles to address people from different cultures;
- greeting people from different cultures in an appropriate way;
- keeping appropriate physical distance;
- exchanging business cards effectively;
- being aware of the taboos in the process of greeting (Dos and Don'ts).

Note: You or your team is asked to prepare a presentation using PowerPoint slides, and write an executive summary using Microsoft Word. You may use appropriate visual aids (e.g., video clips) to support your presentation, and you may also refer to the sample project files online for reference.

Words and Expressions

belligerence	/bə'lɪdʒərəns/	*n.*	斗争性；好战性
boisterous	/'bɔɪstərəs/	*adj.*	喧闹的；欢闹的
buoyant	/'bɔɪənt/	*adj.*	繁荣的
decor	/'deɪkɔː(r)/	*n.*	装饰风格
demeanor	/dɪ'miːnə(r)/	*n.*	风度；举止；行为
knuckle	/'nʌkl/	*n.*	指关节
normative	/'nɔːmətɪv/	*adj.*	规范的；标准的
override	/ˌəʊvə'raɪd/	*v.*	凌驾于；比……更重要
remittance	/rɪ'mɪtns/	*n.*	汇款额；汇款，汇寄
revere	/rɪ'vɪə(r)/	*v.*	尊敬；崇敬
sandal	/'sændl/	*n.*	凉鞋

seismic	/ˈsaɪzmɪk/	*adj.*	地震的；地震引起的
serene	/səˈriːn/	*adj.*	安详的；宁静的
terrestrial	/təˈrestriəl/	*adj.*	陆地的；地球的
unfurl	/ˌʌnˈfɜːl/	*v.*	展开；使……临风招展
purse one's lips			噘嘴
wag one finger			摇晃一根手指

Notes

Scan the QR code for more information about Filipino culture.

Unit 5

Thai Culture, Customs, and Business Etiquette

Thailand: Overview

1.1 Geography and Demographics

Geography

Thailand is made up of two broad geographic areas: the larger main section in the north and a smaller peninsular extension in the south. The main body of Thailand is bordered by Myanmar (Burma) in the west, Laos in the north and east, and Cambodia in the southeast. Thailand's location in the tropical monsoon zone of mainland Southeast Asia and its topographic features have a major influence on the climate of the country, affecting the distribution of rainfall throughout the year.

From May to October, the warm, humid air masses of the southwest monsoon flow northeastward from the Indian Ocean, resulting in heavy rainfall over the whole area, with the peak in September. Between November and February, the winds change direction, and the northeast monsoon brings cool, drier air flowing in a southwesterly direction, allowing most of the country to experience cooler temperatures. March and April are characterized by stagnant air which produces a distinct hot-and-dry inter-monsoonal period.

Population and People

Thailand's population was about 71.7 million in 2022. The vast majority of the inhabitants of Thailand are ethnic Thais, who make up about 80% of the population. There is also a large ethnic Chinese minority, comprising about 14% of the population. Other ethnic minorities include the Malay, Khmer, Mon, and Vietnamese. Northern Thailand also is home to small mountain tribes such as the Hmong, Karen, and Mein, with a total population of less than 800,000.

Language

Thailand's official language is Thai, spoken by approximately 88% of the country's population. It is used as a medium of instruction in schools, by the media, and in all government affairs.

Most of the languages spoken in Thailand belong to one of four major language families: Tai (a subfamily of Tai-Kadai languages), Mon-Khmer (a subfamily of Austroasiatic languages), Austronesian, and Sino-Tibetan. English is also widely used in Thailand for business and many official purposes.

1.2   History, Economy, and World Influence

History in Brief

Evidence of human occupation in Thailand dates all the way back to 40,000 years ago. In the early days, a succession of tribal groups controlled what we now know as Thailand. The Mon and Khmer peoples established powerful kingdoms that included large areas of the country. In 1238, a Tai chieftain declared his independence from the Khmer and established a kingdom at Sukhothai. Thai people regard the founding of the Sukhothai Kingdom as the founding of their country. Sukhothai was succeeded in the 14th century by the kingdom of Ayutthaya.

In 1932, the system of government was changed from absolute monarchy to constitutional monarchy with the prime minister as the head of government and the king as head of state. In the year 1939, the name of the country was changed from Siam, and that is when Thailand got its name.

The 1980s saw the country change course toward a stable democracy, leading to the signing of its first ever constitution in 1997. The year 2001 marked another milestone, with the first government entirely elected by the people. King Rama IX had been the one stable factor throughout the decades of social unrest. This is one of the reasons why he was so beloved by the Thai people. Since 2016, Thailand has a new king, King Vajiralongkorn, son of the deceased King Bhumibol Adulyadej.

Economy in Brief

Thailand is Southeast Asia's second-largest economy which relies heavily on exports. Before the 1960s, the Thai economy was largely agricultural, producing rice and other food and goods for domestic consumption, and rice, rubber, teak, and tin for export. There was then a shift from agriculture to the promotion of the manufacture of textiles, consumer goods, and, eventually, electronic components for export. Thailand was well on its way to industrialization in the 1980s, despite the global economic crisis. In the mid-20th century when the national economy was developing rapidly, one of the most important factors of this growth was foreign investment.

The Thai economy depends mainly on automotive and electronics manufacturing exports (19%), financial services (9%), and tourism (6%). About half of the workforce is employed in the agriculture sector. Thailand is the world's top exporter of rice. The country also exports processed foods such as frozen shrimp, canned pineapple, and canned tuna.

Thailand's currency is called the Thai Baht. Its total GDP is $509 billion (nominal) and $1.2 trillion (PPP) in the year 2020. Its GDP growth rate is 4.1% in the year 2021. Its GDP per capita is $7,380 (nominal) and $18,280 (PPP) in the year 2020.

World Influence

As one of the earliest members of the UN (since 1946), Thailand has actively worked in cooperation with all UN agencies in Thailand, Southeast Asia and other parts of the world. It has been a WTO member since January 1, 1995 and a member of the General Agreement on Tariffs and Trade (GATT) since November 20, 1982.

Thailand is a key player in the ASEAN, an international organization that has 10 member countries in Southeast Asia. It is one of the founding members of ASEAN, together with Indonesia, Malaysia, the Philippines, and Singapore.

The kingdom is also committed to playing an active role in working to address global challenges in various fora including the ASEAN Regional Forum (ARF), the EAS, the APEC, and the Asia-Europe Meeting (ASEM).

1.3   Thailand's Holidays

Thailand is a nation of rich culture and traditions, with a myriad of holidays and festivals. They also celebrate several popular Western holidays. Thai holidays offer a wide variety of celebrations—some commemorate significant events in the country's history, while others are Buddhist observances. Thai holidays attract visitors from all over the world, with people flocking to see the grand spectacles and absorb the local culture of Thailand.

One of the most famous Thai holidays is Chulalongkorn Day. This holiday commemorates the life of King Chulalongkorn. It is celebrated every year on October 23, the anniversary of his birth in 1868. During this holiday, many people visit the countless memorials to Chulalongkorn and leave offerings there in his honor.

Songkran (Thai New Year) is one of the biggest and most important Thai holidays. It is on April 13 every year, but the holiday period extends from April 14 to April 15. This holiday is celebrated with parades, religious ceremonies, and festivities throughout the country. Water plays a big part in this holiday. The tradition of splashing water on people has grown into a multi-day water-fight, where water guns, buckets, and hoses are used to drench everyone in sight. If you are in Thailand during Songkran, be prepared to get wet. Table 5–1 shows a list of main holidays in Thailand.

Table 5–1   A List of Main Holidays in Thailand in 2022

Day	Date	Holiday Name
Saturday	Jan. 1	New Year's Day
Wednesday	Feb. 16	Makha Bucha
Wednesday	Apr. 6	Chakri Day
Wednesday	Apr. 13	Songkran
Sunday	May 1	Labor Day
Wednesday	May 4	H.M. King's Coronation Day
Monday	May 16	Visakha Bucha Day
Friday	June 3	H.M. Queen's Birthday
Wednesday	July 13	Asahna Bucha Day
Thursday	July 28	H.M. King's Birthday
Friday	July 29	Public Holiday
Friday	Aug. 12	H.M. Queen Mother's Birthday
Saturday	Sep. 24	Prince Mahidol Day
Thursday	Oct. 13	The Passing of King Bhumibol
Sunday	Oct. 23	Chulalongkorn Day
Monday	Oct. 24	Chulalongkorn Day (in lieu)
Monday	Dec. 5	King Bhumibol's Birthday
Saturday	Dec. 10	Thailand Constitution Day
Saturday	Dec. 31	New Year's Eve

2. Thai Cultural Orientations

Thai culture is a complex and multifaceted blend of ancient traditions, Buddhist beliefs, and modern influences. Its cultural heritage is shaped by centuries of history and tradition, preserved, and further celebrated in a variety of ways, from the intricately decorated temples and palaces to the vibrant festivals and traditional crafts. The following are brief summaries of Thai cultural orientation with the 6-D Model.

- **Power Distance**

Thailand scores relatively high on power distance, slightly lower than the average Asian countries. It is a society in which inequalities are accepted and a strict chain of command and protocol are observed. Each rank has its privileges and employees show loyalty, respect, and deference to their superiors in return for protection and guidance. This may lead to paternalistic management. Thus, the attitude toward managers is more formal, and the information flow is hierarchical and controlled.

- **Individualism vs. Collectivism**

With a very low score on the individualism dimension, Thailand is a highly collectivist country. This is manifested in a close long-term commitment to the member "group" (a family, extended family, or extended relationships). Loyalty to the in-group is paramount in a collectivist culture and overrides most other societal rules and regulations. The society fosters strong relationships where everyone takes responsibility for their fellow group members. In order to preserve the in-group, Thais are not confrontational and in their communication, a "yes" may not mean an acceptance or agreement. An offense leads to loss of face and Thais are very sensitive not to feel shamed in front of their group. Personal relationships are key to conducting business and it takes time to build such relationships.

- **Masculinity vs. Femininity**

Thailand scores relatively low on masculinity and is thus considered a feminine society. Thailand has the lowest masculinity ranking among the average Asian countries and the world average. This lower level is indicative of a society with less assertiveness and competitiveness, as compared to one where these values are considered more important and significant. This situation also reinforces more traditional male and female roles within the population.

- **Uncertainty Avoidance**

Thailand achieves an intermediate score on this dimension, which indicates a slight preference for avoiding uncertainty. In order to minimize or reduce this level of uncertainty, strict rules, laws, policies, and regulations are adopted and implemented. The ultimate goal of this population is to control everything in order to eliminate or avoid the unexpected. As a result of this high uncertainty avoidance characteristic, the society does not readily accept change and is very risk adverse. Change has to be seen for the greater good of the in-group.

- **Long-term vs. Short-term Orientation**

Thailand's low score on the long-term orientation dimension indicates that Thai culture is more normative than pragmatic. Thai people are normative in their thinking. They exhibit great respect for traditions, a relatively small propensity to save for the future, and a focus on achieving quick results.

- **Indulgence vs. Restraint**

With a relatively low score on indulgence, Thai culture has a preference for restrained lifestyle. The country disallows any form of gambling except for horse races and Thai lottery. Smoking is also forbidden in most public spaces in Thailand. Thais generally have a strong work ethic yet are simultaneously willing to be content with what they have. This attitude is also reflected in "sanuk", the effort to enjoy and be satisfied in whatever one does. It is a guiding principle in a business and work setting, meaning Thais will generally seek to make work a pleasant and enjoyable experience.

Thai Business Practices and Etiquette

3.1 Business Appointments

- When doing business in Thailand, it is imperative to make an appointment first. Face-to-face meetings are preferable to more impersonal forms of communication such as e-mail. At meetings, be sure to introduce the most senior person in your team first.

- It is a good idea to confirm the details of the meeting the day before. Arriving on time shows respect, although Thais often have a more relaxed view of time than is common in the West.

- The standard working week in Thailand is officially from Monday to Saturday, although some companies work until Friday or open only half a day on Saturday. Employees can work up to a maximum of 48 hours per week.

3.2 Business Negotiations

- To Thai businesspeople, negotiating is usually a joint problem-solving process. The buyer is in a superior position; both sides in a business deal own the responsibility to reach an agreement. They expect long-term commitments from their business partners and will focus mostly on long-term benefits.

- The primary negotiation style is cooperative and people may be open to compromising if viewed helpful in order to move the negotiation forward. Maintaining harmonious relationships throughout the process is vitally important.

- While each party is expected to pursue its own best interests, Thais disapprove of competitiveness and strive to find win-win solutions, avoiding confrontation and always leaving a way out for the other.

- The pace of negotiations may seem slow. Don't show any sign of impatience or frustration. In Thailand, the main purpose of the initial meetings is to get to know each other and to build a foundation upon which the relationship can be developed.

- When you are negotiating with Thai counterparts while conducting business, it is essential to be mindful of the importance of personal relations. Take time to build relations with your potential clients and do not settle for a premature business topic. Allow others to understand what your company is all about. Give them in writing about your products, services, and your business goals.

- In your discussions, you should emphasize the benefits your company can offer, but don't expect any quick decisions. Due to the paternalistic-style management, only the most senior managers have authority and responsibility, and the person who makes the decisions may not even be present at the meeting. It is helpful to try to identify exactly who the decision makers are and to cultivate them if possible. Such contacts in high places are essential for cutting through red tape.

- Keep in mind about the communication style, which means you have to be careful about the indirect nature of communication that the Thais prefer.

3.3   Business Entertaining

- Thais are very hospitable people, hence most meetings are organized over a meal or drinks and entertainment. Don't be the first to bring up business matters. Wait for the other party to switch topics at the table.

- Unlike in the West where the "head" of the table is the most important, the host or highest-ranking person usually sits in the middle of the table in Thailand. If you are the honored guest, you will sit opposite the host so that you can converse more easily. It is advisable to wait until you are shown to a seat by a member of your party, rather than choosing a seat yourself.

- If you are seated on bamboo mats on the ground, always position yourself in a way that you can avoid pointing your feet at anyone. Showing someone your feet is considered extremely rude in Thailand.

- If you are dining alone at a restaurant or street stall, it's common for the staff to ask you to sit with another group if the restaurant is busy. Don't be alarmed. It's perfectly normal in Thailand to dine with people you don't know.

- Unlike in many Western countries, you are not expected to finish all of the food on your plate. Finish whatever you can and only stop when you're full. It's never a good idea to waste food, but it's not seen as much of an issue in Thailand when compared to other places you might visit.

- At the end of the meal, don't immediately reach for the bill and don't argue over who will pay. Your host may have already asked for the check, or the group may be planning to split it. It is customary for the host or more senior (often the perceived wealthiest) person at the table to pay. In some instances, particularly in relationships between Thais and foreigners, the foreigner is expected to get the check. Fortunately, food in Thailand is typically very affordable.

3.4 Business Protocol

Greetings

- A general rule to remember is that the junior person offers the "wai" (the hands are raised in a prayer position and the head is slightly bowed) and the more senior person responds. As a foreigner, it is best to see which greeting you are offered and respond to it, rather than initiate the "wai". Foreigners can just smile and nod slightly in respect when they meet someone new.

- "Sawasdee" or "hello" in Thai is the most common and useful Thai greeting to learn. You'll hear a lot of Sawasdee kha/khap in Thailand. Sawasdee can also be used to say good morning, good afternoon, good evening, and even goodbye.

- Courtesy is very important to Thai people. Being polite and respectful to others is considered essential to maintaining good relationships. Speaking softly and smiling warmly will always help to create positive feelings.

- As a whole, Thai culture can be more relaxed than most countries. People may tend to inquire about you, by asking a lot of questions, some of which might be personal. But this is their way of getting to know more about you.

- In a business environment, like greeting your colleagues in the office, handshake is okay because the office culture is mostly borrowed from the West.

- Titles play a very important role in business etiquette. The people of Thailand are very polite and soft-spoken. They address the foreigners with their first names. However, if you are addressing Thai people, use the term "Khun". It is often used as a form of respect for people. Generally, "Khun" precedes a Thai name to show respect for the person.

Gestures

- Smile is ubiquitous to Thai culture. In general, it's always considered polite to return a Thai's smile as it's typically quite genuine. Most Thais believe being too serious is unhealthy and can cause illness, so smile away.

- The head is the most sacred place on the human body and like many cultures of Southeast Asia, it is forbidden to touch someone on their head. This is particularly true for children. A child's "kwan", or individual spirit, is not strong enough to be touched, and some Thais believe the child could become ill or experience nightmares if this taboo is broken.

- When presenting or receiving things, such as money, gifts, food, or business cards, it is respectful to exchange items using two hands, especially with someone you've just met or is older than you. In general, the left hand is considered unclean and is not used to eat, receive gifts, or shake hands.

- Traditionally, giving someone the "thumbs up" gesture is similar to giving them the middle finger—ultimately derogatory in nature. While adults in Thailand today have adopted its more international meaning of approval or a job well-done.

- As in many other Asian countries, you should avoid angering or insulting someone (causing them to "lose face"). Open criticisms and negative responses are seen as an insult to other people and can cause them to think disrespectfully of you. If you must give a negative response, do so indirectly.

- In Thailand, public displays of emotion are best avoided. It is considered inappropriate to show anger or a negative emotion in public.

3.5 Business Gift-Giving

- There are many occasions for celebration in the Thai calendar, and once you have been accepted as a long-term business partner, you are likely to be invited to some of these special occasions. If you are invited to the home of a Thai business associate, take a gift with you.

- Appropriate gifts include some carefully wrapped sweets, chocolate, or a basket of fruit. The royal colors of red and gold are appropriate for both ethnic Thai and Chinese-Thai households. Avoid green, black, or blue as they are associated with funerals.

- A bottle of imported liquor (such as single malt Scotch) is also appropriate for an executive. As in other Asian countries, Thais don't open gifts in the presence of the giver. You should expect the gift to be set aside when you give it to the receiver.

3.6 Business Outfit

- In Bangkok, business attire is more formal and conservative than in other parts of the country. Dark tones are usually acceptable and more expected than bright, vibrant colors. Stick to grays and browns since the color of black is only used at funerals. Businessmen in Thailand usually wear dark suits, white long-sleeved dress shirts with ties.

- It is common for men to wear darker, more conservative clothing. However, you might want to use a more breathable fabric like silk or cotton to combat the extreme temperatures in the country.

- If skirts are worn, they should be knee-length or longer. Shoulders should always be covered. Smart shoes and suitable socks are essential in case the shoes are to be removed.

4 Tips: Making Business Phone Calls

Business communication through phones is crucial for companies to maximize the benefits of live interaction and idea exchanging. The following tips describe how to make phone calls effectively.

- **Prepare for a call.**
  Preparing yourself before you pick up the phone will help you organize your thoughts and know exactly why you want to speak with someone. Use bullet points for the things you need to mention.

- **Research the person whom you need to call.**
  This is especially important if you don't know the caller personally. Know a bit about the person's background through his or her colleagues or via Internet searches. Say "hello", and introduce yourself and where you're calling from. It's polite to start with a bit of chit-chat, and keep it to just a minute or so.

- **Get down to the business of your call.**

  After greetings and introductions, shift to the real purpose of your call. Just don't make the transition too abrupt or obvious. Try making a segue to the purpose of your call, like: "I'm glad to hear that you're doing well. I'm calling to..."

- **Ask questions.**

  Ask questions to make the person feel included and to establish a connection. For instance, try things like: "We're thinking of scheduling a group meeting on the 26th. How does that sound to you, Alex?" or "We're hoping to get all of country managers together to discuss strategy for the next quarter. Do you have any ideas for that, Alex?"

- **Take notes during the call.**

  Jotting things down as you talk to the person has several benefits. It can help you listen attentively to anything the caller says, for instance. It also serves as a record of the call, in case you need to take any follow-up action or report on the call to someone else.

- **Clarify any follow-up actions that are necessary.**

  If you need to find out any information and get back to the person, make a note of this. Make sure to mention this clearly before you end the call. For example, you might say: "So Alex, I'll check with our suppliers about a timeframe for delivery, and get back to you on that, OK?"

- **Speak clearly and smile as you do.**

  Make sure to speak as clearly as possible. Do not speak too fast as the caller may not be able to hear you. Smiling as you speak also helps you sound more natural, even if the person can't see you.

- **End by thanking the person for their call.**

  It's just courteous to thank the person for taking the time to talk to you. Make sure to end with something like "Thanks so much for talking with me. Have a great day!"

If you're looking to make business phone calls more effective, apply the tips discussed above. Try to keep the conversation as light and positive as possible and don't forget about etiquette for making business phone calls.

Exercises

5.1 **Fact Files**

Directions: Complete the following table and find the key facts about Thailand.

Official Name	
Capital City	
Official Language(s)	
Currency	
Population (Year 2022)	
The National Flower	
Current Prime Minister	

5.2 **Compound Dictation**

Directions: Listen to the passage and fill in the blanks with the words or expressions that you hear.

Thailand is the second largest economy in Southeast Asia after Indonesia, bordering the Andaman Sea and the Gulf of Thailand. (1)_____ countries include Burma, Cambodia, Laos, and Malaysia. The (2)_____ consists of a mountain range in the west and a southern Isthmus that (3)_____ the landmass with Malaysia. The government system is a (4)_____ monarchy. The chief of state is the king, and the head of government is the (5)_____. Thailand has a mixed economic system in which there is a variety of (6)_____ freedom, combined with (7)_____ economic planning and government (8)_____. Its economic growth sectors include tourism, automotive, and (9)_____, which are supported by its well-developed transportation system, infrastructure, and communication systems. The tourism industry plays an important role in the Thai economy and (10)_____ an estimated 18.4% to the national GDP. Thailand is a member of the Asia-Pacific Economic Cooperation and the Association of Southeast Asian Nations.

5.3   True or False: Thai Customs and Etiquette

Directions: Put T for true or F for false for each of the following statements.

(   ) 1. When receiving a gift from your Thai counterpart, you should open it in their presence.

(   ) 2. In Thailand, showing emotions and losing one's temper in public is acceptable.

(   ) 3. You shouldn't schedule any meetings at the beginning or end of the day. Avoid these time-slots because of difficulties with transportation to the workplace.

(   ) 4. In Thailand, a welcome topic of discussion is one's occupation. Inquiring about people's job titles is a good icebreaker.

(   ) 5. You shouldn't touch your Thai colleague's head, as it is considered sacred in Thai tradition.

5.4   Multiple Choice: To Know More About Thailand

Directions: Mark the correct answer to each question. Look up the following facts on the Internet or in some reference books and try to get more background information.

1. Which city in northern Thailand is translated as "New Town"?

   A. Chiang Rai.   B. Chiang Mai.   C. Phuket.   D. Pattaya.

2. What is Thailand's main exported crop?

   A. Rice.   B. Corn.   C. Cereal.   D. Sugarcane.

3. How many provinces are there in Thailand?

   A. 56.   B. 76.   C. 74.   D. 62.

4. What is the currency in Thailand?

   A. Dinar.   B. SGD.   C. Kip.   D. Baht.

5. The Thailand New Year is celebrated in _____.

   A. July   B. March   C. April   D. February

5.5 Case Study

Directions: Read the following case and answer the questions.

> Alastair is a manager of a British company, paying a business visit to Thailand. One day, he met a local business associate in a bar after finishing a business meeting. During their conversation, Alastair made a joke about the Thai king and the royal family. The local business associate was embarrassed and quickly said goodbye to Alastair.

1. What went wrong in this case and why?

2. Conduct further research and make a comparison of Chinese and Thai people's attitudes toward the royal family.

6 A Mini Business Project

Directions: Suppose that you are a secretary in the manufacturing department of Shandong Iron & Steel Group Co., Ltd. You are asked to check the tracking information of an order from Brazil. Please explain how to prepare for the international phone call based on the following outline.

- identifying people who are responsible for the tracking information;
- making a list of inquiries before your call;
- introducing yourself and your purpose when you get through;
- taking notes during the call;
- paying attention to your manners during your phone call.

Note: You or your team is asked to prepare a presentation using PowerPoint slides, and write an executive summary using Microsoft Word. You may use appropriate visual aids (e.g., video clips) to support your presentation, and you may also refer to the sample project files online for reference. In addition, create a short dialog using the tips above and rehearse your dialog with your partner.

Words and Expressions

ambiguity	/ˌæmbɪˈɡjuːəti/	n.	模棱两可；不明确
assertiveness	/əˈsɜːtɪvnəs/	n.	自信；魄力
Buddhist	/ˈbʊdɪst/	adj.	佛教的
chieftain	/ˈtʃiːftən/	n.	酋长；首领
commemorate	/kəˈmeməreɪt/	v.	纪念；作为……的纪念
coronation	/ˌkɒrəˈneɪʃn/	n.	加冕礼
derogatory	/dɪˈrɒɡətri/	adj.	贬低的；贬义的
drench	/drentʃ/	v.	使湿透
fora	/ˈfɔːrə/	n.	论坛；讨论会（forum 的复数形式）
hose	/həʊz/	n.	软管，水龙带
Khmer	/kmeə(r)/	n.	高棉人；高棉语
monarchy	/ˈmɒnəki/	n.	君主国；君主制
monsoon	/ˌmɒnˈsuːn/	n.	季风；（印度等地的）雨季；季候风
Myanmar	/ˈmjænmɑː(r)/	n.	缅甸
myriad	/ˈmɪriəd/	n.	无数，大量
observance	/əbˈzɜːvəns/	n.	（节日的）纪念；宗教的仪式
paramount	/ˈpærəmaʊnt/	adj.	至为重要的；首要的
peninsular	/pəˈnɪnsjələ(r)/	adj.	半岛的；半岛状的
propensity	/prəˈpensəti/	n.	倾向；习性
segue	/ˈseɡweɪ/	n.	无间断继续；无间断切换
stagnant	/ˈstæɡnənt/	adj.	（水或空气）不流动而污浊的
teak	/tiːk/	n.	柚木
topographic	/ˌtɒpəˈɡræfɪk/	adj.	地质的；地形学上的
ubiquitous	/juːˈbɪkwɪtəs/	adj.	普遍存在的；无所不在的
Vietnamese	/ˌviːetnəˈmiːz/	n.	越南人；越裔
change course			改变方向；转向
red tape			繁文缛节；官僚作风

Notes

Scan the QR code for more information about Thai culture.

Unit 6

American Culture, Customs, and Business Etiquette

1 America: Overview

1.1 Geography and Demographics

Geography

The United States (US) or the United States of America (USA) is in North America, situated between Canada in the north and Mexico in the south. It stretches from the Atlantic Ocean on the east to the Pacific Ocean on the west. The country is comprised of fifty states, and one federal district, with Washington D.C. (District of Columbia) as its capital city. The two largest states in terms of size are Alaska and Texas.

Mostly lying within the temperate zone, the United States boasts a very wide range of climates and a vast array of natural habitats including forests, deserts, mountains, high flat lands, and fertile plains. The Mississippi and Missouri rivers and their branches drain the center of the country and meander through the vast open plains, flanked by the Appalachian Mountains to the east and the Rocky Mountains to the west. The Mississippi is the longest river in the United States and the fourth longest in the world. Water flows all the way from the source of the Missouri River in the northern Rocky Mountains to the mouth of the Mississippi in the Gulf of Mexico.

Population and People

The population of the United States was approximately 333.3 million in 2022, ranking third in population after China and India. New York is the largest US city, with over 8 million people living within the city boundaries. The United States has been called a melting pot, comprising a huge variety of different ethnic groups, with practically every nation on earth represented. However, constituting 60% of the population, the majority are Caucasians of European origin, including English, French, German, Irish, Scandinavian, Polish, and Russian. African Americans account for 13% of the population, while Asians, Hispanics, and Native Americans constitute approximately 6%, 19%, and 1% of the population, respectively.

Language

Although the most widely used language of the United States is English, there is in fact no "official" language at the federal level. Some states list English as their official language. Spanish is spoken by a large number of people, and more than 300 other languages are spoken.

1.2   History, Economy, and World Influence

History in Brief

Assembled out of former British, French, Russian, and Spanish colonies, the land of the United States had previously been occupied by the indigenous Native Americans and Inuit in the north, who suffered greatly from the influx of Europeans. The United States of America was formed with the signing of the *Declaration of Independence* in 1776, and its Constitution dates back to 1787.

Key events of the 19th century include the Louisiana Purchase in 1803, which added 530 million acres of land purchased from France for $15 million to the United States. The American Civil War (1861–1865) divided the United States as the Northern States fought the secessionist Southern States. The victory of the Northern States united the nation and put an end to slavery. A century later, from 1954 to 1968, the African American Civil Rights movement fought to put an end to racial segregation and discrimination.

The terrorist attacks on the US soil on September 11, 2001 significantly impacted the United States. Less than a month later (October 7, 2001), the United States began the War in Afghanistan. On March 20, 2003, the United States invaded and occupied Iraq. The war lasted for more than eight years before it was officially declared over on December 18, 2011. In 2008, Barack Obama became the first African American to be elected as the President of the United States.

Economy in Brief

The United States is one of world's greatest economic powers in terms of GDP and historically has been among the world's highest-ranking countries in terms of GDP per capita. With less than 5% of the world's population, the United States produces about one-fifth of the world's economic output. It is the most important export destination for one-fifth of countries around the world.

The US dollar is still the most widely used currency in global trade and financial transactions. Therefore, any changes in US monetary policy or investor sentiment may play a significant role in affecting global financing conditions. The United States operates as a free market economy in consumer goods and business services, but it also allows for government intervention for the public good. The major industries in the US include real estate, business services, finance and insurance, health care, manufacturing, wholesale trade, retail trade, and information.

The United States played a leading role in the establishment of the World Bank in 1944 and today is still its largest shareholder, and the only shareholder with veto power over changes in the Bank's structure. As such, the United States plays a unique role in influencing and shaping development priorities. It participates in addressing critical international development challenges.

World Influence

The United States has the world's most powerful military, a huge economy, and a leading role in international institutions. It is a permanent member of the UN Security Council, and a founding member of the North Atlantic Treaty Organization (NATO). Additionally, it is a leading member of the G7 and the G20, a member of the Organization for Economic Co-operation and Development (OECD), and a member of the WTO.

America's influences on the economies and politics of the rest of the world can never be underestimated. Its exports represent more than one-tenth of the world's total. Moreover, its cultural impact through music, movies, television, and video games has been particularly strong.

1.3　American Holidays

Many government offices in the US close on American federal holidays and some private businesses may close as well. If the holiday falls during the weekend, the government may observe it on a different day. Federal employees receive pay and many receive time off for federal holidays. Some holidays are not federal holidays but honor specific groups and events, such as Valentine's Day, Earth Day, Mother's Day, Father's Day, Flag Day, and Halloween.

Christmas is undoubtedly the most popular holiday in the US, celebrated by an estimated 93% of the US population each year. Although Christmas was started to celebrate the birth of Jesus Christ, it has evolved beyond its religious beginnings and is celebrated by many non-Christian Americans as a day to exchange gifts, spend time with family, eat good food, and enjoy yuletide traditions.

Independence Day, or "4th of July", is one of the most widely celebrated holidays in America because it is the day when America declared its independence from Great Britain after being a colony for almost two centuries. People decorate their houses with red, white, and blue flags, wear clothes that are either of those colors or have an American flag printed on them. Table 6-1 shows a list of main holidays in the US.

Table 6-1   A List of Main Holidays in the US in 2022

Day	Date	Holiday Name
Saturday	Jan. 1	New Year's Day
Monday	Jan. 17	Martin Luther King Jr. Day
Monday	Feb. 21	President's Day
Monday	May 30	Memorial Day
Sunday	June 19	Juneteenth
Monday	July 4	Independence Day
Monday	Sep. 5	Labor Day
Monday	Oct. 10	Columbus Day
Friday	Nov. 11	Veterans Day
Thursday	Nov. 24	Thanksgiving Day
Sunday	Dec. 25	Christmas Day
Monday	Dec. 26	Christmas Day (in lieu)

American Cultural Orientations

American culture is a dynamic and diverse blend of global influences, shaped by a rich history of immigration. The country's unique identity is a product of the many cultures that have contributed to its development. The country is also known for its entrepreneurial spirit and innovative mindset. The following section provides a concise overview of the cultural orientations of the United States based on the 6-D Model.

• Power Distance

American culture scores relatively low on power distance. Within American organizations, hierarchy is established for convenience. Superiors are accessible and managers rely on individual employees and teams for their expertise. Both managers and employees expect to be consulted and information is shared frequently.

At the same time, communication is informal, direct, and participative to a degree. The society is loosely-knit in which the expectation is that people look after themselves and their immediate families only and should not rely (too much) on authorities for support. Americans are accustomed to doing business or interacting with people they don't know well. Consequently, they are not shy about approaching their prospective counterparts in order to obtain or seek information.

• Individualism vs. Collectivism

American culture achieves a very high score on being individualist. American culture emphasizes individual initiative and personal achievement. One's position in the US society is determined by one's own achievements as opposed to status or age. Independence and self-reliance are highly valued and extend to the workplace where business is frequently carried out autonomously. In the business world, employees are expected to be self-reliant and display initiative. Also, within the exchange-based world of work, we see that hiring and promotion are based on merit or evidence of what one has done or can do.

• Masculinity vs. Femininity

The score of the US on masculinity is relatively high. This can be explained by the combination of a high masculine drive together with the most individualist drive in the world. In other words, Americans show their masculine drive individually. Behaviors in school, work, and play are based on the shared values that people should "strive to be the best they can be" and that "the winner takes all". As a result, Americans tend to demonstrate their success and talk about their achievements in life. Many American assessment systems are based on precise target setting, by which American employees can show how well a job they did. There exists a "can-do" mentality which creates a lot of dynamism in the society, as it is believed that there is always the possibility to do things in a better way.

• Uncertainty Avoidance

The US scores relatively low on the uncertainty avoidance dimension. There is a fair degree of acceptance of new ideas, innovative products, and a willingness to try something new or different. Americans tend to be more tolerant of ideas or opinions from anyone. At the same time, Americans do not require a lot of rules and are less emotionally expressive than higher-scoring cultures.

• Long-term vs. Short-term Orientation

The United States scores normative on the long-term orientation dimension with a low score. Americans are prone to analyze new information to check whether it is true. American businesses measure their performance on a short-term basis, with profit and loss statements being issued on a quarterly basis. This also drives individuals to strive for quick results within the workplace.

• Indulgence vs. Restraint

The United States scores as an indulgent society. Americans usually work hard and play hard. They stress material comfort and value the balance between life and work. People with a good work-life balance typically do well at work and they also allocate time to maintain a thriving social life and develop healthy habits.

3 American Business Practices and Etiquette

3.1 Business Appointments

- Punctuality is highly emphasized. In some cities, such as Houston, Los Angeles, or New York, extreme traffic can cause delays. Be sure to allow enough driving time to your destination. If you are delayed, call to let your contact know.

- If you are invited to a cocktail party, you can arrive a few minutes late. You do not need to call ahead even if you will be a half hour late.

- The work week is Monday through Friday, 8:30 or 9:00 a.m. to 5:00 or 6:00 p.m. Many people work overtime. Prior appointments are necessary.

3.2 Business Negotiations

- Business is done at a lightning speed in comparison to many cultures. American salespeople may bring final contracts to their first meeting with prospective clients. In large firms, contracts under $10,000 can often be approved by a manager in one meeting.

- American executives begin talking about business after a very brief exchange of small talk, whether in the office, at a restaurant, or even at home. Some common topics of conversation are a person's job, travel, food, exercise, sports, music, movies, and books. Until you know a person well, avoid discussing marriage, money, politics, or other controversial subjects.

- Most businesspeople have business cards, but these cards are not exchanged unless you want to contact the person later. Your card will not be refused, but you may not be given one in exchange. Don't be offended by this. Your card will probably be put into a wallet, which a man may put in the back pocket of his pants. This is not meant to show disrespect.

- Remember that the United States is one of the most litigious societies in the world. There are lawyers who specialize in every industry and segment of society, from corporate tax attorneys to "ambulance chasers".

- Compliments are exchanged very often. They are often used as conversation starters. If you wish to chat with someone, you can compliment something that a person has worn (e.g., clothing) or has done (e.g., a work or sports-related achievement).

3.3 Business Entertaining

- Business meetings are very often held over lunch. This usually begins at 12:00 noon and ends at 2:00 p.m. Lunch is usually relatively light, as work continues directly afterward. An alcoholic drink (usually wine or beer) may be ordered.

- Dinner is the main meal. It starts between 5:30 p.m. and 8:00 p.m., unless preceded by a cocktail party. Business breakfasts are common, and can start as early as 7:00 a.m. On weekends, many people enjoy "brunch", a combination of lunch and breakfast beginning anywhere from 11:00 a.m. to 2:00 p.m. Business meetings can be held over brunch.

- If you are invited out socially, but your host does not offer to pay, you should be prepared to pay for your own meal. This is called "splitting the bill", "getting separate checks", or "going Dutch". If you are invited out for business, your host will usually pay.

- Before going to visit a friend, you must call ahead. Most parties are informal, unless the hosts tell you otherwise. If you are offered food or drink, you are not obliged to accept. Also, your host will probably not urge you to eat, so help yourself whenever you want.

3.4 Business Protocol

Greetings

- The standard greeting is a smile, often accompanied by a nod, a wave, and/or a verbal greeting.

- In business situations, a firm handshake is preferred. Weak handshakes are taken as a sign of weakness. Men usually wait for women to offer their hand before shaking. In casual situations, a smile and a verbal greeting are adequate.

Titles/Forms of Address

- When you meet someone for the first time, use a title and their last name until you are told to do otherwise (this may happen immediately). To show respect, use a title such as Dr., Ms., Miss, Mrs., or Mr. with the last name. If you are not sure of a woman's marital status, use Ms. (pronounced "Miz").

- Sometimes you may not get the last name. In this case, just use the first name or nickname. Nicknames can be formal names shortened in surprising ways (e.g., Alex for Alexandra, or Nica for Monica).

Gestures

- The standard space between you and your conversation partner should be about two feet. Most American executives will be uncomfortable standing closer than that.

- In general, friends of the same gender do not hold hands.

- To point, you can use the index finger, although it is not polite to point at a person. To beckon someone, wave either all the fingers or just the index finger in a scooping motion with the palm facing up. The backslap is a sign of friendship.

- To show approval, there are two typical gestures. One is the "OK" sign, done by making a circle with your thumb and index finger. The other is the "thumbs up" sign, done by making a fist and pointing the thumb upward.

- Direct eye contact shows that you are sincere, although it should not be too intense.

- When sitting, Americans often look very relaxed. They may sit with the ankle of one leg resting on the knee of the other or prop their feet up on chairs or desks. But in business situations, try to maintain good posture and a less casual pose.

3.5   Business Gift-Giving

- Business gifts are discouraged by the law in the United States. If you stay at home of an American host for a few days, a gift is appropriate. You may also write a letter of thanks.

- When you visit a home, it is not necessary to take a gift. However, it is always appreciated if you take some flowers, a plant, or a bottle of wine. If you wish to give flowers, have them sent ahead so as not to burden your hostess with taking care of them when you arrive.

- A good time to give a gift is when you arrive or when you leave. The best gifts are those that come from your country. Business gifts are given after you close a deal. Unless the giver specifies a time to open the gift (as may happen with a gift at Christmas time), gifts are usually unwrapped immediately and shown to all present.

- You may not receive a gift in return right away. Your American friend might wait a while to reciprocate. Taking someone out for a meal or other entertainment is a common gift.

3.6   Business Outfit

- In cities, conservative business attire is the best. In rural areas and small towns, clothing is less formal and less fashionable.

- When you are not working, dress casually. You may see people dressed in torn clothing or in short pants and shirts without sleeves.

- If you wish to wear traditional clothing from your country, feel free to do so.

Tips: Writing a Professional E-mail

Many people in business get more e-mails than they can deal with. To make sure your business e-mails are well received, you need to make them clear, concise, and actionable. In addition, using the appropriate format and knowing what to include in or exclude from a business e-mail can help you and your company build and maintain a professional presence.

- **Start with an opening greeting.**
  Being polite is important in business, and greetings are an important part of this. Also, include the name of your receiver to make your business e-mail more personalized. You can write "Hi, Gabby" (informal), "Hello, Ms. Wallace" (formal), or "Hello, Sales Team" (to groups). If you are not sure who is going to read the e-mail, you can write "To whom it may concern" or "Dear Sir or Madam".

- **Add a social line to engage.**
  The next thing to write is a social line to start the body of your business e-mail before you transit to your main points. It can be in a question form or a statement. The objective is to build rapport and connect to your receiver at the very start. You can write "We met last week at the conference...", "We spoke on the phone earlier..." or "It was great meeting you last week...".

- **Add an introduction section when necessary.**
  The reason why you need to introduce yourself is to break the ice and raise the reader's spirits as you communicate. This should be done before getting to the main body. If your business e-mail is a follow-up e-mail to someone who replied to you, you can start with "Thanks for getting back to me so quickly", or "Thanks for replying to my e-mail", and so on. On the other hand, if you are replying

late to a business e-mail sent to you, offer your apologies in this section: "I'm so sorry for not getting back to you sooner", "I apologize for my late response to your e-mail" and so on.

- **Write the main body for business e-mail.**

What you need to do here is to structure your words well and be as frank as possible. Avoid beating around the bush and get straight to the point. You can start the body with "I am writing because...", "I'm reaching out to you because...", "I have a few questions about...", and so on. If you are responding to your business partners' quests, you can start the body with "Here's the answer to your question about...". The purpose of the e-mail should be stated clearly.

- **Make your business e-mail easier to read.**

To make it easier to read, break up the body of your e-mail into paragraphs. Help the reader find the most important points in the content by using bold text or italics. Readers don't need to go through the body over and over to get the crucial points when you use a list. Avoid overusing the list and combine it with text to make the e-mail body well-structured and meaningful.

- **Close your business e-mail with courtesy.**

This is the last section of your business e-mail. Just as you started the e-mail, you need to finish it the same way. Don't start on a high and end on a low. Just use "All the best" or "Thanks", as they are both friendly and professional. For formal business e-mails, you can use "Sincerely".

- **Add your e-mail signature and any attachments.**

Make sure your signature looks professional and has enough contact information. If you include information or attachments, it's helpful to remind the reader to check it: "I attached the documents for..." or "Please see the attached files...".

- **Review before you send your e-mail.**

Once your e-mail is composed, take a moment to review it. Check for grammar or spelling errors. Double-check dates, times, names, links, attachments, and other specific details. Triple-check that the correct recipients are in the sender fields.

The aim of the e-mail is for the reader to understand what you are saying. Always be courteous to your business partners and make sure your business e-mail is as professional as possible.

Exercises

5.1   Fact Files

Directions: Complete the following table and find the key facts about the US.

Official Name	
Capital City	
Official Language(s)	
Currency	
Population (Year 2022)	
The National Flower	
Current President	

5.2   Compound Dictation

Directions: Listen to the passage and fill in the blanks with the words or expressions that you hear.

The United States of America is a country located in central North America, neighboring Canada and Mexico. There are 50 (1)_____ and 5 major (2)_____ territories in the US. The Americans are a (3)_____ diverse population, which is a result of centuries of (4)_____.

The United States is a constitution-based federal republic. The federal government comprises three branches: the legislative, executive, and judicial branches. Congress is a legislative institution which is divided into the (5)_____ and the (6)_____. Congress makes federal laws, approves treaties and has the power of impeachment. The executive branch is led by an (7)_____ and an appointed cabinet of leaders of federal agencies that administer the laws enacted by the legislative branch. The judicial branch is organized into circuits with the power to review the decisions of the district courts. Ultimate review of lower court decisions is handled by the US (8)_____.

The US accounts for about (9)_____ the global gross domestic product. It also plays an important role in international institutions such as the United Nations, the World Bank, and the (10)_____.

5.3 True or False: American Customs and Etiquette

Directions: Put T for true or F for false for each of the following statements.

(   ) 1. Business cards are infrequently distributed in the US and are not usually exchanged unless you wish to contact the person later.

(   ) 2. When conducting business in the US, it is vital to establish a good, solid relationship with your counterparts to ensure successful future negotiations.

(   ) 3. American companies emphasize personal achievement and independence, which means that one's position in American society depends more on achievement than on age or status.

(   ) 4. Americans are task-centered and tend to communicate in an efficient and direct way.

(   ) 5. Although most American companies recognize that time is money, deadlines are not strictly adhered to in American business culture. Therefore, it is acceptable to postpone deadlines for optimizing the current work.

5.4 Multiple Choice: To Know More About America

Directions: Mark the correct answer to each question. Look up the following facts on the Internet or in some reference books and try to get more background information.

1. Which country gave the Statue of Liberty as a gift to the United States?

    A. Canada.   B. Britain.   C. France.   D. Germany.

2. What do the fifty white stars on the American flag represent?

    A. The American states.   B. The American people.

    C. The American presidents.   D. The American ethnic groups.

3. What is the name of the national anthem of the United States?

    A. Bella Ciao.   B. God Save the Queen.

C. The Star-Spangled Banner.   D. Land of the Free.

4. Who is printed on the US one dollar bill?

   A. George Washington.   B. Thomas Jefferson.

   C. Benjamin Franklin.   D. Abraham Lincoln.

5. The world-renowned Silicon Valley is located in the Bay area of _____.

   A. Los Angeles   B. New York City

   C. Boston   D. San Francisco

5.5   Case Study

Directions: Read the following case and answer the questions.

Jack is a senior programmer who had worked for years for a famous IT company located in the US. A few months ago, he moved to Tokyo and started working for a Japanese Internet corporation. Unfortunately, he felt a bit disappointed with the work schedule and enterprise culture. Last week, he completed a mid-year evaluation form in which he mentioned the challenges that he had encountered. Mr. Tanaka, the department manager, invited Jack for a one-on-one meeting. The following is part of their conversation.

Mr. Tanaka: Good morning, Jack.

Jack: Good morning, Mr. Tanaka.

Mr. Tanaka: Jack, you have worked for our company for several months, and we really appreciate your great work. I saw what you noted in the evaluation form. It seems that you were not satisfied with working long hours and felt stressed in the first few months?

Jack: Well, I like my job, but I never expected that I would have to continue my work at home.

Mr. Tanaka: Oh, actually, that's common practice in Japan, especially in Internet companies like ours. I guess you were told about that before you joined us. I mean no offense, but are you not content with your salary?

Jack: Thank you for explaining the corporate culture in Japan. To be frank, it has nothing to do with the salary, Mr. Tanaka. I was told about working overtime but I did not expect that I would have to work even after I got back home. It's the blurred line between work and personal life that confused me and made me feel stressed. It was quite different when I worked in American companies...

1. What went wrong in this case and why?

2. Conduct further research and make a comparison of Japanese and American business people's attitudes toward working overtime.

6 A Mini Business Project

Directions: Suppose that you are now working overseas for your company in South Africa and you find that your branch company was overcharged by a local telecom company. How can you contact the company and solve the problem regarding the service? Please explain how to prepare a letter of complaint based on the following outline.

- finding out the contact information of the customer service department;
- addressing clearly why you are writing the letter and what your exact complaint is;
- stating specifically what outcome or remedy will satisfy you;
- attaching copies of supporting documents;
- indicating a time limit for resolving the matter.

Note: You or your team is asked to prepare a presentation using PowerPoint slides, and write an executive summary using Microsoft Word. You may use appropriate visual aids (e.g., video clips) to support your presentation, and you may also refer to the sample project files online for reference. In addition, write a letter of complaint based on the outline.

Words and Expressions

admirable	/ˈædmərəbl/	adj.	令人钦佩的；极其出色的
array	/əˈreɪ/	n.	大群；大量
Caucasian	/kɔːˈkeɪʒn/	n.	白种人；高加索人
flank	/flæŋk/	v.	侧面有；位于……的两侧
habitat	/ˈhæbɪtæt/	n.	（动植物的）生活环境，栖息地
Hispanic	/hɪˈspænɪk/	n.	讲西班牙语的美国居民（尤指拉美裔美国人）
indigenous	/ɪnˈdɪdʒənəs/	adj.	本土的；土生土长的
influx	/ˈɪnflʌks/	n.	（人或物的）大量涌入
italics	/ɪˈtælɪks/	n.	斜体字
litigious	/lɪˈtɪdʒəs/	adj.	好诉讼的；好争论的
meander	/miˈændə(r)/	v.	河流（或道路）弯弯曲曲
Missouri	/mɪˈzʊəri/	n.	密苏里（美国州名）
participative	/pɑː(r)ˈtɪsɪpətɪv/	adj.	参与式的
presence	/ˈprezns/	n.	仪态；风度；气质
rapport	/ræˈpɔː(r)/	n.	融洽；和谐
Scandinavian	/ˌskændɪˈneɪviən/	n.	斯堪的纳维亚人
secessionist	/sɪˈseʃənɪst/	adj.	赞成脱离活动的；奉行分离主义的
segregation	/ˌsegrɪˈgeɪʃn/	n.	（对不同种族、宗教或性别的人所采取的）隔离并区别对待
sentiment	/ˈsentɪmənt/	n.	观点，看法；情绪
yuletide	/ˈjuːltaɪd/	adj.	圣诞节期的
beat around the bush			拐弯抹角；说话绕圈子
racial segregation			种族隔离

Notes

Scan the QR code for more information about American culture.

Unit 7

Canadian Culture, Customs, and Business Etiquette

Canada: Overview

1.1 Geography and Demographics

Geography

Canada is the world's second largest country including all its rivers and lakes. Occupying the top half of the North American continent, Canada borders with the United States, to its south and northeast. As you travel north in Canada, the country becomes colder, rockier, snowier, and increasingly uninhabitable, which perhaps explains why so few people live in the northern part of the country. Traveling from west to east, you will discover a diverse geography ranging from lush green valleys to dry and sandy deserts. Traveling north to south, Canada spans more than half of the northern hemisphere.

Canada features a vast array of natural landscapes including lakes and rivers, majestic western mountains, rolling central plains, and forested eastern valleys. Stretching across the north of the country is a hilly region of lakes and swamps known as the Canadian Shield which boasts some of the oldest rocks. The far north of the country stretches into the Arctic, where the landscape is dominated by ice, snow, and glaciers. There are few trees and the environment is unsuitable for farming.

Population and People

Canada had a population of approximately 38.9 million in 2022, of which around 80% are of European background (also referred to as Caucasians or whites), while the remaining 20% comprises a diverse mix of races from all around the globe. By ethnic origin, they are European, North American Aboriginal, other North American, Asian, African, Latin American, Caribbean, and Oceanian.

Language

Canada has two official languages: English and French, making it an officially bilingual country. French predominates in the province of Québec and is also spoken in other provinces or territories such as Newfoundland and Labrador, Ontario and

Manitoba. But in fact, most Canadians only speak English, with fewer and fewer speaking English and French, English and some other language, or only French.

1.2   History, Economy, and World Influence

History in Brief

The country that we call Canada today has been inhabited for thousands of years. When the first explorers came to Canada, they found thriving First Nations and Inuit societies who had their own belief systems, ways of life, and a rich history. The first European explorers called these people "Indians", as they thought they had arrived in the East Indies.

With the arrival of European settlers in the 16th century, the way of life of the indigenous people changed forever. The French explorers arrived in this land first in 1534, then gradually moved westward, claiming much of the middle of North America, but they lost the war against the English in 1760.

Canada became a self-governing member of the British Commonwealth, after gaining its independence in a series of treaties. On July 1, 1867, with passage of the British North America Act, the Dominion of Canada was officially established.

In both World War I and World War II, Canada supported Britain by providing soldiers, food, and manufactured goods. In 1931, Canada was granted full independence from the United Kingdom with the passing of the Statute of Westminster. After World War II, the NATO alliance brought the United States and Canada closer together, and Canada's current configuration was achieved in 1949 when Newfoundland, the last remaining colony, joined the Canadian Confederation. On March 25, 1982, the Canada Act (also called the Constitution Act of 1982) was approved by the British Parliament, and proclaimed by Queen Elizabeth II on April 17, 1982, making Canada wholly independent. It is a landmark document in Canadian history and achieved full independence for Canada by allowing the country to amend its Constitution without approval from Britain.

Economy in Brief

Canada is one of the world's wealthiest nations, due to its wealth of natural resources, forests, minerals, and fossil fuels. The Canadian economy has historically been based on trading natural resources, but is now dominated by manufacturing and service sectors. The economic growth in Canada has been so effective and consistent that today it is among the top ten largest economies in the world based on GDP.

Canada's economy is highly dependent on international trade with exports and imports of goods and services. The United States is Canada's largest trading partner, followed by China and the United Kingdom. Though Canada generally has a free market economy, the government still plays a large role in regulating and subsidizing many industries.

World Influence

Canada has been an influential member of the Commonwealth and has played a leading role in the organization of French-speaking countries known as La Francophonie. It was a founding member of the UN and has been active in a number of major UN agencies and other worldwide operations. Canada is also a member of the G20 and a security partner in NATO.

Canada's promotion of multilateralism as the foundation of the international order has been a hallmark of its foreign policy. Membership of the world's premier multilateral development financing institution has enabled Canada to leverage not only its funds, but also its knowledge and capabilities for its impact on poverty reduction and sustainable development around the world.

1.3 Canada's Holidays

A legal holiday or statutory holiday in Canada is a day when Canadian employers are legally required to give all their workers a day off. There are only two nationwide legal holidays recognized by the Canadian government: Canada Day and Victoria Day. All other legal holidays are set by either the provincial governments, or by a particular worker's contract with their employer. Government workers tend to get more days off than other workers.

There are seven other days that are officially defined as holidays by the federal government—Christmas, New Year's Day, Good Friday, Easter, Labor Day, Thanksgiving, and Remembrance Day—due to the fact that they are public holidays in most provinces. It is generally assumed that the majority of Canadian citizens will not be working on these days.

July 1 has been celebrated as the birthday of the Canadian nation ever since 1867 when the Canadian Constitution was adopted. It is considered as the day "Canada became a country". As Canada Day falls in early summer, it is a perfect opportunity for large outdoor parties, and is usually celebrated with neighborhood or family barbecues, picnics, and fireworks. Many of Canadian's larger cities will organize a variety of official Canada Day festivities, including parades, live music, and outdoor festivals. The streets are usually packed with patriotic revelers from dawn to dusk. Table 7–1 shows a list of holidays in Canada.

Table 7–1   A List of Government and Statutory Holidays in Canada in 2022

Day	Date	Holiday Name
Saturday	Jan. 1	New Year's Day
Monday	Mar. 14	St. Patrick's Day
Monday	Apr. 25	St. George's Day
Monday	May 23	Victoria Day
Friday	July 1	Canada Day
Monday	July 11	Orangeman's Day
Monday	Sep. 5	Labor Day
Friday	Sep. 30	National Day for Truth and Reconciliation
Sunday	Dec. 25	Christmas Day
Monday	Dec. 26	Boxing Day

Canadian Cultural Orientations

Canadian culture is a dynamic and inclusive collage of traditions, customs, and values. The country's rich history of colonization and immigration has resulted in a unique blend of indigenous, European, and global influences. The six cultural orientations presented below may have contributed to the formation of its distinct cultural identity, influencing the country's values, beliefs, and overall way of life.

• Power Distance

Scoring relatively low on this dimension, Canadian culture is characterized by interdependence among its inhabitants, while egalitarianism is still valued. This is also reflected by the lack of overt status and/or class distinctions in society. As in other cultures that also have low scores on this dimension, the hierarchy in Canadian organizations is established for convenience, superiors are accessible, and managers rely on individual employees and teams for their expertise. It is usual for managers and staff members to consult one another and share information freely. In communication, a straightforward exchange of information is valued.

• Individualism vs. Collectivism

Canada scores relatively high on the dimension of individualism, meaning that it can be characterized as an individualist culture. This results in a loosely-knit society in which people are expected to look after themselves and their immediate families. Similarly, in the business world, employees are expected to be self-reliant and to display initiative. Within the exchange-based world of work, hiring and promotion decisions are based purely on merit or evidence of what one has done or can do, rather than on connections.

• Masculinity vs. Femininity

Canada achieves an intermediate score on masculinity, which means that it can be characterized as a moderately "masculine" society. While Canadians strive to attain high standards of performance in both work and play (sports), the overall cultural tone is more subdued with respect to achievement, success, and winning. Canadians also tend to have a good work-life balance and take time to enjoy their personal interests, family gatherings, and life in general. Despite this, Canadians are still hard workers who are likely to strive to attain high standards of performance in all of their endeavors.

• Uncertainty Avoidance

The Canadian culture scores relatively low on this dimension, which indicates that it is more "uncertainty accepting". This is indicative of an easy acceptance of new ideas, innovative products, and a willingness to try new or different things, whether it is technology, business practices, or consumer products. Canadians also tend to be tolerant of ideas or opinions from anyone, and allow freedom of expression. At the same time, Canadian culture is not rules-oriented and Canadians tend to be less emotionally expressive than cultures which score higher on this dimension.

- **Long-term vs. Short-term Orientation**

    With a low score on the long-term orientation dimension, Canada can be considered as a normative society. As such, Canadians tend to be normative in their thinking. They show great respect for traditions, have a relatively small propensity to save for the future, and often focus on achieving quick results.

- **Indulgence vs. Restraint**

    A high score on the indulgence dimension means that Canadian culture is classified as indulgent. People in societies which have a high indulgence score tend to exhibit a willingness to act on their impulses and desires with regard to enjoying life and having fun. They have a positive attitude and tend to be optimistic. In addition, they place a higher degree of importance on leisure time, act as they please and spend money as they wish. Canada is regarded as a giant playground, with beaches and lakes for water sports, and hills, mountains, and plains for hiking, biking, running, and winter sports. Most Canadians are what you'd call "outdoorsy".

Canadian Business Practices and Etiquette

3.1   Business Appointments

- Punctuality is important in Canada. Be sure to be on time for all business-related meetings.

- In the French-speaking areas of Canada, people may be less punctual, but individual businesspeople vary. As a foreigner, you will be expected to be prompt, even if your Canadian counterpart is not.

- In general, it is acceptable to be 15 minutes late for evening social occasions.

- Mornings are preferable for business appointments.

- Business hours are generally 9:00 a.m. to 5:00 p.m., Monday through Friday.

- Shop hours are generally 10:00 a.m. to 6:00 p.m., Monday through Saturday, but many shops are open until 9:00 p.m.

3.2 Business Negotiations

- Negotiating styles tend to be very similar to those in the United States, although they may be at a slightly slower pace.

- To Canadians, negotiating is usually a joint problem-solving process. French-Canadians, however, tend to be somewhat more aggressive in debate for reaching a mutually agreeable solution. Never inflate a product's benefits as it could generate claims of illegal promotion.

- Canadian negotiators usually spend time gathering information and discussing details before the bargaining stage. They may share a lot of information as a way to build trust. They value information that is straightforward and to the point.

- When dealing with French Canadians, be sure to have all material written in French and English. Acknowledge Canadians' desire for a "Canadian identity". French Canadians generally exhibit less reserve than English Canadians. Their gestures are often more expansive, they may stand closer together while speaking, and they are more likely to touch each other during a conversation. In business conversations, Canadians usually get down to business immediately. In French-speaking Canada, they may talk briefly about general topics (travel, traffic, weather, etc.).

- Canada is a multiethnic nation, and the etiquette of businesspeople from different ethnic backgrounds may differ. It is important to be aware of such possible differences.

- Canadians listen to the speaker and do not interrupt. They are polite and wait for their turn to speak. While usually friendly and polite, communication in Canada is often quite direct. Canadians dislike vague statements and may openly share their opinions and concerns. Too much diplomacy can confuse and irritate them and give the impression of insincerity.

3.3   Business Entertaining

- Business meals are popular in Canada, although the concept of the breakfast meeting is a relatively new practice.

- Most entertaining takes place in public establishments, such as restaurants or nightclubs.

- Traditionally, dinners were considered social occasions—if business was discussed at all, it was at the end of the meal. This is changing, but it is better to let your Canadian counterpart bring up business first.

- It is not common to receive an invitation to dine at a Canadian home except in the western provinces where outdoor barbecues are now popular.

3.4   Business Protocol

Greetings
- The standard greeting is a smile, often accompanied by a nod, wave, and/or verbal greeting such as "Hello".

- In business situations, it is usual practice to greet people with a handshake. Among Canadians of British descent, the handshake tends to be firm, and a weak handshake may be considered as a sign of weakness. Men usually wait for women to offer their hands before shaking.

- French Canadians also have a firm handshake, and tend to shake hands more often: upon greetings, introductions, and departures, even if the person has been greeted earlier that day.

- Good friends and family members sometimes embrace. This is even more common among the French who also often kiss cheeks. Note that the French Canadians do not finish an embrace with a pat or two on the back, as is common in the United States.

Titles/Forms of Address
- While many Canadians quickly address others by their first names, it is safest to wait for your Canadian counterpart to suggest it.

- To show respect, use a title such as Dr., Ms., Miss, Mrs., or Mr. followed by the last name. When you meet someone for the first time, it is polite to use the person's title and surname until you are told to do otherwise (this may happen immediately).

- Note that although they often use first names over the telephone, French Canadians may use surnames when communicating in person.

Gestures

- When speaking with someone, the standard space between you should be two feet. British Canadians are uncomfortable standing closer, but French Canadians may be comfortable standing slightly closer.

- Canadians, and especially those of British descent, are not known for frequent or expansive gesturing.

- Generally speaking, friends of the same gender do not hold hands in Canada. Only French Canadians commonly touch each other during conversation.

- To point, you can use your index finger, but don't point at people as it is considered impolite. To beckon someone, wave all the fingers in a scooping motion with the palm facing up.

- The backslap is a sign of close friendship among British Canadians, but is rare among French Canadians. To wave goodbye, move your entire hand, facing outward.

- Direct eye contact is a sign of sincerity, but don't be too intense. Some minorities look away to show respect.

3.5 Business Gift-Giving

- Business gifts should be modest rather than ostentatious.

- It is usual to bring a gift when you visit someone's home. The most common gifts are flowers, candy, and alcohol.

- Gifts are exchanged at Christmas. For business associates, give gifts that are useful in the office or alcohol. Most stores will wrap your gifts.

- A good time to present a gift is on arrival or departure. Gifts from your country are a good choice.

- Business gifts are given when you close a deal. As a rule, gifts are unwrapped immediately and shown to everyone, unless otherwise specified.

3.6   Business Outfit

- Canadians tend to have a disdain for new clothing. Older, classic clothes that are neat and clean are respected among businesspeople, while new and trendy clothes may not be well-received.

- Men and women should wear dark, conservative business suits with ties, especially in cities. Conservative colors such as navy and gray, and shirts in white and light blue are preferred.

- Quality leather shoes are important to complete your look.

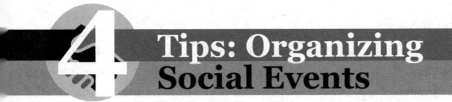

4 Tips: Organizing Social Events

Social events make great networking and bonding opportunities, and they come in all types and sizes. Planning a business-related social event, whether a weekend picnic or formal business dinner, requires a meticulous plan. There are speakers to hire, venues to rent, guests to invite, and food to supply. Getting all of this done may seem impossible, but if you start organizing yourself right away and delegating tasks to a competent team, you can make your event run smoothly and tackle anything the day might throw at you.

- **Establish your overall event budget.**

  Set a preliminary budget by determining how much you can spend on food, entertainment, room rental, invitations, and any other additions that you would like to make for the event. Consider your spending limit when choosing the important elements. Plan in advance for the best availability for your venue, and keep in mind that some venues may be more expensive, due to last-minute reservations.

- **Make a schedule to keep yourself organized.**

  Schedule six months or more for large events, such as fundraisers, workshops and opening ceremonies that may host 200 or more. Smaller events, such as networking mixers, game nights, and social parties require less time and money. You may find that you can get the venue donated and only need to pay for food and activities for guests.

- **Create the guest list.**

The number of guests and the type of guests would be dependent on the event you have planned. Deciding on the target audience would be what would help you allocate your resources effectively and efficiently. Whom do you want to invite for the corporate event—will it include executives, managers, longtime clients, business partners, and community members? Picking the right audience would be quite helpful in choosing your speakers, catering, and other services.

- **Hire competent speakers.**

Get to know your audience and tailor the event message and content to them. The people who attend your event are your customers, so you need to know them well in order to provide them with an experience that meets their expectations. Make sure that you get a great keynote speaker who can kick off the event in the right way. If you want to inspire your audience with a compelling story, then make sure you find a motivational speaker who has the experience to hold your audience's attention. In addition, you may schedule a Q & A period after each presentation or session.

- **Prepare invitations for the event.**

Create and send out your invitations via traditional mail or electronically. Include details about the location, time, and dress code for the event. Give instructions for any special meeting areas or activities they need to know about.

Create a plan for the overall visual look of your event. Secure the supplies needed for decorating your space, your centerpieces, and the seating.

Set up the decorations, signs, tables, and chairs.

- **Plan a menu that matches the event.**

Arrange for catering when you can, and be sure that food is prepared on time and presented before your guests arrive. Consider food restrictions and allergies in your menu. Your main meal options are a buffet meal and a sit-down dinner.

- **Finalize preparations on the day of the event.**

Arrive early to the venue with your team members and volunteers. Check that everyone is present and all electronic equipment is in working order. Double check speakers' biographies and copies of slides. Review the names of guests, spouses, and significant others, as well as company affiliations. Take care of last-minute details.

- **Greet your guests.**

  As your first guests arrive, greet them at the door. Introduce newcomers all around the room until the number of guests gets too large. When that happens, introduce newcomers only to the people who are closest at hand.

- **End the event.**

  The party should be over an hour after dessert is finished. As people begin to leave, station yourself at the door. Distribute any souvenirs or other publications to relevant people. Accept their compliments, thank them for coming, and wish them a good evening. Clean up the venue when the event is over. Take down the banners, break down the tables, and pick up everything you brought in.

- **Express gratitude to people involved in the event.**

  Thank all the team members, especially sponsors and volunteers. Collate feedback from the evaluation forms. Take notes on the pros and cons of the event for improvements next time. Put learning materials on the website or produce a post-conference publication to send to delegates, and let them know you'll keep them in mind for future events.

  Above all, stay calm and remind yourself that even if things don't go perfectly, your event will still be super special.

Exercises

5.1 Fact Files

Directions: Complete the following table and find the key facts about Canada.

Official Name	
Capital City	
Official Language(s)	
Currency	
Population (Year 2022)	
The National Flower	
Current Prime Minister	

5.2 Compound Dictation

Directions: Listen to the passage and fill in the blanks with the words or expressions that you hear.

Canada is located on the continent of North America, north of the United States. Although many theories were (1)_____ regarding the etymology (词源) of the country's name, it has been widely accepted today that the word "Canada" was first used by a French explorer, Jacques Cartier. It (2)_____ from the word "kanata", St. Lawrence-Iroquoian language for the village.

Canada can get as cold as it does on the surface of Mars. On February 3, 1947, a small village of Snag had a (3)_____ of −63℃ or −81.4 ℉ which is about the same temperature as the surface of Mars. Sixty percent of polar bears in the world or (4)_____ 25,000 can be found in Canada. In Churchill, people leave their cars unlocked for pedestrians to use as a (5)_____ refuge if they encounter polar bears. In the Northwest Territories, (6)_____ are shaped as polar bears.

Canada's border with the United States is the longest border or (7)_____

_____ in the world with a length of 8,891 kilometers or 5,525 miles. Canada is rich in (8)_____. It has the third largest (9)_____ in the world after Saudi Arabia and Venezuela, with an estimated 176.8 billion barrels of oil, which is four times more than Kazakhstan and six times greater than Russia. (10)_____ is the great benefit of having 563 lakes.

5.3 True or False: Canadian Customs and Etiquette

Directions: Put T for true or F for false for each of the following statements.

(   ) 1. The predominant language in Québec of Canada is English. One should make sure all the documents are written in English for businesspeople in Québec.

(   ) 2. Canadians act on problems more from the perspective of the people involved, attaching great importance to the opinions of others.

(   ) 3. Facts are accepted as the primary evidence in negotiations.

(   ) 4. In Canada, residents believe in experts from various backgrounds.

(   ) 5. Family and personal affairs are good topics for small talk before business negotiations in Canada.

5.4 Multiple Choice: To Know More About Canada

Directions: Mark the correct answer to each question. Look up the following facts on the Internet or in some reference books and try to get more background information.

1. Canada is a former _____ colony.

   A. British   B. Indian   C. Spanish   D. American

2. Canada achieved its independence from the United Kingdom through _____.

   A. third-party involvement   B. a war of independence

   C. a series of gradual treaties   D. armed revolution

3. When did Montreal host the Olympics?

   A. 1964.   B. 1976.   C. 1980.   D. 1984.

4. What is Canada's most populous city?

   A. Calgary, Alberta.   B. Winnipeg, Manitoba.

   C. Québec City, Québec.   D. Toronto, Ontario.

5. What is the largest lake entirely in Canada?

    A. Lake Huron.   B. Great Bear Lake.

    C. Great Slave Lake.   D. Lake Erie.

5.5 Case Study

Directions: Read the following case and answer the questions.

> Xiao Hua is an intern at a Canadian company based in Beijing. She has a colleague named Cindy, a Canadian woman. One day, when she and Cindy were waiting in line at the snack bar downstairs to buy food, Cindy found that she had no cash with her. Not knowing how to use WeChat or Alipay, she was ready to return to the company to get her purse. Xiao Hua took out her cell phone and told Cindy that she could pay for her, but Cindy insisted on going back to the company to get some cash. Upon her return a few minutes later, Xiao Hua, standing at the front of the queue, beckoned to her, "Hey, Cindy. Come and join me." To Xiao Hua's surprise, Cindy turned her down again.

1. What went wrong in this case and why?

2. Conduct further research and make a comparison of Chinese and Canadian people's attitudes toward "paying one's bills" and "waiting in line".

A Mini Business Project

Directions: Suppose you are the organizer of the 20th International Conference on Web-based Learning, how would you arrange the conference? Please explain your plan based on the following outline.

- defining the purpose and theme of the conference;
- choosing the date and location of the conference;
- knowing your prospective participants and target audience;
- drafting your budget;
- forming a team and assigning tasks;
- proposing a tentative conference agenda including speakers and their topics.

Note: You or your team is asked to prepare a presentation on how to arrange the conference using PowerPoint slides, and write an executive summary using Microsoft Word. You may use appropriate visual aids (e.g., video clips) to support your presentation, and you may also refer to the sample project files online for reference.

Words and Expressions

aboriginal	/ˌæbəˈrɪdʒənl/	*n.*	原住民；土著居民
ambiguous	/æmˈbɪgjuəs/	*adj.*	模棱两可的，有歧义的
bilingual	/ˌbaɪˈlɪŋgwəl/	*adj.*	会说两种语言的
camaraderie	/ˌkæməˈrɑːdəri/	*n.*	同事情谊；友情
Caribbean	/ˌkærɪˈbiːən/	*n.*	加勒比人
Commonwealth	/ˈkɒmənwelθ/	*n.*	英联邦
Confederation	/kənˌfedəˈreɪʃn/	*n.*	加拿大联邦
configuration	/kənˌfɪgəˈreɪʃn/	*n.*	布局；构造；配置
distain	/dɪsˈteɪn/	*v.*	轻蔑；鄙弃
etymology	/ˌetɪˈmɒlədʒi/	*n.*	词源学；词源
hemisphere	/ˈhemɪsfɪə(r)/	*n.*	（地球的）半球

inflate	/ɪnˈfleɪt/	v.	夸大；吹嘘
lush	/lʌʃ/	adj.	茂盛的；草木繁茂的
multilateralism	/ˌmʌltiˈlætərəlɪzəm/	n.	多边主义
Oceanian	/ˌoʊʃiˈɑːniən/	n.	大洋洲人
predominate	/prɪˈdɒmɪneɪt/	v.	（数量上）占优势；以……为主
remembrance	/rɪˈmembrəns/	n.	纪念；怀念
reveler	/ˈrevələ(r)/	n.	欢宴者，狂欢者；饮酒狂欢者
uninhabitable	/ˌʌnɪnˈhæbɪtəbl/	adj.	不宜居住的；无法居住的
from down to dusk			从早到晚
poverty reduction			减贫

Notes

Scan the QR code for more information about Canadian culture.

Unit 8

English Culture, Customs, and Business Etiquette

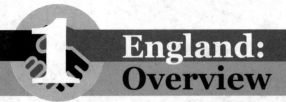

England: Overview

1.1 Geography and Demographics

Geography

England is located in the southern part of the island of Great Britain, which is part of the country of the United Kingdom (a sovereign country including England, Scotland, Wales, and Northern Ireland). It has an extensive coastline along the Celtic Sea, the North Sea, the Irish Sea, and the English Channel. The longest river in England is the Thames. It runs through a large part of south-eastern England. England's climate is rainy and temperate. Winters are mild while summers are cool. Rain falls in almost all seasons.

Population and People

The population of England reached 57.7 million in 2022. It has a high population density. According to the 2019 England population data, the region with the highest population is the South East and the London region as the second. London is the largest city and one of the most heavily populated regions in England. Other large urban areas in England include West Midlands, Greater Manchester, and West Yorkshire. The people of England are a mixture of many different ethnic groups. There is a large immigrant community primarily from India, Pakistan, and Bangladesh.

Language

The official language of England is English. There are also many regional dialects spoken across England, including recently introduced languages spoken by immigrants. The most common of these are Polish, Punjabi, and Urdu. The English language has been influenced by Latin and Greek (languages used at the time of the Romans, and used in religion and education until recent times), German (the language of the Angles, Saxons, and Jutes), French (the language of the Normans), Gaelic or Scottish (Celtic languages), etc.

1.2   History, Economy, and World Influence

History in Brief

England has a long history of human civilization dating back to prehistoric times. The earliest known humans arrived in these lands around 900,000 years ago. Prehistory stretches from then until the Roman invasion in 43 CE. The Romans maintained control of their province of Britannia until the early 5th century. This is one of the most important periods in English history—the Early Middle Ages. A kingdom of England emerged in these centuries with a new "English" identity and language, and became an independent kingdom in 927.

William of Normandy (the Conqueror) was crowned King of England in 1066. This marked the dawn of a new era—Norman Conquest. This was also a period of upheaval and change. The Stuart period (1603–1714) witnessed the shift of power from the monarchy to the parliament. Meanwhile, discoveries and innovations transformed science, architecture, and everyday life.

In 1800, the United Kingdom of Great Britain (consisting of England, Scotland, and Wales) and Ireland was founded. From 1837 to 1901, Queen Victoria ruled England for over 60 years. During this long reign, the country acquired unprecedented power and wealth. England began Colonization and Exploration with the Age of Discovery as European powers raced across the group to establish new trading posts that transformed into colonies. England's first permanent settlement overseas was in Jamestown, Virginia in 1607, and several other colonies followed. At the height of the British Empire, just after World War I (1914–1918), an island smaller than Kansas controlled roughly a quarter of the world's population and landmass.

The 20th century saw two world wars in England which catalyzed enormous social change across the country. The 1970s brought the oil crisis and the collapse of the British industry. Conservative Prime Minister Margaret Thatcher was elected in 1979 and stayed until 1990. She privatized the railways and shut down inefficient factories, but also increased the gap between the rich and the poor by cutting on the social security. Her methods were so harsh that she was nicknamed the "Iron Lady". Nowadays, the English economy relies heavily on services. The main industries are travel, education, music, prestige cars, and fashion.

Caroline Elkins, a Harvard historian, contends that Britain's use of systematic violence was no better than that of its rivals, such as Hitler's Germany and Hirohito's Japan. Taking the Opium War (1840–1842) as an example, it left an indelible scar on China. On August 29, 1842, the Treaty of Nanking was signed, five ports (Canton, Xiamen, Fuzhou, Ningbo, and Shanghai) in China were forced to open to foreigners and Hong Kong was ceded to the British. It was on July 1, 1997, after about 155 years of cession, that the whole territory of Hong Kong was eventually handed over to China. In Elkins's account, the British paramilitary cadre, many of them trained by Tudor's Toughs, became the basis of an increasingly violent ruling culture that sought to reassert control in the aftermath of World War II, when the Empire needed colonial resources to rebuild a depleted economy and to bulk up a waning geopolitical status.

Economy in Brief

The economy of England is the largest and a highly industrialized economy of the four countries that make up the United Kingdom. It is the principal financial, industrial, and agricultural region of the UK. Major industries include banking, finance, insurance, oil and natural gas, music and arts, tourism, pharmaceuticals, digital technology, and steel. It is also an important producer of textiles and chemical products. A significant proportion of the country's income comes from the City of London. Since the 1990s, the financial services sector has played an increasingly significant role in the English economy and the City of London is one of the world's largest financial centers. Banks, insurance companies, commodity and futures exchanges are heavily concentrated in the City. The British Pound Sterling is the official currency of England and the central bank of the United Kingdom, the Bank of England, is in London. Besides London, other English cities such as Birmingham, Manchester, Liverpool, Sheffield, Leeds, Bradford, and Newcastle also portray themselves as great tourist destinations.

In England, there is an active contribution from both the private and the government sectors. England leads the world in aerospace, arms, and the manufacturing segment of the software industry. The service sector of the economy is now the largest in England, with manufacturing and primary industries in decline. The only major secondary industry that is growing is the construction industry, fueled by economic growth provided mainly by the growing services, administrative and financial sectors.

World Influence

England is globally recognized in various sectors and fields, such as the English language, culture, education, the Commonwealth of Nations, healthcare, governance, business, trade, and environmental sustainability. England's capital, London, is the world's largest financial center.

Since Britain has been a colonizer all around the globe for hundreds of years, it has influenced its colonies with its culture—from industries to governments. One of its most obvious worldwide influences is the modern English language. Approximately 1.35 billion people speak English around the world.

1.3 England's Holidays

English people celebrate many holidays, some of which are unique to the United Kingdom and England, including Saint George's Day (the National Day of England) and Bonfire Night. Some holidays are shared with many Western countries or Christian countries such as Christmas and Easter.

The National Day of England occurs on April 23, also called Saint George's Day, the Patron Saint of England. Traditionally, April 23 is the day for a red rose to be worn in the buttonholes of people's shirts. However, for the majority of people today, Saint George's Day is a normal day.

Bonfire Night (or sometimes called Guy Fawkes Night) occurs on November 5 in remembrance of the Gunpowder Plot of 1605 after a failed attempt to blow up Parliament in London by Guy Fawkes and a group of Catholic followers. Bonfires are lit during the night and it is a time to meet family and friends.

In England, a bank holiday is a public holiday when banks and many other businesses close for a day. If a bank holiday occurs on a weekend, a "substitute" weekday becomes a bank holiday, usually the following Monday. Table 8–1 is a list of bank holidays in England.

Table 8–1   A List of Bank Holidays in England in 2022

Day	Date	Holiday Name
Saturday	Jan. 1	New Year's Day
Friday	Apr. 15	Good Friday
Monday	Apr. 18	Easter Monday
Monday	May 2	Early May Bank Holiday
Thursday	June 2	Spring Bank Holiday
Friday	June 3	Platinum Jubilee
Monday	Sep. 19	Day of National Mourning
Sunday	Dec. 25	Christmas Day
Monday	Dec. 26	Boxing Day

2 English Cultural Orientations

English culture is a vibrant and intricate mosaic of traditions, customs, and values, shaped by its long and complex history. Literature, music, and the arts are central to English culture, reflecting a deep appreciation for creativity and expression. The monarchy, tea, and pub culture are also significant aspects of English culture, reflecting a love of community and socialization. The following six cultural orientations indicate its unique identity that continues to evolve with the times.

• Power Distance

England has a low ranking on the power distance index. This signifies that English people prefer power to be more equally distributed. For example, English organizations have relatively flat structures, thus, a boss will not have a lot more power than the employees and sometimes will be "one of the team". Meetings are likely to be participative, and even junior members usually have a say in decisions. However, there is a difference in England between historical classes. Although they are becoming less important, they are still long-standing in English society. These classes are the upper class, the middle class, and the working class.

• Individualism vs. Collectivism

England has a high score on the dimension of individualism, which indicates that England is a highly individualistic culture. English people focus more on their own lives than on the lives of others, as other people should consider their own needs. Children are taught from an early age to think for themselves and to find out what their unique purpose of life is. There is also a culture of personal achievement, with respect goes for those who individually contribute to and benefit society.

• Masculinity vs. Femininity

England is a more masculine society. Although politeness and modesty are highly regarded in England, the fundamental value system is success-oriented. People tend to value their achievements and success and are comfortable with expressing ambitions.

• Uncertainty Avoidance

England has a low score on uncertainty avoidance. This suggests that English society is quite comfortable with uncertainty about the future and adapts to a situation as it presents itself. The phrases "going with the flow" and "muddling through" are very British ways of expressing this.

• Long-term vs. Short-term Orientation

England has no dominant orientation on the long-term orientation dimension, and both past and future are fairly important. It means that English society equally values its own past while dealing with the challenges of the present and future. English people are adherent to their customs and traditions, in which they often take great pride. On the other hand, they value constant innovation and change in technology, literature, finance, and regulation.

• Indulgence vs. Restraint

England scores high on the indulgence dimension and can be classified as an indulgent culture. English people seem to have relatively weak impulse control and a tendency to try to realize their desires. In addition, they place more importance on leisure time, flexible working, and work-life balance.

3 English Business Practices and Etiquette

3.1　Business Appointments

- Schedule your appointments in advance, and then confirm your appointments when you arrive in England.
- The standard working week is from Monday to Friday, where working hours vary between 8:00 a.m. and 5:30 p.m.
- Executives' hours vary widely depending on the company.
- Whether it is getting to work, a meeting, or a deadline, punctuality is critical.

3.2 Business Negotiations

- The best way to contact English businessmen and women is through a third-party organization. If you do not have a contact, it is necessary to liaise with the company to assess who the best contact is for your business.

- English people do not make extravagant claims about products or plans. Do not take a "hard sell" approach.

- The primary negotiation style is cooperative, and the English may be open to compromise if viewed helpful in moving the negotiation forward.

- Decision-making can be slow in England. It is not a good idea to rush English people toward a decision.

- Do not be too direct about asking personal questions such as family. English people dislike discussing personal topics with people they do not know well.

- The English are polite and will apologize often. It is important to reciprocate this politeness. Avoid talking about the royal family in a humorous or negative manner.

- Try not to talk too much. The English do not appreciate long lectures, vague messages and descriptions, or meaningless conversations.

3.3 Business Entertaining

- Business entertaining should be done at restaurants or at formal events. To gain the attention of a waiter in a restaurant, raise your hand and establish eye contact. Do not call out or click fingers as this is considered rude.

- Inviting colleagues or business counterparts to lunch, dinner, or an event is appreciated. It is not required. If you invite someone out, you are expected to pick up the tab. It's a courteous gesture.

- Having a drink after work is commonplace and part of standard business practices. It's called "pub culture" in England. It is always a good idea to buy a round of drinks for your colleagues after work.

- After work, it is best not to continue discussing work. English people may find this boring or even an attempt to interrupt their "free time". Wait for the early morning of the next day for business matters unless it is urgent.

- As a host, offer the best seat to the most senior person of their company. If the most senior member offers it back to you instead, accept it thankfully. English men, traditionally, hold the door open for women.

- Being overly inquisitive about the food the host has ordered is not advised. It is too casual to try other people's food in a business situation.

3.4   Business Protocol

Greetings

- The standard practice of greeting in England is a handshake. It is standard for both formal and informal situations. A handshake may vary in strength depending on the person and return the handshake as you receive it.
- Personal space is highly valued in England. In a crowded place, preserving personal space is a way of showing respect to your English business partner.

Titles/Forms of Address

- Address English hosts using Mr. for a man and Mrs. for a woman, followed by a surname, where Miss is used for an unmarried woman.
- Find out if your hosts have an honorific title such as Sir. or Dr. when introduced, say "Hello, nice to meet you" while shaking hands.

Gestures

- Do not leave your hands in your pockets when talking in a formal business situation as it is considered rude.
- English people do not always hold eye contact when talking. Do not take this as a negative gesture.
- Indicate with your whole hand pointed rather than pointing with a finger. It is better not to sit with one leg resting on the knee. This can be seen as casual or rude.
- Touching another person in England is uncommon as it can make the other person uncomfortable.
- The English find loud voices, shouting, big gestures, and overly expressive body language intrusive and rude.
- In England, two fingers up in a V shape with the back of your hand toward the other person (the "V" sign) is offensive and rude.
- Tapping the side of your head means someone is stupid in England.

3.5　Business Gift-Giving

- Gift-giving is not generally a part of business and negotiation in England.

- If you give a gift, it is important to ensure that the price of the gift is not sufficient to be considered a bribe or too cheap to be considered insulting.

- If you receive a gift in public, it is recommended that you open it immediately and thank the gift-giver.

- Instead of gift-giving, it is better to invite your English hosts to go out to a formal event such as for a meal at a restaurant.

- When you are invited to an English person's home, it is appropriate to bring alcohol (champagne on special occasions), flowers, or chocolates.

3.6　Business Outfit

- Conservative dress is important in England, as is the case for Europe in general, both for men and women.

- Men usually wear formal laced shoes, preferably black or brown. Women usually wear formal shoes. It is not acceptable to wear casual shoes or sports shoes in business settings.

- If men's shirts have a pocket, they should be empty.

- Clothes should be of excellent quality, but they do not necessarily have to look new.

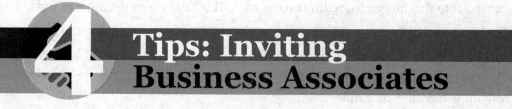

4 Tips: Inviting Business Associates

Business invitations are perfect opportunities to share details of important occasions with your work colleagues, business associates, or important potential new customers. Business invitations can be informal or formal. Although invitations have traditionally been sent through the mail, informal invitations such as e-mails and phone invitations are becoming more acceptable today. Here are some tips for you to compose your business invitations.

- **Choose a proper invitation timing.**

  For most informal occasions, it's best to invite guests three to four weeks in advance. If you choose to invite your guests by phone, remind them again in writing at least one week before the gathering.

- **Use appropriate invitation phrases.**

  The following invitation phrases are for your reference. For instance, "You are cordially invited to…" or "Our company requests the honor of your presence at…" and so on.

- **Mention the purpose of your invitation.**

  State the reason why you request the presence of the guests. For instance, it is an event for introducing someone, launching a new product, or celebrating an occasion.

- **State the exact date, time, and location clearly.**

  Write out the date and time of the event completely. The most formal style is to write "Friday, the twenty-seventh of July at six-thirty o'clock", while the least formal is "Friday, July 27, at 6:30 p.m." The address of where the event will be held should be stated next. Provide a map (a snapshot) as an attachment if the venue is difficult to find or if your guests haven't been there before. Inform the guests whether there is a reserved parking space for the visitors.

- **Explain the event to the guests.**

  Indicate whether the event is a breakfast, lunch, dinner, cocktail party, or other occasion. Mention if there are any special requirements in dress code or if the recipient needs to bring anything. Include a brief description of the event. Let the recipient know if they can bring guests, and mention how many accompanies they can bring. You can also extend the invitation to specific other family members.

- **Express your anticipation of the guest's acceptance.**

  You can also use "please reply if you can attend" or "let us know at your earliest convenience" to request a confirmation for participation. Formal business invitations are most commonly printed in black, navy, dark gray, or brown ink on white or off-white high quality paper which can uphold and promote the company's image. Nowadays, informal invitation letters are also acceptable through e-mails or via social media like WeChat in China.

There are many occasions when you may send out an invitation. For instance, you may want to showcase a new product line or service, launch a brand-new business venture, congratulate your team for their hard work on an important project, get together with your colleagues at an annual general meeting, or simply organize an informal business lunch. Refer to the above suggestions and make your invitation professional and successful.

 Exercises

5.1 Fact Files

Directions: Complete the following table and find the key facts about England.

Official Name	
Capital City	
Official Language(s)	
Currency	
Population (Year 2022)	
The National Flower	
Current Prime Minister	

5.2 Compound Dictation

Directions: Listen to the passage and fill in the blanks with the words or expressions that you hear.

England is an indispensable part of the United Kingdom of Great Britain and Northern Ireland (UK for short). There are several interesting facts about the UK. The prime minister lives at 10 Downing Street, near the Houses of Parliament. The head of state is the king. The king's image is on (1)_____, stamps and coins. He usually lives in (2)_____, a very popular place for tourists in London. Other famous towns and cities in England are York, with its beautiful cathedral, called York Minster, and its narrow streets; Stratford-upon-Avon, the birthplace of (3)_____; Liverpool, once a very important port and the home of The Beatles; Cambridge and Oxford, both famous for their (4)_____ and their bicycles.

The (5)_____ is a crucial part of England. In the (6)_____ of the northwest of England, there are beautiful hills and lakes. A lot of British people come here on holiday and over 24 million foreign tourists come to Britain every year. They visit lots of places, usually including one of the most (7)_____ monuments, (8)_____ in Wiltshire, England. At (9)_____ Station in London, trains go through the (10)_____ to Paris, in France, and to Brussels, in Belgium.

5·3   True or False: English Customs and Etiquette

Directions: Put T for true or F for false for each of the following statements.

(   ) 1. During the negotiation process, English business professionals are aggressive, and they prefer to interrupt so as to achieve their goals.

(   ) 2. When entering an English meeting room, those of a higher rank are supposed to enter first.

(   ) 3. It is considered polite to enquire about an individual's salary during an initial meeting in England.

(   ) 4. When invited to an English home, it is customary to arrive at least 10 to 20 minutes earlier before the agreed time.

(   ) 5. The English value their personal space. Respect other participants' need for personal space by keeping a fair distance apart when in conversation.

5·4　Multiple Choice: To Know More About England

Directions: Mark the correct answer to each question. Look up the following facts on the Internet or in some reference books and try to get more background information.

1. Who was elected Lord Mayor of London in 2016?

    A. Nicholas Lyons.　　　　　　　　　B. Gordon Brown.

    C. Theresa May.　　　　　　　　　　D. Sadiq Khan.

2. Which of the following dishes originated in England and is popular in numerous other countries?

    A. Black pudding.　　　　　　　　　B. Haggis.

    C. Fish and chips.　　　　　　　　　D. Roast duck.

3. In which year were the First Olympic Games held in London?

    A. 1908.　　　　B. 1948.　　　　C. 1916.　　　　D. 1932.

4. Which is the largest lake in the United Kingdom?

    A. Lough Neagh.　　B. Lough Morar.　　C. Loch Awe.　　D. Lock Ness.

5. In which city was the 1960s band "The Beatles" formed?

    A. Birmingham.　　B. Liverpool.　　C. London.　　D. Bristol.

5·5　Case Study

Directions: Read the following case and answer the questions.

> Maomao was born in Jiangsu Province, China. She started her first overseas job recently in London. Two weeks after her arrival, she was invited to have tea at her English colleague's home. She was told to arrive around 5:00 p.m.
>
> Maomao thought afternoon tea usually starts around 3:00 p.m., so she decided to arrive early and help her colleague out. When Maomao arrived at her colleague's home, her colleague seemed rather surprised and a bit embarrassed. She asked Maomao to sit in the living room and said, "I'm afraid the tea's not ready yet."

1. What went wrong in this case and why?

2. Conduct further research and make a comparison of etiquette for visiting someone's home in China and Britain.

6 A Mini Business Project

Directions: China Import and Export Fair, also known as the Canton Fair, is a comprehensive international trading event in China. The official website has released related information about the event. Suppose that you are one of the organizers for this international event. Please prepare an introductory presentation for inviting an international exhibitor based on the following outline.

- introducing the international business event;
- including the details like venue, date, and time of the event;
- indicating the potential business opportunities for exhibiting at the event;
- providing an exhibitor's guide for exhibiting their products or services at the event.

Note: You or your team is asked to prepare a presentation on how to write an invitation letter using PowerPoint slides, and write an executive summary using Microsoft Word. You may use appropriate visual aids (e.g., video clips) to support your presentation, and you may also refer to the sample project files online for reference.

Words and Expressions

bonfire	/'bɒnfaɪə(r)/	*n.*	篝火；营火
cadre	/'kɑːdə(r)/	*n.*	骨干（队伍）
catalyze	/'kætəlaɪz/	*v.*	催化；刺激

Celtic	/'keltɪk/	adj.	凯尔特人的；凯尔特语的
inquisitive	/ɪn'kwɪzətɪv/	adj.	过分好奇的；爱打听的
liaise	/li'eɪz/	v.	与……联络，联系
monarchy	/'mɒnəki/	n.	君主制；君主国
off-white		adj.	米色的；米黄色的
paramilitary	/ˌpærə'mɪlətri/	adj.	准军事的；辅助军事的
pharmaceutical	/ˌfɑːmə'sjuːtɪkl/	n.	药物；制药
reconcile	/'rekənsaɪl/	v.	调和；使协调一致；（使）和解
referendum	/ˌrefə'rendəm/	n.	公民投票；全民公决
sovereign	/'sɒvrɪn/	adj.	（国家）有主权的；完全独立的
temperate	/'tempərət/	adj.	温带的；（气候）温和的
upheaval	/ʌp'hiːv(ə)l/	n.	激变；剧变
liaise with			与……联络；保持联系
pick up the tab			承担费用

Notes

Scan the QR code for more information about English culture.

Unit 9

French Culture, Customs, and Business Etiquette

France: Overview

1.1 Geography and Demographics

Geography

France, officially the French Republic (French: *République Française*), is located in Western Europe. Geographically, France is approximately hexagonal in shape and is bordered by the English Channel and the Atlantic Ocean in the west, and by the Mediterranean Sea in the southeast. It shares boundaries with its six neighboring countries: from north to south, Belgium, Luxembourg, Germany, Switzerland and Italy in the east, and Spain in the southwest. The capital and also the most populous city of France is Paris, a world-famous city that is considered one of the most beautiful cities in the world.

Population and People

In 2022, France's population was roughly 67.9 million. Although the French tend to be strongly conscious of belonging to a single nation, they are in fact far from constituting a unified ethnic group. Traveling from the Middle East and Africa across the Mediterranean Sea, and from Central Asia and the Nordic lands through Europe, for centuries, different groups of migrants came to France where they settled permanently. The Celtic tribes, whom the Romans called Gauls, spread from central Europe in the thousand-year period from 500 BCE to 500 CE, forming the major component of the population of France, particularly in the central and western regions of the country. In addition to these earlier migrations, France was subject to numerous battles and prolonged occupations over the centuries. The 19th and especially the 20th century saw more foreign immigration into Europe, adding further to the ethnic melting pot, the population of France.

Language

The national language of France is French, and it is spoken and taught throughout the country, although brogues and dialects are widespread in the rural regions. Many people, especially those on the frontiers, aim to conserve their regional linguistic customs by maintaining the use of their regional dialects. Examples include Alsatian and Flemish (Dutch) which are Germanic languages spoken in the eastern and northern part of the country; the Latin-influenced Occitan, Corsican, and Catalan spoken in the south; Breton, which is a Celtic language related to languages spoken in some western parts of the British Isles (notably Wales); and the language isolate, Basque. In addition to French and the regional dialects, recent immigration has brought with it a variety of non-European languages, most notably Arabic.

1.2   History, Economy, and World Influence

History in Brief

The original Celtic inhabitants of France were collectively referred to as the Gauls. The Roman Emperor Julius Caesar conquered the Gauls in 51 BCE, bringing with him the Latin language, a version of which was to become modern French. Caesar also imposed a uniform system of law.

After the withdrawal of the Romans in the 5th century CE, France was ruled by the Franks, who were Germanic tribes originally from Pomerania, on the Baltic. In the late 5th century, the Frankish King Clovis I united most of Gaul under his rule, beginning a period of Frankish domination of the region which lasted for centuries.

After becoming the Frankish King in 768, Charlemagne (Charles the Great) united most of Western Europe for the first time since the Roman Empire, then after his death in 814, France became one of the empire's successor kingdoms and eventually developed into the strongest of the unified continental monarchies.

During the four-year French Revolution beginning in 1789, the monarchy was overthrown and the First Republic was established. In 1804, Napoleon Bonaparte began to rule over the First Empire, and successive governments since then eventually led to the Fifth Republic which was established in 1958 and still exists today.

Economy in Brief

France ranks along with China, the United States, Japan, Germany, Italy, and the United Kingdom as one of the major global economic powers. For much of the postwar years from the mid-1940s to the mid-1970s, a period frequently referred to as the "Trente Glorieuses" ("thirty years of glory"), France experienced an extended period of unprecedented growth which is the basis of its current financial position. For example, between the years of 1960 and 1973, there was an average annual increase in GDP of close to 6%. However, following the oil crises of the 1970s, this economic growth decreased considerably and France experienced a substantial increase in unemployment. However, the end of the 1980s saw a rebound, and a trend of strong expansion continued into the 21st century.

World Influence

France is one of the most powerful nations in the world, particularly in terms of its "soft power". According to the comprehensive annual Soft Power Index by Portland Communications, France ranked No.1 as the leading soft power nation in 2019. With the election of President Emmanuel Macron as head of a centrist government in 2017, France was propelled to the top of the Soft Power league table, taking first place ahead of other countries including the United Kingdom, the United States, Germany, and Canada. President Macron has a distinctive perspective on diplomacy, which has seen him gift a live horse to China's President Xi Jinping and lend the Bayeux Tapestry to the United Kingdom for the first time in history. He was reelected in 2022, becoming the first French president in two decades to win a second term.

1.3   French Holidays

Bastille Day is France's National Day, celebrated on July 14 and marks the birth of the French Republic. If it falls on a Sunday, the following Monday is a holiday, and if it's on a Thursday, many people take the Friday off, creating a "pont" (bridge) to the weekend. Bastille Day is generally considered as a celebration of the storming of the Bastille, a key event in the popular uprising against the Monarchy after years of misrule and increasing taxes and food prices. It was an effort by the French people to take control of their own country.

On the morning of July 14, there is a military parade, known as "Le Défilé" (the parade), along the Champs Élysées. It is the oldest and biggest military parade in Europe. Every year, more than 4,000 servicemen take part, and the French President and other VIPs attend. The first parade was held in 1870 to improve national morale after France's defeat in the Franco-Prussian War. In addition to the parade, there are parties, fairs, and fireworks held all around the country in celebration of Bastille Day. Table 9-1 shows a list of holidays in France.

Table 9–1   A List of Public Holidays in France in 2022

Day	Date	Holiday Name
Saturday	Jan. 1	New Year's Day
Monday	Apr. 18	Easter Monday
Sunday	May 1	Labour Day
Sunday	May 8	V-E Day
Thursday	May 26	Ascension Day
Monday	June 6	Whit Monday
Thursday	July 14	Bastille Day
Monday	Aug. 15	Assumption Day
Tuesday	Nov. 1	All Saints' Day
Friday	Nov. 11	Armistice Day
Sunday	Dec. 25	Christmas Day

French Cultural Orientations

French culture could be described as an intricate and delicate tapestry of traditions, customs, and values, woven from a rich and complex history that spans thousands of years. It is characterized by a deep appreciation for beauty, creativity, and innovation, which is reflected in their world-renowned art, music, and fashion. The French language and literature are integral to their cultural identity, with a literary tradition that spans centuries and has produced many influential and world-famous works. The following section shows six critical dimensions of French cultural orientations.

• Power Distance

With a relatively high score on this dimension, France is a society in which a fair degree of inequality is accepted. Power is not only centralized in companies and government, but also geographically, with all roads leading to Paris. Many studies have shown that French companies tend to have one or two hierarchical levels more than comparable companies in Germany and Britain. French superiors have privileges and are often inaccessible. The CEO of big companies is called Mr. PDG, meaning President Director General (Président Directeur Général in French), which is a more prestigious abbreviation than CEO. These PDGs have frequently attended the most prestigious universities called *grandes écoles*, or "big schools".

• Individualism vs. Collectivism

France scores high on the dimension of individualism, which indicates its inclination to be independent. However, French people prefer to be dependent on the central government, an impersonal power center which cannot so easily invade their private life. French people need a strong leadership in times of crisis. In spite of that, when the crisis is resolved, the president should make space for much weaker leadership. Many French have the need to become a "patron" or "boss", whether as mayor of a small village or as the chairman of the bridge club. The French are self-motivated to be the best in their trade. They, therefore, expect respect for what they do, after which they are very much willing to serve you well.

• Masculinity vs. Femininity

France scores low in the dimension of masculinity and is a somewhat feminine culture. It may be indicated by its famous welfare system, the 35-hour working week, five weeks of holidays per year and its focus on the quality of life. French culture in terms of the model has, however, another unique characteristic, which indicates that people in the working class face more competitions and need to keep striving harder for success.

• Uncertainty Avoidance

French culture scores very high on uncertainty avoidance. French businesspeople don't like surprises or uncertainty. Structure and planning are required in France. Before meetings and negotiations, they like to receive all the necessary information. There is a strong need for laws, rules, and regulations to structure life. This, however, doesn't mean that most French people will try to follow all these rules, the same as in other Latin countries. Given the high score on power distance, this means that power holders have privileges and power holders don't necessarily feel obliged to follow all those rules. At the same time, commoners may also try to relate to power holders so that they can also claim the exception to the rule.

- **Long-term vs. Short-term Orientation**

    France has a rather high score on the long-term orientation dimension, meaning that the French tend to be a pragmatic people. In societies with a pragmatic orientation, people show an ability to easily adapt traditions to changing conditions, and have a strong propensity to save and invest. They also exhibit thriftiness, as well as perseverance in achieving results.

- **Indulgence vs. Restraint**

    France scores somewhere near the middle between indulgence and restraint. Considering the high score on uncertainty avoidance, this seems to imply that the French are less relaxed and less likely to enjoy life than others tend to assume. Indeed, France does not score particularly high on the happiness indices.

French Business Practices and Etiquette

3.1 Business Appointments

- It is normal to make business appointments ahead of time in France.
- As a visitor to France, you should always be punctual, but don't be surprised if your French business associates are late, as the French tend to have a relatively casual concept of time. It is generally acceptable in French culture to arrive 10 to 20 minutes late for a scheduled appointment.
- Business hours are from 8:30 or 9:00 a.m. to 6:30 or 7:00 p.m., although a company's top executives may stay a little later.
- Business lunches usually start at 12:00 p.m. or 1:00 p.m. and may last for two hours or more.

- Dinner time is relatively late, usually starting around 8:00 p.m., and some special events last until midnight.

3.2　Business Negotiations

- Your business cards should ideally be printed in both French and English. Once you have exchanged business cards with your counterpart, you should examine their card carefully before putting it away. If you are considering printing your business cards in French, make sure to include your position within your organization in French and your level of education, for example, if it is at the master's or doctoral level.

- Make sure you state your business intentions directly and clearly since meetings follow a rigid format with a detailed agenda. During your first business meeting, try to remain respectful and welcoming, bearing in mind that your French counterparts need time to build trust in you and your organization.

- It is strongly recommended that you learn basic French phrases and use them in your meetings whenever possible. Your French language efforts will be much appreciated and remembered. If you can't speak French, it is advisable to confirm if counterparts are fluent in your language or in English to facilitate communication and, if necessary, consider using an interpreter.

3.3　Business Entertaining

- The French are renowned for their hospitality, so you can expect to attend a variety of social events during your business dealings. When you are invited to an event, pay attention to the dress code, or ask for information about how you are expected to dress. Dressing appropriately will help you feel more confident and comfortable during the event.

- Food is an integral part of French culture, and the French are very enthusiastic and proud of their cuisine. You should therefore show your appreciation when taken out to a business lunch or dinner and be sure to compliment both the food and drink.

- It is usual in France to drink wine with meals. Knowing some of the basics of French wine and the proper way to drink it can be a credit to your business. French people don't urge others to drink more than they want to, so if you have had enough, just turn your glass upside down during the meal.

- During the meal, the food will be served gradually in smaller amounts, so don't fill up too soon as there may be more to come. When you finish, place your fork and knife across your plate.

3.4 Business Protocol

Greetings

- The most common greeting in French business settings is the handshake. You should shake hands when you are introduced or when you meet someone, and again when you leave.

- Men should wait for women to offer their hands. Note that the French handshake is not as firm as it usually is in the United States.

- It is a good idea to know the proper titles of your business associates and to greet them appropriately, using their correct title and surname. If you are not sure how to address your business counterparts, ask them how they would like to be addressed. If you don't speak French, ask for the pronunciation of your partners' names and confirm it with them.

Gestures

- The "thumbs up" sign in French culture is used to show your approval of something.

- Slapping an open palm over a closed fist is a very rude gesture in France and must be avoided.

- To call for the check in a restaurant, make a writing gesture.

- It is not acceptable to chew gum in public.

- You should stand up or at least make a move to stand up whenever a visitor or a superior enters the room.

3.5 Business Gift-Giving

- Giving business gifts is not part of French business culture. You should avoid giving gifts when you first meet your business partners, and don't give anything too expensive when you do offer a gift.

- French people usually have good taste, so books or music albums in French make appropriate gifts.

- If you are invited to dinner at your host's home, choose some flowers to take with the advice of a florist, or you could ask a shopping guide to help you select some fine chocolates. France is famous for its wines, so do not take wine as a gift.

- It is a good idea to write a thank-you note after the dinner and you can invite the host out to reciprocate.

3.6　Business Outfit

- French people pay great attention to their appearance and tend to dress conservatively in business settings.

- You should aim to wear well-tailored clothes and quality shoes in order to make a good impression.

- In line with their conservative tendency, it is not the practice of French businessmen to loosen their ties or take off their jackets in the office.

- Women should dress in formal business suits, and avoid bright or gaudy colors.

- Signs of ostentation, such as wearing flashy jewelry or accessories should be avoided in business settings.

4 Tips: Conducting Successful Business Negotiations

Negotiation is a process where two or more parties with different needs and goals discuss an issue to find a mutually acceptable solution. In business, negotiation skills are important in both informal day-to-day interactions and formal transactions such as negotiating conditions of sale, lease, service delivery, and other legal contracts. To successfully negotiate a business deal, you have to be prepared, observant, and professional.

- **Be aware of essential qualities of a good negotiator.**

  Strong negotiators usually need to master written, verbal, and nonverbal communication skills. Successful negotiation requires several essential qualities of negotiators. A good negotiator should be a confident speaker and a patient listener. Therefore, remain calm, professional, and patient during the negotiation and show your respect for the other parties. If there are disagreements, don't become emotional or make it personal, and avoid becoming angry, hostile, or frustrated. Remember to stick to the issue. Sometimes, a sense of humor can help overcome an awkward situation, and you may also need to rely on your creativity for achieving your desired outcome. Strive for mutually beneficial solutions and prepare for compromises. Pay attention to details and consider seeking legal advice if necessary. Put things in writing if there is a settled agreement.

- **Use an aggressive or assertive communication style.**

  Using an assertive style will help increase your chances of negotiating successful outcomes for your business. Assertive communicators are both confident and considerate. These communicators are more likely to keep discussion going and facilitate mutually beneficial outcomes. They adopt a strong, steady tone of voice. They are factual, rather than emotional or critical. They describe their views by starting sentences with "I" rather than directing criticisms by starting with "you".

- **Master the cultural differences in international negotiations.**

  Understanding a foreign counterpart's culture is like peeling an onion. At the core of the cultural onion are the deeply held beliefs or values within the culture. People's negotiating behaviors reveal their attitudes and reflect the norms of their culture, and all of these are founded on their beliefs or values. Do your homework about your counterpart's culture and be aware of how others may perceive your culture. Show respect to cultural differences and find ways to bridge the cultural gap. Negotiation involves give and take. You should aim to create a courteous and constructive interaction that is a win-win for both parties.

5 Exercises

5.1 Fact Files

Directions: Complete the following table and find the key facts about France.

Official Name	
Capital City	
Official Language(s)	
Currency	
Population (Year 2022)	
The National Flower	
Current President	

5.2 Compound Dictation

Directions: Listen to the passage and fill in the blanks with the words or expressions that you hear.

France is one of Europe's largest countries. It is bordered by six countries: Germany, Belgium and Luxembourg to the northeast, Switzerland and Italy to the southeast and Spain to the southwest. The United Kingdom borders France via the English Channel. France is considered to be the (1)_____ to Europe as it has several large international airports (two of these can be found in Paris), (2)_____ terminals and rail services.

France is one of the most popular tourist destinations in the world. Why do so many people enjoy visiting this diverse country? The reasons are various: the natural beauty, the amazing climate, the outdoor (3)_____ activities, the art museums and galleries, and so on. There are many different activities that outline the history of the country which are enjoyable to visitors, especially considering its (4)_____ past.

France is well-known for its (5)_____ and wines. French people love to cook and love their food. Meals in France are joyous and long events with families drawn close together for conversation. The (6)_____ French meal offers three to four courses which include cheese before dessert. Meals are (7)_____ by freshly baked bread and wine. Popular foods in France include chicken in a red wine sauce, known as *Coq au Vin* and (8)_____ cooked in butter, or *Coquilles Saint-Jacques*. The food on the menu can be quite diverse and varies from region to region.

People in France are (9)_____ and formal. They are also known for being chic, taking great pride in their personal appearance and clothing. France is viewed by some as an (10)_____ country because of these characteristics, although the French themselves attribute this to simply being fashionable and cautious about their appearance.

5.3   True or False: French Customs and Etiquette

Directions: Put T for true or F for false for each of the following statements.

(   ) 1. It is a rude gesture to slap your open palm over a closed fist in France.

(   ) 2. If you are invited for dinner at a French business associate's home, the best gift for the host is a bottle of wine.

(   ) 3. The French maintain an air of formality, and business titles are often used in business settings.

(   ) 4. In France, interrupting during business meetings or negotiations is always a sign of disrespect. You should remain silent until your counterpart has finished speaking.

(   ) 5. You shouldn't rush or display signs of impatience with your French counterparts. The French take their time before arriving at a decision.

5.4   Multiple Choice: To Know More About France

Directions: Mark the correct answer to each question. Look up the following facts on the Internet or in some reference books and try to get more background information.

1. Which of these countries does not border France?

   A. Austria.   B. Italy.   C. Germany.   D. Luxembourg.

2. On what day of the year do the French celebrate their national holiday?

   A. September 2.   B. October 23.   C. July 14.   D. March 10.

3. Which of these countries was never a French colony?

   A. Kenya.   B. Vietnam.   C. Haiti.   D. Dominica.

4. What is the westernmost region on the French mainland?

   A. Normandy.   B. Brittany.   C. Occitanie.   D. Corsica.

5. About what percentage of France's electricity comes from nuclear power?

   A. 30%.   B. 10%.   C. 70%.   D. 50%.

5.5   Case Study

Directions: Read the following case and answer the questions.

> Mr. Wang was the owner of a Chinese company. He went to France to attend a business negotiation. During the negotiation, Oliver, the owner of the French company, constantly interrupted Mr. Wang's presentation. Mr. Wang felt upset by these interruptions and thought Oliver was rude. Oliver, however, didn't seem to be sorry for his interruptions.

1. What went wrong in this case and why?

2. Conduct further research on the interruption strategies in international business negotiations and compare people's different perceptions of interruption in business negotiations from a cross-cultural perspective.

 6 A Mini Business Project

Directions: Suppose that your company is going to purchase 50 laptops with a limited budget, and there is a Lenovo model labeled RMB 8,900 that meets the parameters for purchasing. However, the price for one computer is still too high, making the total amount of purchase surpass the budget. Please define your BATNA (Best Alternative to a Negotiated Agreement) based on the following aspects.

- The price of each computer should be less than RMB 8,000;
- The price should also include licensed software, such as the latest Windows system and Microsoft Office;
- The price should also include a two-year free maintenance service;
- Some discount coupons for future purchases;
- Prospective purchase in the future.

Note: You or your team is asked to prepare a presentation using PowerPoint slides, and write an executive summary using Microsoft Word. You may use appropriate visual aids (e.g., video clips) to support your presentation, and you may also refer to the sample project files online for reference.

Words and Expressions

brogue	/brəʊg/	n.	口音；（尤指讲英语的爱尔兰或苏格兰人的）土腔
morale	/məˈrɑːl/	n.	士气；斗志
patron	/ˈpeɪtrən/	n.	赞助人；资助者
a centrist government			中间派政府
nuclear power plant			核电站

Notes

Scan the QR code for more information about French culture.

Unit 10

German Culture, Customs, and Business Etiquette

Germany: Overview

1.1 Geography and Demographics

Geography

The Federal Republic of Germany, simply as Germany, occupies an important position at the very heart of Europe. Although it is not the largest country in Europe, it is considered to be the economic powerhouse of the European Union. To the north, Germany is bounded by two seas, the North Sea, and the Baltic Sea. Its neighboring countries are Denmark to the north, Poland and the Czech Republic to the east, Austria and Switzerland to the south, and France, Luxembourg, Belgium, and the Netherlands to the west. Germany's capital city is Berlin. It is the political, economic, and art center of Germany. Germany is a beautiful and varied country that boasts a long history and fascinating culture. It has also had a profound influence on the way the modern world thinks and acts.

Population and People

In 2022, the German population was roughly 84.1 million. Over the centuries, and as the territory changed, the Germans intermingled with numerous other peoples. Up until the 1950s, few ethnic minorities lived in Germany, other than Jews. In the mid-1950s, "guest workers" and their families began to immigrate to Germany, of whom the largest group is of Turkish ancestry. Later, people from countries such as Sri Lanka and Vietnam also added to the cultural mix of Germany. By the beginning of the 21st century, nearly 10% of the population, or about eight million people, were ethnically non-German. In 2015 alone, more than one million migrants entered Germany.

Language

German is the official language of Germany. There were once distinct dialectal divisions in the German language which represented significant ethnic and cultural distinctions. In recent years, however, mass education and communication as well as internal migration have had a leveling and standardizing influence on German language. These factors have led to a trend among the younger, better-educated, and more mobile ranks of society to speak a standard, "accent-less" German. Dialectal differences in the language spoken can still be found, though, most notably among those living in rural areas, as well as among longtime native inhabitants of the cities.

There are three major dialectal divisions of German, which coincide almost identically with the major topographical regions: the North German Plain (Low German), the Central German Uplands (Central German), and the Southern Jura, Danube Basin, and Alpine districts (Upper German). Each of these dialects has its own local variations.

1.2   History, Economy, and World Influence

History in Brief

The original Germans mainly arrived in two waves of migration around the year 2,300 BCE. First came the Celtic people and after them the Southern Russians. German history is considered to have truly begun in the 8th century when Charles the Great, the Roman Emperor, conquered the region and consolidated the Germanic tribes living there.

The Thirty Years' War, from 1618 to 1648, was a significant event in German history. It was a German civil war. During the war, the Holy Roman Emperor's authority in Germany was greatly reduced, but it was not until 1806 that it was finally dissolved by Napoleon Bonaparte.

In 1815, Napoleon Bonaparte was defeated by the Prussian troops and their Allies at the Battle of Waterloo. In 1871, Bismarck, the Chancellor of Prussia, declared Prussia's Wilhelm I Kaiser (Emperor) of a united Germany with its capital in Berlin. A new German Empire was created.

On January 30, 1933, Adolf Hitler was appointed Chancellor of Germany and the head of government. A national referendum held on August 19, 1934, confirmed Hitler as the sole Führer (leader) of Germany. All power was centralized in Hitler's person and his word became the highest law. Genocide, mass murder, and large-scale forced labor became hallmarks of the regime. Starting in 1939, hundreds of thousands of German citizens with mental or physical disabilities were murdered in hospitals and asylums. Einsatzgruppen paramilitary death squads accompanied the German armed forces inside the occupied territories and conducted the genocide of millions of Jews and other Holocaust victims. After 1941, millions of others were imprisoned, forced to work to death, or murdered in Nazi concentration camps and extermination camps. This genocide is known as the Holocaust. The Third Reich, under the rule of Hitler and the Nazis, ended in May 1945 after just 12 years when the Allies defeated Germany, ending World War Ⅱ in Europe.

After World War Ⅱ, Germany was partitioned into two separate countries: the Western Federal Republic of Germany and the Eastern Democratic Republic of Germany, divided by the Berlin Wall. It was not until 1989 that the Berlin Wall finally came down, and the next year the two countries were reunited as the Federal Republic of Germany, which is today's Germany.

Economy in Brief

Germany has a mixed economy, which allows a free market economy in consumer goods and business services, but at the same time the government imposes regulations to protect its citizens. Germany has a command economy in defense as everyone in the country receives the benefit, and those who earn more pay higher taxes. The government provides health care insurance and education. In this system, citizens pay according to their income and receive benefits according to their needs.

The most important sectors of the German economy in 2020 were industry (23.4%). Public administration, defense, education, human health and social work activities account for 19.4% of its economy. Wholesale and retail trade, transport, accommodation, and food service activities are about 15.8% of the economy.

Intra-EU trade accounts for 53% of Germany's exports (France 8% and the Netherlands 7%), while outside the EU 9% go to the United States and 8% to China. In terms of imports, 64% come from EU Member States (the Netherlands 14%, France, Poland, and Belgium 6%), while outside the EU 8% come from China and 5% from the United States.

World Influence

Germany is a firm supporter of international cooperation to address the global challenges of conflict, poverty, food security, preserving the environment, and climate change. As such, Germany supports multilateral efforts to establish peace, promote a stable global economy, and encourage the use of renewable resources and environmentally friendly production.

Germany has long played a role in the international economy, joining the International Bank for Reconstruction and Development (IBRD) in 1952, which is now today known as the World Bank. It is one of the 15 signatory countries for the International Development Association in 1960, which has become the leading source of concessional lending to the world's poorest countries. Germany became a member of the International Finance Corporation in 1956, and in 1961, it was the first European country to establish a development ministry. It joined the International Centre for Settlement of Investment Disputes in 1969 and the Multilateral Investment Guarantee Agency in 1988. Today, Germany is the fourth largest shareholder of the World Bank. As one of the founding European Union Member States, they have 96 member seats in the European Parliament (705 members in total).

1.3   German Holidays

German Unity Day (Tag der Deutschen Einheit) is held on October 3 to mark the anniversary of the nation's unification. It commemorates October 3, 1990, the day the Federal Republic of Germany in the west and the Democratic Republic of Germany in the east united to create a single and federal Germany. Many people have a day off and there are big public celebrations including speeches by various leaders, concerts, communal meals, food, and cultural presentations from different regions of the country, as well as fireworks displays. Each year, the national celebrations are hosted by different cities, and there is a festive, welcoming, and safe atmosphere. Many government offices close on public holidays and some private businesses may close as well. Table 10–1 shows a list of main holidays in Germany.

Table 10–1   A List of Main Holidays in Germany in 2022

Day	Date	Holiday Name
Saturday	Jan. 1	New Year's Day
Friday	Apr. 15	Good Friday
Monday	Apr. 18	Easter Monday
Sunday	May 1	Labour Day
Thursday	May 26	Ascension Day
Monday	June 6	Whit Monday
Monday	Oct. 3	German Unity Day
Sunday	Dec. 25	Christmas Day
Monday	Dec. 26	St. Stephen's Day

2 German Cultural Orientations

With a history spanning centuries, German culture is an enduring and intricate combination of traditions, practices, and values. The German people are known for their precision, attention to detail, and love of efficiency, which is reflected in their world-renowned engineering, science, and technology. German language, literature, and philosophy have made significant contributions to the world, with many famous writers and thinkers emerging from Germany. The following section highlights six key dimensions of German cultural orientations, exploring how these dimensions shape the country's values, beliefs, and behaviors.

• Power Distance

Highly decentralized and supported by a strong middle class, Germany has a relatively low score on this dimension, making it one of the lower power-distant countries. Co-determination rights are extensive, and management must take them into account. A direct and participative communication and meeting style is common. There is a dislike of control in German corporations. The leadership is challenged to show expertise, and is best accepted when based on expertise.

• Individualism vs. Collectivism

The German society is a truly individualist culture, scoring relatively high on the dimension of individualism. Small nuclear families with a focus on the parent-children relationship rather than extended families are most common. There is a strong belief in the ideal of self-actualization. Loyalty is based on personal preferences for people as well as a sense of duty and responsibility. This is defined by the contract between the employer and the employee. Germans are very direct in their communication, according to the ideal of "being honest, even if it hurts". In this way, the recipient can learn from his or her mistakes.

• Masculinity vs. Femininity

Scoring above the intermediate score on the masculinity dimension, Germany can be considered as a masculine society. Performance is highly valued and early required. The school system in Germany separates children into different types of schools as early as the age of 10. People "live in order to work" and their self-esteem tends to come from work. Managers are expected to be decisive and assertive. Status is often displayed, especially by way of cars, watches, cell phones, etc.

• Uncertainty Avoidance

Germany is among the uncertainty avoidant countries with a relatively high score on this dimension. It means that Germans have a preference for avoiding uncertainty. In line with the philosophical heritage of Kant, Hegel, and Fichte, there is a strong preference for deductive rather than inductive approaches, whether it be in thinking, presenting, or planning. The systematic overview has to be given in order to proceed. This is also reflected in the legal system. Details are equally important to create certainty that a certain topic or project is well thought out. In combination with their low power distance, where the certainty about one's own decisions is not covered by the larger responsibility of the boss, Germans prefer to compensate for their higher uncertainty by strongly relying on expertise.

• Long-term vs. Short-term Orientation

Germany scores very high on the long-term orientation dimension, indicating that it is a very pragmatic country. People in such societies tend to believe that truth depends very much on the situation, context, and time. They show an ability to adapt traditions easily to changed conditions. German people have a strong propensity to save and invest. They are thrifty and persevere in order to achieve results.

• Indulgence vs. Restraint

With quite a low score on the indulgence dimension, it can be said that German culture is restrained in nature. Such societies have a tendency toward cynicism and pessimism. Also, in contrast to indulgent societies, restrained societies do not put much emphasis on leisure time, and control the gratification of their desires. People with this orientation tend to feel that their actions are restrained by social norms and that indulging themselves is somewhat wrong.

3 German Business Practices and Etiquette

3.1 Business Appointments

- Germans are extremely punctual people, so make sure that you are on time for every appointment, no matter whether it is for business or social engagements. Arriving even four or five minutes late is very impolite, especially if you are in a subordinate position to the person whom you are meeting.

- Be sure to make appointments to meet people well in advance. You should provide at least one week's notice for an appointment made by phone. If you are pressed for time, a short preliminary meeting can sometimes be arranged with only a few days' notice.

- Be aware that if you send an e-mail to an executive who is on vacation, you may need to wait for a long time for a reply as most Germans take at least six weeks of vacation per year.

- When arranging appointments, avoid Friday afternoons as some offices close early on Fridays. Also be aware that many people take long vacations in the months of July, August, and December, and that during regional festivals such as the Oktoberfest or the three-day carnival before Lent, little work gets done.

- Note an important difference in specifying time. Whereas an Englishman might refer to 9:30 a.m. as "half-nine", a German may say "half-ten", so be sure to clarify if you are in doubt.

3.2 Business Negotiations

- The pace of German corporate decision-making tends to be methodical and much slower than the norm in the US or UK. It can be very hard for outsiders to understand the decision-making process in German firms. German companies often have a parallel "hidden" series of advisers and decision-makers whose approval of proposals and plans is also necessary.

- Germans tend to be direct and may even bluntly criticize your product or company. This is acceptable in German business practice, so don't take it personally. Make sure that you have plenty of data such as case studies and examples to back up any claims you make about your company or your products as Germans hate hype and exaggeration. Be prepared to provide a lot of detailed information at short notice. Although their requests may seem trivial to you, they are important to your German associates.

- Germans have a reputation for quality, and this is partly the result of slow and methodical planning. Every aspect of a proposal you make will be examined in great detail by various executives. Don't expect to speed up the process, as it will extend through all the steps due to the belief that a proper job takes time.

- Be patient in your dealings as it takes time to establish a close business relationship with Germans, but over time as you get to know them, they are likely to become much friendlier and more talkative. Germans may or may not socialize before beginning to discuss business with you. Don't be surprised if the business discussion starts right after you introduce yourself, without any preliminary small talk.

- Make sure that all of your company's promotional materials and instruction manuals are translated into German, even if your business associates speak your language.

- If a problem occurs, you should explain it clearly, in detail, and unemotionally. You may need to do this in writing, as Germans are not accustomed to informally passing on information to others.

- Since work and family life are kept separate in Germany, don't ask your German business associates personal questions. They will tell you about their family life if they want to.

- Sports are a suitable topic of conversation, as Germans tend to be passionate soccer fans, and also enjoy a variety of other sports including skiing, hiking, cycling, and tennis, as well as some lesser-known sports such as ice skating, curling, and gliding.

3.3   Business Entertaining

- When doing business in Germany, it is common to have business lunches, but not business breakfasts.

跨文化沟通与商务礼仪综合教程
Intercultural Communication and Business Etiquette

- Business may be discussed before and (sometimes) after lunch, but not while you are eating. If you are invited out for a meal, you can offer to pay, but your host will most likely decline your offer. You can insist on paying when you make the invitation yourself.

- Be sure to arrive on time for social events. Drinks are served before the meal, usually with a few appetizers, and the meal starts soon after.

- Germans do not often entertain business associates at home, so if you are invited to someone's home, consider it an honor.

- Always use utensils when eating. In Germany, very few items are eaten with the hands. Place your utensils vertically side by side on the plate when you have finished eating.

- If you smoke, check first if you are allowed to smoke, and if you are, offer a cigarette to everyone else.

3.4 Business Protocol

Greetings

- Shaking hands is the norm in German business situations, at the beginning and at the end of meetings. Note that the German handshake may be accompanied by a subtle nod of the head.

- As in many cultures, it is usually the eldest or the highest-ranking person who enters the room first.

- Although you may feel uncomfortable, you are expected to maintain extended, direct eye contact during conversations. If not, you may be considered as untrustworthy.

- It is considered rude to speak to someone with your hands in your pockets. You may take something out of your pocket, but don't leave your hands in there.

Titles/Forms of Address

- Traditionally, only family members and close friends address each other by their first names, so it is quite possible that you may never have a close enough relationship with older German colleagues to use their first names, although you may with younger Germans.

- For those without a professional title, use Mr. (Herr), Mrs. or Ms. (Frau), or Miss (Fräulein) followed by their surname, where Fräulein is only used for young women under 18, and Frau is used for all businesswomen, regardless of their marital status.

- Education is highly respected in Germany. It is very important to know your German associates' professional titles. Professionals such as attorneys, engineers, and pastors should be addressed as "Herr" or "Frau" plus their title, and PhDs as Herr (or Frau) Doctor/Professor.

Gestures

- Germans are usually open and generous with close friends, but more formal and reserved in public. Don't expect to see many smiles or displays of affection in public places.

- To get someone's attention, rather than waving or beckoning, raise your hand, palm facing out, with the index finger extended.

- When sitting, you may cross one knee over the other, but don't rest your ankle on your knee, and don't rest your feet on anything other than a footstool.

3.5 Business Gift-Giving

- Note that German civil servants cannot accept gifts of any kind. Expensive gifts are not given when doing business in Germany. Small, good quality, and inexpensive gifts are preferred. These could include good quality pens, reasonably priced electronics, or imported liquor. A good choice is a gift from your home region or country, such as an illustrated book. The only acceptable article of clothing that can be offered as a gift is a scarf. Other clothing, perfume, and soap are considered as being too personal for business gifts.

- If you are invited to a German associate's home for dinner, you should treat it as an honor. If you send flowers ahead of time to your host, there should be an odd number of flowers (but not 13). You should not include certain flowers in the bouquet, such as white carnations, white chrysanthemums, or calla lilies, which are usually reserved for funerals.

- Be careful when choosing alcohol as a gift. While an imported liquor is appropriate, presenting a locally available wine might not be appreciated. A good wine from your home country which is not available in Germany or a top-quality imported red wine is a good choice. Since Germans produce some of the finest beers in the world, a gift of foreign beer is not likely to impress your host.

3.6 Business Outfit

- When doing business in Germany, you should dress very conservatively. Dark suits, unobtrusive ties, and white shirts are the norm. Blue blazers and gray flannel pants are acceptable for formal occasions. Women should also dress conservatively in dark suits, pantsuits, and blouses of a neutral color.

- When the weather is hot, wait to see if your German associates remove their jackets or ties before removing yours. They may well remain fully dressed, no matter how hot the weather is. Clean, tidy, and comfortable shirts and jeans are the most common casual wear, and German men tend to wear sandals in summer.

- For most formal social events, such as parties, dinners, and the theater, it is also appropriate to wear a business suit. If you go to the theater, you have to check your coat, so be sure to take a sweater with you if you are worried about being cold. When attending the opening night of an opera, concert, or play, men should wear their best dark suit or tuxedo, and women should wear a long evening gown.

4 Tips: Observing Proper Table Manners

A business lunch or dinner is a great opportunity to let your professionalism shine. Table manners are a set of rules that govern the expectations of social and dining behavior in a workplace, group, or society. Different cultures observe different rules for table manners. While business dining etiquette rules can vary from country to country, the general guidelines remain the same. Practice good manners and use common sense.

- **Arrive on time.**
  Arriving on time is appreciated, 5 to 15 minutes late for an invitation is generally fine, but do not arrive any more than 30 minutes late for a party or a big gathering. Shake hands with everyone already seated at the table. If necessary, introduce yourself. Remain standing until your host is seated. Once

seated, place your napkin on your lap only after everyone else is seated and your host has moved his or her napkin. If someone comes to the table after you do, it's polite to stand up to greet them.

- **Dress appropriately.**
Take a moment to look at the guest list and determine whether it is an informal gathering or a formal, business-oriented event. Dress appropriately according to the dress code provided by the event organizers or ask if it is not specified in the invitation.

- **Focus on the person at the table.**
Turn off your cell phone and keep it in your pocket. It's a sign of respect to fully focus on the person in front of you. If you check text messages or take calls, the other person may think that they're not important enough for your full attention. If you cannot miss a call, turn your phone on silent and excuse yourself if you have to take the call in another room.

- **Behave properly while eating.**
Follow your host's lead and choose something similar to what he or she has ordered. When eating, make sure to keep your plate tidy and not make it messy. It is necessary to use the knife and fork in an appropriate manner. Eat in small bites and slowly. Do not hold food on your fork or spoon while talking.

- **Finish your meal politely.**
When you have finished eating, signal your server to clear your place setting by resting your fork (tines up) and knife blade inward, with the handles resting at five o'clock and the tips pointing to ten o'clock on your plate. Napkins should be placed unfolded on the table when the meal is finished. Leaving a very small amount of food on the plate is considered acceptable, while leaving a large amount is considered a sign of disrespect.

- **Choose right topics at the table.**
Do not talk about business unless your host brings it up. Avoid talking about controversial topics. Safe topics include weather, sports, current events, and common interests. If someone else brings up a topic you're uncomfortable with during the meal, politely try to change the subject as subtly as possible.

- **Make the goodbye brief but cordial.**
When it's time to leave, don't delay your host with a lengthy goodbye, make your departure brief but cordial. Be sure to kindly thank your host for the meal. Shake hands and maintain good eye contact before leaving.

5 Exercises

5.1 Fact Files

Directions: Complete the following table and find the key facts about Germany.

Official Name	
Capital City	
Official Language(s)	
Currency	
Population (Year 2022)	
The National Flower	
Current Federal Chancellor	

5.2 Compound Dictation

Directions: Listen to the passage and fill in the blanks with the words or expressions that you hear.

Germany is situated at the heart of the European continent. It is Europe's most populous nation and the largest economy, which has a (1)_____ business culture. Therefore, before doing business in Germany, it's necessary to learn German business (2)_____ .

First is about politeness. Be polite and use (3)_____ when you are addressing, introducing or writing to a business person. Put "Herr" and "Frau" (4)_____ before a man's and a woman's title or last name when you address them. And one's (5)_____ is held in high regard in German culture.

Second is (6)_____ . Be on time for every appointment, whether for business or (7)_____ . To be five or ten minutes late for the appointment is considered disrespectful. Being too early can be considered just as (8)_____ as being late.

Third concerns the code of business dress. Dress (9)_____ when meeting with German businesspeople. If you are a man, do not (10)_____ your jacket unless your counterpart does so.

5.3   True or False: German Customs and Etiquette

Directions: Put T for true or F for false for each of the following statements.

(   ) 1. German executives prefer to keep their office doors open to create a sense of openness and mutual trust.

(   ) 2. Waving or shouting at each other from a distance for a greeting is acceptable in Germany.

(   ) 3. If you work in Germany, to show your friendliness, you can keep smiling at the customers and co-workers.

(   ) 4. You can hype the products to draw the attention of the companies so that the business can be conducted successfully.

(   ) 5. Germans are interested in sports, which is a great topic for conversation.

5.4   Multiple Choice: To Know More About Germany

Directions: Mark the correct answer to each question. Look up the following facts on the Internet or in some reference books and try to get more background information.

1. Oktoberfest Munich in Germany is the world's largest celebration of Bavarian culture—the area of Bavaria being the southeast corner of Germany famous for _____.

   A. bread   B. beer   C. cheese   D. wine

2. After World War Ⅱ, Germany was divided into two parts. When did the two halves of Germany reunite?

   A. January 22, 1990.   B. October 3, 1990.

   C. August 10, 1990.   D. July 15, 1990.

3. In the European Union, Germany has _____.

   A. the largest population

B. the biggest national land area

C. the most developed agriculture

D. the third largest economy in terms of GDP

4. What is an inappropriate topic for the first conversation with a German?

    A. Sports.   B. Private messages.

    C. Rigorous data.   D. Beers.

5. Where is BMW headquartered in Germany?

    A. Berlin.   B. Munich.   C. Stuttgart.   D. Hamburg.

5.5   Case Study

Directions: Read the following case and answer the questions.

> Mr. Wang, a Chinese businessman, was on a business trip in Germany. On the first day after the business meeting, Hans Weber, a German senior executive, invited Mr. Wang to dinner. Mr. Wang was very happy about the opportunity to strengthen his relationship with Mr. Weber. The following is their dialog at the dinner table:
>
> Wang: Hans, thank you for inviting me, and I hope we can have better cooperation. Well, by the way, can I ask you a question? What is your salary as an executive in Germany?
>
> Hans: (Hans was a little embarrassed) Well, I think that's my private business.

1. What went wrong in this case and why?

2. Conduct further research on the inappropriate conversational topics that can invade privacy in international business settings and provide advice on how to respect privacy in conversations.

6 A Mini Business Project

Directions: Suppose that you are entertaining your German business partner in a restaurant this evening. Please introduce your preparation based on the following aspects.

- getting to know your partner's favorite dishes and eating taboos;
- getting familiar with the menu in the restaurant ahead of time;
- dressing appropriately and arriving on time;
- choosing safe topics to discuss during the meal;
- learning Western table manners.

Note: You or your team is asked to prepare a presentation using PowerPoint slides, and write an executive summary using Microsoft Word. You may use appropriate visual aids (e.g., video clips) to support your presentation, and you may also refer to the sample project files online for reference.

Words and Expressions

bluntly	/ˈblʌntli/	adv.	坦率地；直率地
carnival	/ˈkɑːnɪvl/	n.	狂欢节
Chancellor	/ˈtʃɑːnsələ(r)/	n.	（德国、奥地利）总理
consolidate	/kənˈsɒlɪdeɪt/	v.	使巩固；使加强
cordial	/ˈkɔːdiəl/	adj.	热情友好的；和蔼可亲的
curling	/ˈkɜːlɪŋ/	n.	冰壶，冰上溜石（将重石片滑向一目标）
deductive	/dɪˈdʌktɪv/	adj.	推论的；演绎的
festive	/ˈfestɪv/	adj.	节日的；喜庆的；欢乐的
footstool	/ˈfʊtstuːl/	n.	脚凳（坐时搁脚的矮凳）
genocide	/ˈdʒenəsaɪd/	n.	种族灭绝；大屠杀
gliding	/ˈɡlaɪdɪŋ/	n.	滑翔运动
Holocaust	/ˈhɒləkɔːst/	n.	大屠杀

impose	/ɪmˈpəʊz/	v.	推行，采用（规章制度）；强制实行
inductive	/ɪnˈdʌktɪv/	adj.	归纳的
intermingle	/ˌɪntəˈmɪŋgl/	v.	使（人、思想、色彩等）混合
Lent	/lent/	n.	大斋节
methodical	/məˈθɒdɪkl/	adj.	有条理的；井然有序的
pessimism	/ˈpesɪmɪzəm/	n.	悲观主义
Prussia	/ˈprʌʃə/	n.	普鲁士
Prussian	/ˈprʌʃən/	adj.	普鲁士的
subordinate	/səˈbɔːdɪnət/	adj.	隶属的；从属的；下级的
be partitioned into			被划分为……
calla lily			马蹄莲
communal meal			公共膳食
concessional lending			优惠贷款
Nazi concentration camp			纳粹集中营
Third Reich			第三帝国（指希特勒统治下的德国）

Notes

Scan the QR code for more information about German culture.

Unit 11

Russian Culture, Customs, and Business Etiquette

Russia: Overview

1.1 Geography and Demographics

Geography

The Russian Federation covers nine time zones and all climate zones except tropical, with land that stretches almost halfway around the planet. In fact, by jet from Moscow, it takes about eight hours to reach Vladivostok on the Pacific Ocean coast. If you were to take the trip on the Trans-Siberian Railroad, you can count on your journey taking at least four days.

Russia has 16 cities with a metro population of more than one million. The most populated cities are Moscow, St. Petersburg, Novosibirsk, Yekaterinburg, and Nizhny Novgorod. Moscow, the capital, with over 12 million (metro) residents, is the country's major economic and political center, and the seat of the President, the government, and the State Duma.

Population and People

In 2022, the population of Russian Federation was about 143.6 million. Russia is one of the countries with the largest number of ethnic groups in Europe. It has over 185 ethnic groups or nationalities. Various ethnic groups or nationalities spread across the country and are represented at all levels of government. Some of the largest ethnic groups in Russia include Russians, Tatars, Ukrainians, and Bashkirs.

Language

Russian is the official language and also the primary language spoken by the overwhelming majority of people in Russia. It is also used as a second language in other former republics of the Soviet Union. Russian dialects are divided into the Northern group, the Southern group, and the Central group. Modern literary Russian is based on the Central dialect of Moscow, having basically the consonant system of the Northern dialect and the vowel system of the Southern dialect.

1.2   History, Economy, and World Influence

History in Brief

The earliest human settlers in Russia arrived around 500 CE, as Scandinavians (what is now Norway, Denmark, and Sweden) moved south to areas around the upper Volga River. These settlers mixed with Slavs from the west and built a fortress that would eventually become the Ukrainian city of Kiev.

Kiev evolved into an empire that ruled most of European Russia for 200 years, then broke up into Ukraine, Belarus, and Muscovy. Muscovy's capital, Moscow, remained a small trading post until the 13th century, when Mongol invaders from Central Asia drove people to settle in Moscow.

In the 1550s, Muscovite ruler Ivan IV became Russia's first tsar, or emperor, after driving the Mongols out of Kiev and unifying the region. In 1682, 10-year-old Peter the Great and his older brother, Ivan, both became tsars (though Peter's aunt and Ivan's mother, Sophia, was in charge). Soon after, Sophia was overthrown, and Peter was considered by most to be the real tsar, though he allowed his brother to keep his official position. For 42 years, Peter worked to make Russia more modern and more European.

In 1762, Peter III (1728–1762), a grandson of Peter the Great, took a trip to Germany, and his wife, Catherine, named herself the sole ruler of Russia. Just six months later the tsar died, and Catherine the Great, the empress, continued to modernize Russia, support arts and culture, and expand its territory, claiming Ukraine, Crimea, Poland, and other places. She ruled for 34 years.

In 1917, Russians who were unhappy with the leadership, overthrew Tsar Nicholas II and formed an elected government. Just a few months later, the Bolsheviks seized power. Their leader, Vladimir Lenin, created the Union of Soviet Socialist Republics (USSR), uniting Russia and 11 other countries.

The USSR, also known as the Soviet Union, lasted from 1917 through 1991. On December 25, 1991, it ceased to exist. The Russian Federation is still the largest and most powerful of the former republics.

Economy in Brief

The basis of the Russian economy is the extraction, processing, and export of various types of mineral raw materials, including oil and natural gas, coal, iron ore, apatites, potassium salts, phosphorites, diamonds, gold, silver, nickel, platinum, copper, etc. Russia is one of the world leaders in production of oil and natural gas. The total reserves of coal were more than 200 billion tons (more than 5% of the world's reserves) in 2016.

Russia has about 10% of all arable land in the world. It is a major exporter of agricultural products, and the world leader in wheat exports. The main crops are cereals, sugar beet, sunflower, soybean, and vegetables.

The main types of livestock products produced in Russia are meat, milk, eggs, wool, and honey. The food industry is relatively well-developed and is mainly oriented to the domestic market. Russia is one of the world leaders in power generation. Electricity is produced at thermal, nuclear, and hydroelectric power stations.

The transport system in Russia is one of the most extensive in the world, including more than 120,000 km of railways, 1 million km of roads, 230,000 km of main pipelines, and 100,000 km of inland waterways. The huge territory and severe climate predetermined the paramount importance for Russia of all-weather types of land transport, including railways and pipelines.

Today's Russia has one of the most developed markets of mobile communication in the world. It is the largest country in Europe in terms of the number of Internet users.

Russia occupies one of the leading places in the world in the field of international tourism. Several famous places include resorts on the Black Sea coast of the Caucasus (Sochi), a group of resorts of the Caucasian Mineral Waters. Other popular destinations of international and domestic tourism are St. Petersburg and the surrounding area, Moscow, Kazan, the cities and towns of the Golden Ring of Russia, the Volga River, Lake Baikal and so on.

World Influence

The Russian Federation succeeded to the Soviet Union's seat, including its permanent membership on the Security Council in the UN after the 1991 dissolution of the Soviet Union, which originally co-founded the UN in 1945. The Russian Federation has also been a member of the WTO since August 22, 2012. Russian President Vladimir Putin signed the bill ratifying the country's accession to the WTO after 18 years of complicated negotiations. Russia's accession to the WTO strengthened the multilateral trading system, making the WTO a more universal organization.

For much of the post-Cold War era, Russia's ability to project its influence on a global scale was constrained by internal challenges and limited resources, but since Vladimir Putin returned to the presidency in 2012, Moscow has engaged in a broad campaign to expand its international reach. Russia's more assertive foreign policy is making the Kremlin an important player in an expanding array of countries and regions.

1.3 **Russian Holidays**

Russians love to celebrate, and Russia's public holidays should not be treated lightly. On the most important holidays, such as New Year's Day, Christmas, and the May holidays, many shops close completely and city streets become strangely quiet. All government offices are closed on public holidays, and so are most overseas embassies.

The first holiday of the year is New Year's Day. People welcome the New Year at midnight on December 31 with champagne and listen to the Kremlin chimes striking 12 o'clock. There are many New Year traditions in Russia. In every home, there is a New Year's tree glittering with colored lights and decorations. Children always wait for Father Frost to come and give them a present. Table 11–1 is a list of main holidays in Russia.

Table 11–1   A List of Main Holidays in Russia in 2022

Day	Date	Holiday Name
Saturday	Jan. 1	New Year's Day
Sunday to Monday	Jan. 2–3	New Year's Holiday (Bridge Day)
Tuesday to Saturday	Jan. 4–8	Orthodox Christmas Holiday
Friday	Jan. 7	Orthodox Christmas
Wednesday	Feb. 23	Defence of the Fatherland Day
Tuesday	Mar. 8	International Women's Day
Sunday	May 1	Day of Spring and Labor
Monday	May 2	Public Holiday
Tuesday	May 3	Day of Spring and Labor Holiday

(continued)

Day	Date	Holiday Name
Monday to Tuesday	May 9–10	Victory Day Holiday
Sunday to Monday	June 12–13	Russia Day
Friday	Nov. 4	Day of Unity

2. Russian Cultural Orientations

Russia's cultural identity has been shaped by a mix of Slavic, Nordic, and Asian cultures, resulting in a unique and multifaceted mosaic. Russian language, literature, and art reflect a deep appreciation for beauty, emotion, and intellectual pursuits. Russian music and dance, from classical ballet to traditional folk dances, showcase a range of styles and influences. Russian architecture is similarly diverse, with influences from Byzantine, baroque, neoclassical, and modernist styles. The following section briefly describes Russian cultural orientations based on the 6-D Model.

- **Power Distance**

  Russia, scoring very high on this dimension, is a nation where power holders are very distant in society. This is underlined by the fact that the largest country in the world is extremely centralized. About two-thirds of all foreign investments go into Moscow, where 80% of all financial potential is concentrated. The huge discrepancy between the less powerful and the more powerful people leads to an emphasis on status symbols. Behavior must reflect and represent the status roles in all areas of business interactions. The approach should be top-down, with clear mandates for each task.

- **Individualism vs. Collectivism**

  Russians demonstrate notably higher manifestations of collectivism than individualism, but their collectivism takes a different form. If Russians plan to go out with their friends, they would literally say "We with friends" instead of "Me and my friends". If they talk about brothers and sisters, it may well be cousins. Family, friends, and even the neighborhood are extremely important for coping with everyday life's challenges. Relationships are crucial in obtaining information, getting introduced, or achieving successful negotiations.

• Masculinity vs. Femininity

Russia has a relatively low score for masculinity, and it may be surprising with regard to its preference for status symbols. At second glance, one can see that Russians at workplace as well as when meeting a stranger tend to understate their personal achievements, contributions, or capacities. They talk modestly about themselves. Scientists, researchers, or doctors are most often expected to live on a very modest standard of living. Dominant behavior might be accepted when it comes from the boss, but is not appreciated among peers.

• Uncertainty Avoidance

Scoring very high on this dimension, Russians feel very much threatened by ambiguous situations. This mentality is evident in Russians' well-prepared and extremely detailed business presentations during the key stage of negotiations. Russians also prefer to have context and background information. As long as Russians interact with people who are considered to be strangers, they appear very formal and distant. At the same time, formality is used as a sign of respect.

• Long-term vs. Short-term Orientation

With a very high score on long-term orientation, Russia is definitely a country with a pragmatic mindset. In pragmatic societies, people show an ability to easily adapt traditions to changing conditions, a strong propensity to save and invest. Thrift and perseverance are valued by Russian people to achieve success.

• Indulgence vs. Restraint

The restrained nature of Russian culture is easily visible through its very low score on indulgence. Societies with a low score on this dimension have a tendency to cynicism and pessimism. Also, in contrast to indulgent societies, restrained societies do not put much emphasis on leisure time and control the gratification of their desires. People with the orientation of restraint have the perception that their actions are restrained by social norms and feel that indulging themselves is somewhat wrong.

3 Russian Business Practices and Etiquette

3.1 Business Appointments

- Obtaining an appointment can be laborious in Russia. Be patient and persistent. Once your appointment is scheduled, make every effort to avoid a cancellation.

- Business hours in Russia are generally from 9:00 a.m. to 5:00 p.m., Monday through Friday. Do not schedule business on holidays when Russian people observe and celebrate. Many government offices also close on holidays.

3.2 Business Negotiations

- It is said that Russians are great "sitters" during negotiations. Russians regard compromise as a sign of weakness and morally incorrect.

- Be certain that all members of your negotiating team know and agree on exactly what you want from the deal. Write it down and bring it with you. Do not show the Russians anything other than the unity of your team.

- "Final offers" are never final during initial negotiations. Be prepared to wait. The offer will be made more attractive if you can hold out.

- Get your own expert in Russian law. Don't be surprised when something you did yesterday is disallowed tomorrow. Many laws are nebulous, and their interpretation is subject to change.

3.3 Business Entertaining

- Always have a good supply of soft drinks, tea, coffee (not in plastic cups!), cookies, snacks, and so forth, on the meeting table. Russians try hard to provide a variety of refreshments when conducting business, and will appreciate your reciprocating in kind.

- At Russian hotels and restaurants, the doormen may let in only certain people. Don't be surprised if they are not friendly.

- In restaurants, you may have a long wait for food. Ignore the menus, as only a third of the items listed may actually be available. You must ask the waiter what is being served that day. Restaurants tend to have large tables set for many people. If your party consists of only two or three people, you may have to share a table with others.

- It is a great honor to be invited to a Russian home. Russian tradition demands that you be served a lunch or dinner that far exceeds everyone's appetite. For example, caviar might be served with huge spoons.

- In a restaurant or nightclub, Russians may invite you to dance or to join them at their table. It is best to accept graciously.

3.4   **Business Protocol**

Greetings

- Only during greetings do Russians display affection in public. Relatives and good friends will engage in a noisy embrace and kiss each other on the cheeks.

- Except at formal or state occasions, Russians usually greet a stranger by shaking hands and stating their names, rather than uttering a polite phrase (such as "How do you do?"). Respond in the same way.

Titles/Forms of Address

- Russian names are listed in the same order as in the West, but the Russian middle name is a patronymic (a name derived from the first name of one's father). Thus, Fyodor Nikolaievich Medvedev's first name is Fyodor, his last name is Medvedev, and his middle name means "son of Nikolai".

- Russian women add the letter "a" on the end of their husband's surnames. For instance, Medvedev's wife would be Mrs. Medvedeva.

- Unless invited to do so, do not use first names. If a Russian has a professional title, use the title followed by the surname. If he or she has no title, use Mr., Miss, Mrs., or Ms. plus the surname.

- Among themselves, Russians use a bewildering variety of diminutives and nicknames. They also address each other by first name and patronymic, which can be quite a mouthful. As you establish a relationship with them, you will be invited to call them by one of these. This is the time to invite them to call you by your first name.

Gestures

- Whistling is not taken as a sign of approval in a concert hall. It means you did not like the performance. American "OK" sign will be interpreted as vulgar. The "thumbs up" gesture indicates approval among Russians.

- Do not sit with the legs splayed apart or with one ankle resting upon the knee. Some common traditions or superstitions include sitting for a minute before leaving a home, and knocking three times on wood to avoid bad luck.

3.5 Business Gift-Giving

- Not surprisingly, items in demand make prized gifts. These items often include baseball caps, ballpoint pens, picture books or art books, perfume, good soaps, and lighters.

- Other good gifts include solar-powered calculators, well-made business cardholders, watches, and inexpensive jewelry. Take flowers, liquor, or a food item in scarce supply if invited to a Russian home.

3.6 Business Outfit

- If you go to Russia during the winter, bring very warm clothes or buy Russian-style hats and gloves upon arrival. In addition, bring a pair of shoes or boots with no-slip soles.

- Bring your own shoe polish, since Russian streets can be muddy all year round. Women in high heels will have a difficult time if they have to run around outside on many errands. Business attire is usually conservative.

- Since Russian buildings are usually well heated, it is best to dress in layers so that you can take off clothes to be comfortable while inside.

4 Tips: Giving Gifts Appropriately

A gift can serve as a symbol of thanks and gratefulness in any setting. Gift-giving is the norm among business associates. Giving gifts to business connections can also be very sensitive, so it is imperative to follow proper etiquette. You need to make sure the gift is appropriate and follows the customs and norms of your industry. The following are several useful tips for giving gifts in international business settings.

- **Consider your client's interests.**

  Here are some basic gift ideas: a book from your home country or hometown, handmade or gourmet chocolates, candy or sweets, a calendar, pens and other writing instruments, a coffee mug, or office memorabilia. Find out what sports, hobbies, or pastimes your clients enjoy. Perhaps your client has a favorite food or beverage. If you can't determine this on your own, contact an assistant or associate. Make your gift stand out just as you want your company to stand out.

- **Choose a mindful gift.**

  A mindful gift means a gift that does not offend the person or their culture. Gifts chosen for a business associate or client should be creative and relevant to the occasion, for example, buy something from your home country before your trip to make it special and unique. However, always avoid anything too personal that may be misinterpreted as a bribe, or could offend or embarrass the recipient. Sometimes a gift given in innocence can be taken the wrong way. Don't give a business associate intimate apparel, expensive perfume, or jewelry that is not related to the business. Examples of appropriate business gifts may also include a fruit basket, a box of candy, a bouquet of flowers, a book by the recipient's favorite author, items manufactured by your company, or tickets to events and performances.

- **Wrap your gift beautifully.**

  Have your gift wrapped and presented in a festive way. The wrapping is part of the present, and even more important than the gift itself. The wrapping is the first thing they see when you present a gift to somebody—much like a first impression. Make an effort to wrap your gift with crisp folds and elegantly placed tape. Many countries have lucky colors. In China, it's red or gold. In India, it's red, yellow, or green. When you travel internationally for business, find out if the country you're going to has a lucky color and if so, wrap your gift in that color. This will add an extra element of joy for your recipient when they receive your gift.

- **Follow the corporate guidelines.**

Before you leave for an international business trip, research that country's culture, and also the company policy to find out if you can offer a gift and if the gift you would like to offer would be suitable. In some countries, you really have to be careful what type of gift you offer because some gifts may be considered a bribe or may not be allowed at all. Some companies have strict policies about what kinds of gifts, if any, their employees may receive.

- **Present your gift with two hands.**

In Asia, presenting your gift with two hands is a must to convey respect to the other person. Offer your gift in the same manner when you do business in other countries; when you offer a gift with both hands, you show that you hold that person in high regard and it can really make them feel special.

- **Choose the right time to give gifts.**

The common times to give gifts in the business are as follows: after the completion of a project, to show appreciation after someone has gone above the call of duty, to celebrate something business-related such as acquiring a new client or a promotion, or during the holidays.

Appropriate gift-giving in the business world is a task that requires nuance and thoughtfulness. It is a common business practice of improving relationships with prospects, customers, employees, and vendors. Researching the ethics and etiquette of gift-giving in different cultures is essential to achieving success in international business settings.

Exercises

5.1　Fact Files

Directions: Complete the following table and find the key facts about Russia.

Official Name	
Capital City	
Official Language(s)	
Currency	
Population (Year 2022)	
The National Flower	
Current President	

5.2　Compound Dictation

Directions: Listen to the passage and fill in the blanks with the words or expressions that you hear.

Russia, or the Russian Federation, is the largest country in the world. It covers (1)_____ of the earth's inhabited land area, spans nine time zones and incorporates climate zones ranging from the Arctic north to the generally (2)_____ south. In the vast (3)_____ of Russian territory, there are still too many (4)_____ sites waiting to be discovered. Though many of them are either too cold or too barren (贫瘠的) to be inhabited by humans, they are perfect (5)_____ for wild animals.

The Russian economy ranks as the fourth largest in Europe and the eighth largest in the world by (6)_____ as of 2022. Russia's extensive (7)_____ resources are the largest in the world, making it one of the leading producers of oil and (8)_____ globally.

Russia hosts the world's ninth largest UNESCO World Heritage Site and is among the most popular tourist (9)_____. Over 180 different ethnic groups or nationalities live in Russia and most of them have distinctive traditions including (10)_____.

5.3　True or False: Russian Customs and Etiquette

Directions: Put T for true or F for false for each of the following statements.

(　　) 1. The number of flowers must be odd if they are intended to be given as a present to Russians.

(　　) 2. Russians view compromise in business negotiations as a sign of weakness.

(　　) 3. Russian people admire veterans and the elderly, and it is almost a national practice to help them as much as possible.

(　　) 4. During a business dinner with your Russian counterparts, you should not keep talking while eating or drinking.

(　　) 5. If your Russian clients greet you with a large round loaf of bread on a towel with a salt shaker on top, as a guest you should say thanks but never touch or eat the bread.

5.4　Multiple Choice: To Know More About Russia

Directions: Mark the correct answer to each question. Look up the following facts on the Internet or in some reference books and try to get more background information.

1. Which one is Russia's Mother River and the cradle of Russian civilization?

　　A. Yenisei River.　　　B. Volga River.　　　C. Ob River.　　　D. Lake Baikal.

2. When is Russia's Victory Day?

　　A. October 10.　　　B. May 9.　　　C. June 12.　　　D. November 5.

3. What animal is printed on the Russian coat of arms?

　　A. Eagle.　　　B. Bear.　　　C. Dragon.　　　D. Tiger.

4. _____ is to Russia what the White House is to America.

　　A. Buckingham Palace　　　　　　B. The Kremlin complex

　　C. Number 10 Downing Street　　　D. The Winter Palace

5. Which of the following novels tells the story of several families within the frame of grand historical events, the war of the Russian Empire against Napoleonic France?

　　A. *Dead Souls* by Nikolai Gogol.

　　B. *The Brothers Karamazov* by Fyodor Dostoevsky.

　　C. *War and Peace* by Leo Tolstoy.

　　D. *Crime and Punishment* by Fyodor Dostoevsky.

5.5   Case Study

Directions: Read the following case and answer the questions.

> Ivan is a Russian business executive seeking cooperation with Chinese companies. Ming is the executive manager of a Chinese manufacturing company. One day, a business meeting was arranged for the two parties.
>
> Ming, in order to show his respect and sincerity, arrived at the conference room 15 minutes early. But Ivan and his colleagues arrived 30 minutes late. Ming felt a bit offended, but Ivan didn't seem sorry for their late arrival.
>
> During the meeting, Ivan showed his resolution and refused to make any concessions for the prospective deal. Ming appeared impatient and he thought that a little concession would mean sincerity and cooperation. Ivan and Ming ended up feeling unhappy with each other at the first meeting.

1. What went wrong in this case and why?
2. Conduct further research on the negotiation styles of Chinese and Russian businesspeople and provide suggestions for ensuring a successful negotiation if you were in the above situation.

6 A Mini Business Project

Directions: Suppose that you are going to visit your Russian client Mr. Mikhail Khodorkovsky, a middle-aged gentleman with deep interest in Chinese culture. Please explain how you would prepare an appropriate gift for him.

- understanding the gift-giving culture in Russia;
- presenting gifts with Chinese characteristics;
- selecting a suitable gift for the client;
- useful expressions for giving gifts and sending best wishes.

Note: You or your team is asked to prepare a presentation using PowerPoint slides, and write an executive summary using Microsoft Word. You may use appropriate visual aids (e.g., video clips) to support your presentation, and you may also refer to the sample project files online for reference.

Words and Expressions

apatite	/'æpətaɪt/	n.	磷灰石
apparel	/ə'pærəl/	n.	衣服，服装
arable	/'ærəbl/	adj.	适于耕种的
bewildering	/bɪ'wɪldərɪŋ/	adj.	令人困惑的
caviar	/'kæviɑ:(r)/	n.	鱼子酱
chime	/tʃaɪm/	n.	钟声；铃声
consonant	/'kɒnsənənt/	n.	辅音
diminutive	/dɪ'mɪnjətɪv/	n.	（单词，尤指名字的）非正式缩略形式
discrepancy	/dɪs'krepənsi/	n.	差异；不符合；不一致
fortress	/'fɔ:trəs/	n.	要塞；设防的地方
hydroelectric	/ˌhaɪdrəʊ'lektrɪk/	adj.	使用水力发电的
imperative	/ɪm'perətɪv/	adj.	必要的；紧急的；极重要的
innocence	/'ɪnəsəns/	n.	单纯；清白
mandate	/'mændeɪt/	n.	正式命令；授权
Mongol	/'mɒŋgl/	n.	蒙古人
multilateral	/mʌltɪ'lætərəl/	adj.	多边的；多国的
nebulous	/'nebjələs/	adj.	模糊的；不清楚的
nuance	/'nju:ɑ:ns/	n.	细微差别
pastime	/'pɑ:staɪm/	n.	消遣；休闲活动
patronymic	/ˌpætrə'nɪmɪk/	n.	从父名衍生出的名字
phosphorite	/'fɒsfəraɪt/	n.	磷灰石；磷矿
ratify	/'rætɪfaɪ/	v.	正式批准；使正式生效
thermal	/'θɜ:ml/	adj.	热的；热量的
tsar	/zɑ:(r)/	n.	沙皇（旧时俄国皇帝的称号）
vendor	/'vendə(r)/	n.	小贩；卖主
vowel	/'vaʊəl/	n.	元音
vulgar	/'vʌlgə(r)/	adj.	粗俗的；通俗的
iron ore			铁矿石

non-slip soles	防滑鞋底
potassium salt	钾盐
run on errands	跑腿办差事
splay apart	张开
sugar beet	甜菜
table set	成套餐具

Notes

Scan the QR code for more information about Russian culture.

12

Unit 12

Australian Culture, Customs, and Business Etiquette

Australia: Overview

1.1 Geography and Demographics

Geography

Australia, officially the Commonwealth of Australia, is a sovereign country comprising the mainland of the Australian continent, the island of Tasmania, and numerous smaller islands. While Australia is the world's smallest continent, it is the world's largest island. Lying between the Indian and Pacific Oceans, nearly 40% of Australia's total coastline length comprises island coastlines. Canberra is Australia's capital city.

Australia is classified as arid or semi-arid because 70% of its territory receives less than 500 millimeters of rainfall annually. Nearly 20% of Australia's land mass is classified as desert. In addition to the low average annual rainfall, rainfall across Australia is also variable. The rainfall pattern is concentric around the extensive arid core of the continent, with high rainfall intensity in the tropics and some coastal areas. Climate zones range from tropical rainforests, deserts, and cool temperature forests to snow-covered mountains. Within this climate, plants and animals have evolved on a geographically isolated continent through a period of slowly drying climate combined with continued high variability.

Population and People

In 2020, Australia's population was roughly 25.7 million. Australia has one of the world's highest urbanization rates, with 85% of its population living in cities. Australia's population is concentrated along the coastal region of Australia from Adelaide to Cairns, with a small concentration around Perth, Western Australia. Central Australia is sparsely populated. The most populous states are New South Wales and Victoria, with their respective capitals, Sydney and Melbourne, the largest cities in Australia.

Aboriginal people constitute only a very small percentage of the Australian population. Immigration continues to be largely from Europe (Europeans still make up about 90% of the population), although significant numbers are arriving from Asia (about 5% of the population) and other regions of the world.

Language

Australia legally has no official language. However, English is spoken by 95% of the population and is essential for economic participation and social cohesion. Australian grammar and spelling are a mix of British and American patterns.

1.2　History, Economy, and World Influence

History in Brief

The first known inhabitants of the continent, the Aborigines, were hunters and gatherers and are believed to have migrated from some unknown point in Asia to Australia at least 38,000 years ago. Many of these people retain their traditional culture and live separately from the rest of the population. In recent decades, efforts have been made by the Australian government to be more responsive to Aboriginal rights.

Captain Cook is credited with the European discovery of Australia in 1770. However, it was not until 1788 that Australian penal colonies were established; thus, the first settlers in the country were convicts and soldiers. Free settlers arrived later when word spread of the opportunities available "down under". The numbers increased greatly when gold was discovered in 1851. The transportation of convicts to the eastern colonies was abolished in 1852 and to the western colonies in 1868.

Australia became a member of the British Commonwealth in 1901. In 1942, the Statute of Westminster Adoption Act was passed, officially giving Australia complete autonomy in both internal and external affairs. British authority was finally removed in 1986.

Economy in Brief

Underpinning Australia's strong economy is its open and transparent trade and investment environment, a pro-business regulatory approach, and trade and economic links with emerging economies, particularly in Asia. Australia's economy is considered one of the strongest, most stable and diverse, and also one of the largest in the world in terms of its GDP.

The service sector is the largest part of the Australian economy, accounting for 60% of GDP and four out of five jobs. Australia is an important and growing financial center, with a sophisticated financial service sector and strong regulation. A continuing process of reform to further open up the economy and strengthen its competitiveness has been a key ingredient of Australia's success.

World Influence

Australia is an open market with minimal restrictions on the import of goods and services. The process of opening up has increased productivity, stimulated growth, and made the economy more flexible and dynamic. Australia plays an active role in the WTO, APEC, the G20, and other trade forums. Australia's Free Trade Agreement (FTA) with China came into force in 2015, adding to existing FTAs with other Asian countries, as well as with New Zealand and the US.

Australia continues to negotiate bilateral agreements with Indonesia, as well as larger agreements with its Pacific neighbors and the Gulf Cooperation Council countries, and an Asia-wide Regional Comprehensive Economic Partnership that includes the 10 ASEAN countries and China, Japan, Korea, New Zealand, and India.

1.3 Australian Holidays

Australian national public holidays are New Year's Day, Australia Day, Good Friday, Easter Monday, Anzac Day, Christmas Day, and Boxing Day. All other public holidays such as Queen's Birthday and Labor Day, are individually declared by the state and territory governments.

Australia Day, January 26, is a day to reflect on what it means to be Australian, to celebrate contemporary Australia and to acknowledge its history. It is about acknowledging and celebrating the contribution that every Australian makes to the contemporary and dynamic nation. People call this country home, including Aboriginal and Torres Strait Islander, those who have lived here for generations, and those who have come from all corners of the globe.

More than half of all Australians participate in Australia Day celebrations, attending events organized by state governments, local councils, community groups or getting together with family and friends. In addition, over 16,000 new Australians become citizens on Australia Day. Table 12–1 shows a list of main holidays in Australia.

Table 12-1   A List of Main Holidays in Australia in 2022

Day	Date	Holiday Name
Saturday	Jan. 1	New Year's Day
Wednesday	Jan. 26	Australia Day
Friday	Apr. 15	Good Friday
Monday	Apr. 18	Easter Monday
Monday	Apr. 25	Anzac Day
Sunday	Dec. 25	Christmas Day

Australian Cultural Orientations

Australia's culture is rich and dynamic in nature, shaped by a diverse range of indigenous and immigrant traditions that have evolved over centuries of history. The country's identity is characterized by a deep connection to the land, a laid-back and friendly lifestyle, and a strong sense of community. Australian culture reflects a unique blend of indigenous and Western influences. The section below provides a brief overview of Australian cultural orientations based on the 6-D Model.

- **Power Distance**

    Australia has a relatively low ranking on the power distance dimension. Leadership in Australian organizations are accessible to be consulted (and they are expected to be accessible). They facilitate individuals and teams with their expertise, and share information frequently with subordinates. Communications between the leaders and the subordinates are informal, direct, and participative.

- **Individualism vs. Collectivism**

    Australia has a high score in individualism, indicating that Australia is a highly individualistic culture. Australians tend to look after themselves and their immediate families foremost. In business, hiring and promotion are often based on ability or evidence of what one has done or can do. Employees are also expected to be self-reliant and display initiative.

• Masculinity vs. Femininity

While not very masculine, Australians are proud of their successes and achievements in life. Starting from school, Australians are encouraged to "strive to be the best they can be". Work and play are also based on these values, which are also the basis for hiring and promotion decisions in the workplace.

• Uncertainty Avoidance

Australia scores intermediate on this dimension. Australians try to control their future as much as possible through things such as financial planning and life insurance. However, when unexpected situations arise, Australians tend to adapt well.

• Long-term vs. Short-term Orientation

Australia scores very low on the long-term orientation dimension, indicating that Australia is a normative culture. Australians have a great respect for tradition and a strong focus on achieving quick results.

• Indulgence vs. Restraint

With a high score on indulgence, Australia is a relatively indulgent country. Australians tend to place a high value on leisure time, fulfilling their impulses and desires to enjoy life and have fun. They like to act as they please and spend money as they wish. They generally have a positive attitude and are optimistic.

Australian Business Practices and Etiquette

3.1 Business Appointments

• The best time to visit is from March to November since the peak tourist season is December through February. Christmas and Easter are especially hectic and many executives will be on vacation.

- Business hours are from 9:00 a.m. to 5:00 p.m., Monday through Friday, and 9:00 a.m. to noon on Saturdays.

- Appointments are relatively easy to schedule at all corporate levels. Most executives are friendly and easy to approach and they will be glad to meet with you to discuss business. Plan for meetings one month in advance by telephone or e-mail.

- Be punctual for meetings. To Australian businesspeople, tardiness signals a careless business attitude.

3.2 Business Negotiations

- Before business meetings, spend a brief period of time in small talk (sports or current news). This social time can be short, but will establish a familiar rapport, which is important to Australians.

- Modesty and casualness are Australian characteristics. A business presentation filled with hype and excitement will not impress Australians. Instead, it will inspire them to deflate the presenter with caustic humor.

- Australians are very direct and love to banter. If you are teased, take it in good humor and tease back without insulting anyone.

- Australians generally do not like negotiations or high-pressure sales. They value directness. Therefore, present your case in a forthright manner, articulating both the good and the bad.

- Do not digress or go into too much detail. Australians consider brevity a virtue.

- Australians are wary of authority and of those who consider themselves "better" than others. Be modest in your interactions and downplay your knowledge and expertise. Let your accomplishments speak for themselves.

- Decision-making takes place with the consultation of top management. This takes time and will generally be slower than in other countries. Be patient.

3.3　Business Entertaining

- Australians don't invite strangers into their homes right away. They take their time getting to know someone before an invitation is made. Barbecues are a favorite reason for gathering.

- If you are invited out for a drink to establish a friendly relationship, don't talk about business unless your host brings it up. Work and play are taken equally seriously in Australia and are not to be confused.

- Australians do not make unannounced visits and always call ahead.

- To avoid confusion, remember that "afternoon tea" is around 4:00 p.m., "tea" or "dinner" is the evening meal served between 5:00 p.m. and 8:00 p.m., and "supper" is a late-night snack.

- In an Australian pub, it is vital to remember that each person pays for a round of drinks. Missing your turn to "shout for a round" is a sure way to make a bad impression.

- Good conversation topics are sports, which are very popular, and sightseeing, as Australians are very proud of their country. Remember that Australians respect people with opinions, even if those opinions conflict with their own. Arguments are considered entertaining, so do not be afraid to express your own opinions.

3.4　Business Protocol

Greetings

- Australians are friendly and easy to get to know. It is acceptable for visitors to introduce themselves in social situations.

- Australians greet each other with "Hello" or an informal "G'day", but they tire of hearing tourists overusing the latter.

- It is customary to shake hands at the beginning and end of a meeting. Women may shake hands with one another. In an informal setting, a peck on the cheek or a hug may be used as a greeting.

- It is appropriate to present a business card when introducing yourself, but don't be surprised if you do not get one in return since many Australians do not have them.

- Full names are used for initial greetings. Australians are quick to go to a first-name basis. Wait for them to initiate this as a cue for you to do the same. If not invited to use the first name, use "Mr.", "Mrs.", or "Ms.". Follow the lead of others in using titles. In Australia, a title, whether academic or job-related, is downplayed in public.

Gestures

- The thumbs-up sign signifies "OK", or "good".
- It is inappropriate for a man to wink at a woman, even in a friendly way.
- Men should not be too physically demonstrative with other men.

3.5 Business Gift-Giving

- Australians generally do not give gifts in a business context. If you are invited to a home for dinner, however, you may want to bring a small gift from home such as flowers, wine, chocolates, or folk crafts.
- As a foreigner, an illustrated book from your home area also makes a good gift.

3.6 Business Outfit

- Australia is in the southern hemisphere, so its seasons are opposite to those of the northern hemisphere. Northern Australia is tropical, with a wet season in the summer months. Southern Australia has hot summers and cold winters. During winter months, warmer clothes and rain gear are needed.
- Business dress is conservative. Men wear a suit, generally with a long-sleeved shirt. Jackets are removed in summer and ties are not required. Women may wear a skirt or pants and blouse, or a dress. Fashions follow North American trends, although women wear pants much less than in the United States.

4 Tips: Preparing Your Business Attire

Business attire refers to the clothing that employees wear to work. Appropriate business attire can vary from company to company and even from job to job.

- **Get to know different types of business attire.**

There are generally four types of business dress codes: business formal, business professional, business casual, and casual.

Business formal: This is the highest level of professional dress attire and it means tailored suits and ties for men, and a pantsuit or skirt suit paired with conservative accessories and shoes for women. Employees are expected to maintain a high standard in their appearance.

Business professional: This is a step down from business formal, but it's still conservative and traditional. You will start to see more flexibility in colors and patterns in business professional. Men tend to wear suits and ties with more patterns and colors, and women tend to wear a suit or skirt, top, and jacket paired with jewelry that is more noticeable—such as chunky watches or statement pieces.

Business casual: However, if your employee handbook says that you can dress business casual, that means you don't have to wear a suit, pumps, and stockings every day. However, you should still keep a certain level of professionalism, no matter how casual the dress code is. Men tend to wear button-ups while women can wear skirts, slacks, or khakis with a cardigan or jacket. Employees are allowed more freedom with their jewelry and other accessories.

Casual: As the least formal, the trickiest part might be making sure you are still maintaining a level of professionalism. Clothes should still be pressed, neat, and appropriate for the type of work you do. For men, you can expect casual pants and slacks with collared polos or crew-neck sweaters. Women have the freedom to wear nicely-fitted tops and blouses, slacks or skirts. Fun patterns and colors are acceptable with a casual dress code.

- **Choose the right business attire.**

  You might use different styles of business attire for different settings or occasions. Pay attention to the dress code, if applicable. If not, look to other people's style of dress or ask around if needed.

  If you work in an office, pay close attention to the way people dress. While the office may be casual, you might notice that people in leadership positions dress slightly more formally. You may choose to dress similarly to the people who hold the position you would like to reach.

  If you're going to an interview, check the company's "About Us" page and social media profiles for clues about their culture. They might have pictures or videos about their offices where you can see how employees typically dress. If you're still unsure, ask your recruiter or other contact what they recommend you to wear to be successful in the interview.

  If you're going to a business meeting, ask your colleagues who may know or have met with this same person about how their offices operate and how you can appear respectful and professional during your meeting with them.

  In any setting, avoid overly large or busy accessories, heels that are four inches or higher, and any clothing with profanity or possibly offensive images or phrases.

- **Benefits of business attire.**

  Business attire conveys to your colleagues, bosses, and customers or clients your level of professionalism and dedication. When you keep your focus on your performance rather than your fashion sense, you make a good impression and send a message about your priorities at work. Cultivating your image can help you present yourself in the best light, and wearing the appropriate business attire is part of that image.

  By following these guidelines, you can look professional in your selected business attire at your workplace.

Exercises

5.1 Fact Files

Directions: Complete the following table and find the key facts about Australia.

Official Name	
Capital City	
Main Language(s)	
Currency	
Population (Year 2022)	
The National Flower	
Current Prime Minister	

5.2 Compound Dictation

Directions: Listen to the passage and fill in the blanks with the words or expressions that you hear.

Australia is a country that covers an entire continent. It offers a vibrant array of (1)_____ options with immaculate beaches and natural paradises never too far away. From the thriving arts (2)_____ of Melbourne to the high-flying (3)_____ culture of Sydney, there's always a place to call home. The following are two of the best places to visit in Australia.

Cairns is well known for being the gateway to the (4)_____. Tropical weather, a relaxed lifestyle and coastal living are the drawcards for visitors who come for a holiday and stay for a lifetime. Cairns isn't as cheap as it once was, but it is another great escape from the (5)_____ cost of living in Australia's major capital cities.

Cairns also has a good mix of public and private schools. James Cook University is one of the most renowned (6)_____ institutions in the world. Another positive to the Cairns lifestyle is that it is very bike friendly. Cairns is completely flat and has (7)_____ so that riding to any location is safe.

Home to some of the most beautiful beaches in Australia, it's no wonder the Gold Coast is one of the most popular holiday destinations in the world. Its vibrant and young (8)_____ , along with the sunny climate and the quality of life, makes it a top destination for expats. The Gold Coast is surrounded by (9)_____ , mountains, and a few national parks.

The Gold Coast is also home to dozens of public and private schools, many built relatively recently to cater for the booming population. Housing (10)_____ of four Australian universities, the Gold Coast has around 30,000 university students and is probably the best Australian city for partying and enjoying a thriving nightlife.

5.3   True or False: Australian Customs and Etiquette

Directions: Put T for true or F for false for each of the following statements.

(   ) 1. Australian grammar and spelling are a mix of British and American patterns.

(   ) 2. Australians tend to express their opinions directly since directness is important to them.

(   ) 3. If you are teased by Australians, don't tease back.

(   ) 4. Australians like people with ability, but hate it when you show off your expertise.

(   ) 5. Australians are not wary of authority or those who consider themselves "better" than others.

5.4   Multiple Choice: To Know More About Australia

Directions: Mark the correct answer to each question. Look up the following facts on the Internet or in some reference books and try to get more background information.

1. Australian tea (meal) refers to _____ .

  A. meal served around 4 p.m.

  B. meal served between 5:00 p.m. and 8:00 p.m.

  C. a late-night snack

  D. a drink before bedtime

2. Australia covers _____ time zones.

    A. 2   B. 3   C. 4   D. 5

3. The best topic for conversation in Australia is _____.

    A. sports   B. politics   C. religion   D. the military

4. The original inhabitants of the continent, the indigenous Aboriginal peoples, were

    _____.

    A. bishops and priests   B. convicts and soldiers

    C. hunters and gatherers   D. refugees

5. Australia became a member of the British Commonwealth in _____.

    A. 1901   B. 1942   C. 1986   D. 1991

5.5 Case Study

Directions: Read the following case and answer the questions.

Xiao Wang owned a garment factory in China. When he heard that Chinese-made clothes were popular in Australia, he asked a professional photography team to record an online presentation to promote his products. In the video, Xiao Wang bragged that he had one of the most famous designers in China working for him and then passionately introduced the process of making clothes in his factory. In addition, in order to prove the popularity of his products, Xiao Wang asked his employees to make compliments about the clothes made in the factory. To Xiao Wang's dismay, after his video advertisement was sent to the potential buyers by e-mail, none of the Australian buyers responded.

1. What went wrong in this case and why?

2. Conduct further research and find out strategies for marketing in Australia. Provide suggestions to Xiao Wang for designing an effective commercial for his products.

6 A Mini Business Project

Directions: Suppose that you are the leader of a business delegation attending an international business conference in Sydney in October this year. How can you dress professionally for the conference? Please explain your preparation based on the following outline.

- the weather in Sydney during your conference;
- dress codes for men and women at business conferences in Australia;
- more details for businesspeople at social events.

Note: You or your team is asked to prepare a presentation using PowerPoint slides, and write an executive summary using Microsoft Word. You may use appropriate visual aids (e.g., video clips) to support your presentation, and you may also refer to the sample project files online for reference.

Words and Expressions

antiauthoritarian	/ˈæntɪɔːˌθɒrɪˈteərɪən/	*adj.*	反独裁主义者的；反权威主义的
banter	/ˈbæntə(r)/	*v.*	无恶意的玩笑；打趣
caustic	/ˈkɔːstɪk/	*adj.*	刻薄的；挖苦的
chunky	/ˈtʃʌŋki/	*adj.*	粗短的；厚实的
digress	/daɪˈgres/	*v.*	离题
immaculate	/ɪˈmækjələt/	*adj.*	洁净的；无瑕疵的
khakis	/ˈkɑːkiz/	*n.*	卡其裤
profanity	/prəˈfænəti/	*n.*	亵渎；不敬的言语
semi-arid	/ˌsemiˈærɪd/	*adj.*	半干旱的
button-up			系扣衬衫
crew-neck sweater			圆领套头毛衣
statement piece			点睛饰物

Notes

Scan the QR code for more information about Australian culture.

13

Unit 13

New Zealand Culture, Customs, and Business Etiquette

1 New Zealand: Overview

1.1 Geography and Demographics

Geography

New Zealand is situated approximately 1,600 km from both Australia and Polynesia. It consists of three main islands: the North Island, the South Island, and Stewart Island. The terms "deep south" for Southland and "far north" for Northland indicate just how long the main islands are. The country's long, narrow shape is also represented in the Māori names for the islands—the North Island is known as Te Ika a Māui (the fish of Māui), while the South Island is called Te Waka o Māui (the canoe of Māui). The capital city of New Zealand is Wellington, and the largest and most populous city is Auckland. Both cities are located on the North Island.

While New Zealand has three main islands, it is in fact an archipelago consisting of more than 700 offshore islands, most of which are small and lie within 50 km of the main islands. These islands are the visible surface of an extensive submarine plateau, which allows New Zealand to enjoy a huge exclusive economic zone (fishing grounds).

Population and People

The recent estimate of the New Zealand population was just over 5.1 million in 2022. New Zealand today celebrates a wide and varied heritage, with its inhabitants hailing from the Pacific, Europe, Asia, Africa, and America. It was first discovered by Europeans in 1642, approximately 400 years after Polynesian navigators had landed there. In the late 18th century, settlers began to arrive from England, Scotland, and Ireland after a long, arduous, and uncomfortable journey. From the 20th century onwards, groups and individuals from around the world have migrated to New Zealand in order to escape war or other troubles, while others have chosen New Zealand for a change of lifestyle.

Prior to the Second World War, most immigrants to New Zealand were from Britain, but in the post-war years of the 1950s and 1960s, more people were helped to migrate including many Dutch as well as more English and Scots. Starting in the mid-1960s, work opportunities attracted immigrants from the Pacific Islands including Samoa, Tonga, and the Cook Islands. In 1975 and again in 1987, New Zealand changed its immigration policies to admit people based on their qualifications rather than their ethnicity, which led to an influx of immigrants from Asia, as well as some from Africa.

These policy changes led to New Zealand becoming much more multicultural. By 2006, approximately 67% of New Zealanders identified as Pākehā, meaning that they have a European background, with the rest of the population largely comprised of Māori, Pasifika, and Asian New Zealanders.

"Kiwi" is a common self-reference used by New Zealanders, though it is also used internationally. Unlike many demographic labels, its usage is not considered offensive; rather, it is generally viewed as a symbol of pride and affection for most people of New Zealand. However, not all New Zealanders prefer to self-identify with the name.

Language

New Zealand has three official languages: English, Māori and New Zealand Sign Language. English is the most widely spoken language in the nation. It is the primary language used in parliament, government, the courts, and the education system, and is spoken by over 96% of the population. The Māori language has been an official language by statute since 1987, as defined by the "Māori Language Act 1987". New Zealand Sign Language has been an official language by statute since 2006. New Zealand was the first country to grant official status to a sign language.

1.2　History, Economy, and World Influence

History in Brief

The earliest known inhabitants of New Zealand were the Māori, who came by boat from the Polynesian islands around 900 BCE. The first European explorers to arrive in New Zealand waters in 1642 were the Dutch, who continued to visit while on whaling and trading expeditions. Captain James Cook led the first British exploration of New Zealand in 1769, on the first of his three Pacific voyages. Cook thought highly of the islands and the local Māori that he encountered. Britain annexed New Zealand in 1838 in response to increased colonization and missionary activity.

The chiefs of a few Māori tribes signed a treaty accepting British sovereignty in 1840 in return for legal protection and land ownership. However, much of their land was taken away after the Anglo-Māori wars of the 1860s. The colony was granted internal self-government in 1852. New Zealand became an independent dominion within the British Commonwealth in 1907.

New Zealand has become a culturally diverse country. Particularly since the 1980s, a wide range of ethnic groups have been encouraged to settle here, and New Zealand is now much more multicultural.

Economy in Brief

New Zealand has a highly developed free market economy. The country has one of the most globalized economies and depends greatly on international trade, mainly with Australia, Canada, China, the European Union, Japan, Singapore, South Korea, and the United States. It makes up around 60% of New Zealand's total economic activity.

The national economy is dominated by the service sector, followed by the industrial sector, and agriculture, with international tourism as a significant source of revenue. The foundation of New Zealand's economy is exporting agricultural commodities such as dairy products, meat, forest products, fruit and vegetables, and wine. New Zealand is the world's twelfth largest agricultural exporter by value and the second leading dairy product exporter. Prior to the COVID-19 pandemic, tourism made a huge contribution to the New Zealand economy, contributing 20.1% of total exports. Although New Zealand constitutes only about 0.1% of the world's population, its economy is still able to produce approximately 0.3% of the world's material output.

World Influence

New Zealand ranks highly in terms of national performance such as quality of life, education, protection of civil liberties, government transparency, and economic freedom in comparison with other countries. It enjoys a distinctive and rather relaxed way of life with its moderate climate, open environment, reasonable public services, and relative safety from war and terrorism. Early in 2020, the New Zealand government established the Infrastructure Reference Group (IRG) to work with local councils and businesses to identify a pipeline of projects to support the economy. New Zealand belongs to a number of international organizations including the United Nations, the Commonwealth of Nations, ANZUS (Australia, New Zealand

and the United States), the OECD, ASEAN Plus Six, the APEC, the Pacific Community and the Pacific Islands Forum.

1.3 **New Zealand's Holidays**

New Zealand's national day, February 6, is called Waitangi Day. It commemorates the signing of the Treaty of Waitangi by representatives of the British Crown and over 500 Māori chiefs in 1840. This treaty paved the way for the British colonization of New Zealand.

Traditionally, Waitangi Day commemorations always took place at Te Tii Marae (meeting house) and the Treaty Grounds at Waitangi. The celebrations included a dawn service, pōwhiri (welcome ritual), launching of waka (canoes), sports, Māori cultural performances and a naval salute. In the early 21st century, community concerts and gatherings have been held around the country so as to widen participation and emphasize the positive aspects of Waitangi Day. Table 13−1 shows a list of main holidays in New Zealand.

Table 13−1   A List of Main Holidays in New Zealand in 2022

Day	Date	Holiday Name
Saturday	Jan. 1	New Year's Day
Sunday to Tuesday	Jan. 2−4	New Year's Holiday
Sunday	Feb. 6	Waitangi Day
Friday	Apr. 15	Good Friday
Monday	Apr. 18	Easter Monday
Monday	Apr. 25	Anzac Day
Monday	June 6	Queen's Birthday
Friday	June 24	Matariki
Monday	Oct. 24	Labour Day
Sunday	Dec. 25	Christmas Day
Monday	Dec. 26	Boxing Day

2 New Zealand Cultural Orientations

New Zealand's culture is an intriguing and complex blend of indigenous and immigrant traditions that have evolved over centuries, resulting in a unique and multifaceted identity. The country's identity is featured by a deep respect for the natural environment, a relaxed and inclusive way of life, and a strong sense of community. Using the 6-D Model as an analytical framework, the upcoming section offers a concise introduction to the cultural orientations of New Zealand.

• Power Distance

New Zealand has a very low score on power distance. Within New Zealand organizations, hierarchy is established for convenience, superiors are always accessible, and managers rely on individual employees and teams for their expertise. Both managers and employees expect to be consulted, and information is frequently shared. Communication tends to be informal, direct, and participative.

• Individualism vs. Collectivism

New Zealand has a relatively high individualism score, meaning that it is without a doubt an individualistic culture. This results in a loosely knit society in which people are expected to look after themselves and their immediate families. At work, employees are expected to be self-reliant and to display initiative, and within the exchange-based world of work, hiring and promotion decisions are based on merit or evidence of what one has done or can do, rather than on relationships.

• Masculinity vs. Femininity

New Zealand scores intermediately on masculinity and can be considered as a slightly masculine society. New Zealanders are proud of their successes and achievements in life, and these values offer a basis for hiring and promotion decisions in the workplace, and conflicts are resolved by fighting them out.

• Uncertainty Avoidance

New Zealand gains an intermediate score on uncertainty avoidance. On one hand, people in New Zealand develop and implement laws driven toward sustainable development and prevention of uncertainty. On the other hand, they also embrace unconventional practices and are comfortable with uncertainty.

• Long-term vs. Short-term Orientation

New Zealand is a normative country with a low score on long-term orientation. People are normative in their thinking. They exhibit great respect for traditions, a relatively small propensity to save for the future, and a focus on achieving quick results.

• Indulgence vs. Restraint

New Zealand's relatively high score on indulgence indicates that its culture is one of indulgence. People in New Zealand exhibit a willingness to realize their impulses and desires with regard to enjoying life and having fun. They possess a positive attitude and have a tendency toward optimism. In addition, they place a higher degree of importance on leisure time, doing as they please and spending as they wish.

New Zealand Business Practices and Etiquette

3.1 Business Appointments

- The best times to visit New Zealand for business are February through May, and October to November. December and January are the summer months, when many people are on vacation, and offices may be closed.

- Always be on time or a little early for appointments. Being late is considered rude, and social events usually start on time.

- If possible, it is best to arrange meetings by telephone or e-mail several weeks prior to your arrival.

3.2 Business Negotiations

- New Zealanders value their egalitarian society and are very emphatic about equality. They respect people for who they are, and have little regard for wealth or social status. It is thus vital to emphasize honesty and forthrightness in your negotiations, and avoid hype and ostentation.

- Initial meetings are usually held in an office environment. After that, you may suggest meeting over lunch at a restaurant or hotel.

- Lunch appointments are generally for conducting business. If you receive an invitation for dinner, however, this will be a more relaxed social event with spouses. Note that dinner is not the time or place to discuss business.

3.3 Business Entertaining

- New Zealanders love to entertain in their homes, so don't be surprised if you are invited to their home for a meal. Note that there is a difference between "tea" and "afternoon tea". Afternoon tea is usually served between 3:00 p.m. and 4:00 p.m. and consists of tea and coffee with light snacks, while tea is the evening meal served between 6:00 p.m. and 8:00 p.m. Supper is a late-night snack.

- Don't expect much conversation during the meal, as most socializing takes place after the meal.

- Good conversation topics are sports. New Zealanders love the outdoors and many are very keen on activities such as hiking, fishing, or sailing, as well as organized sports, including the national sports of rugby and cricket.

- Avoid discussing race relations and particularly the treatment of Māori. New Zealanders strive to establish a separate and distinct identity from Australia. There is a strong but friendly rivalry between the two countries. Avoid praising Australia or Australians to New Zealanders, and try never to confuse the two nations.

3.4 Business Protocol

Greetings

- New Zealanders are usually very friendly and polite but can be quite formal in the work environment. They may wait to be approached but are warm after an initial meeting.

- Men shake hands upon introduction and when preparing to leave. The handshake should be firm and accompanied by direct eye contact.

- Men in New Zealand may wait for a woman to extend her hand. Women generally shake hands with other women and often with men as well.

- The formal greeting of "How do you do?" is used until a friendlier relationship is established. After that, "Hello" or the New Zealand "G'day" can be used on informal occasions.

Titles/Forms of Address

- The order of names for European-descended New Zealanders is first name followed by surname.

- At first meetings with New Zealanders, address them by their titles or "Mr." for men and "Ms." for women plus their surname.

- Once a relationship is established, New Zealanders like to progress to a first-name basis as quickly as possible. However, you should continue to use titles and surnames until a more informal tone has been set or until you are invited to address someone by their first names.

Gestures

- Chewing gum or using a toothpick in public is considered impolite, as is spitting.

- New Zealanders usually keep their speech soft and find loud voices annoying and uncultured. They do not open their mouths wide when they speak and may even seem to be speaking through clenched teeth.

- New Zealanders generally maintain more of the traditional British reserve than do Australians, especially on formal occasions.

3.5   Business Gift-Giving

- If you are invited to a New Zealander's home for dinner, you may bring a modest gift. Chocolates, flowers, wine, or a good bottle of whiskey would be appreciated.

- Gifts should be simple and practical.

3.6 Business Outfit

- Business attire is conservative. Men may wear a dark suit and tie. Businesswomen should wear a suit, pantsuit, dress, or a skirt and blouse with a jacket.

- New Zealand is located in the southern hemisphere. The climate is temperate, not tropical. You will need warm clothes and rain gear no matter what season of the year.

Tips: Gestures and Body Language

Our body language is everything from our appearance, facial exporessions, dress code, postures, eye contact, personal space, to gestures. It makes up the largest part of our nonverbal communication. Body language is important in international business, and sets the foundation for people to communicate with others on a deeper level. Here are some tips for using body language in business communications:

- **Focus on posture.**
  Posture is crucial when it comes to demonstrating things like confidence and assertiveness. Research indicates that we're more attracted to people who have open stances. For instance, open arms, straight spine, and no crossed limbs. When you cross your arms and legs or hunch your shoulders, you convey an air of anxiety and isolation. These actions naturally encourage other people to take a step back, rather than inviting them to interact with you on a deeper level.

- **Address your facial expressions.**
  Smiling is a crucial part of body language in business, whether you're interacting with colleagues or consumers. Smiles instantly remove some of the friction from any conversation. Another good rule of thumb to follow is to try and mirror the facial expressions of the person you're speaking to. If the person you're talking to is laid back and relaxed, act the same way and you'll

be more likely to enjoy your discussion. On the other hand, if you're speaking to someone with a very serious demeanor, sharing the same body language will show that you're treating the matter at hand with care.

- **Maintain eye contact.**

  Eye contact is another important element when it comes to body language in business communication. Once you've perfected a welcoming smile and good posture, it's crucial to keep a close eye on the people you're communicating with. Eye contact indicates that you're giving your full attention and respect to the other person in the room. Try to make eye contact regularly, but don't stare at other people in a conversation constantly, as this can make them nervous.

- **Practice your handshake.**

  Many business experts agree that a handshake says a lot about a person. People with firm and confident handshakes are generally more outgoing and positive—the kind of people that others want to work with. Most people know that a good handshake is essential when they're preparing for a job interview. However, a handshake is also crucial for other aspects of growing a business. Every time you meet with a new client, investor, or even a colleague, your handshake will help them make a snap judgment about you and your business. Practice your handshake frequently and get feedback from your friends and family to help you perfect it.

- **Go global.**

  Thanks to the rise of the Internet, the "global" business space is bigger than ever, and many brands are continuously looking for ways to build feelings of trust with overseas partners, investors, and customers. If you work in a space that requires you to manage and maintain relationships with overseas experts, then it's important to brush up on the role that body language can play in your conversations. Regular eye contact is a sign of respect in Western countries, but can cause problems between members of opposite genders in the Middle East. Many hand gestures have cultural overtones. For example, the "OK" sign with thumb and forefinger together creating a circle is regarded as a positive gesture in the US, while it has very different meanings in other countries. In France, it means "worthless" or "zero". In Japan, it stands for money, and in other parts of the world it represents an indecent comment.

The importance of body language in international business communication

can't be overstated. You can connect with your international business partner more easily if you use the right body language gestures.

Exercises

5.1 Fact Files

Directions: Complete the following table and find the key facts about New Zealand.

Official Name	
Capital City	
Official Language(s)	
Currency	
Population (Year 2022)	
The National Flower	
Current Prime Minister	

5.2 Compound Dictation

Directions: Listen to the passage and fill in the blanks with the words or expressions that you hear.

New Zealand is located in the Southwestern Pacific Ocean. It is one of the most beautiful countries in Oceania. In addition, New Zealand is ranked by the World Bank as one of the most (1)_____ countries in the world. Its economy has successfully (2)_____ from being dominated by agriculture to an industrialized free-market economy with (3)_____. Before conducting business in New Zealand, it is necessary to learn some business etiquette:

First, it is about the way of greetings. New Zealanders are very friendly but tend to be formal in a work environment. They may wait to be (4)_____ but are warm after an initial meeting. The handshake (5)_____ is the formal way of greeting in New Zealand. The handshake should be firm and accompanied by (6)_____.

Second, always make appointments in advance. Punctuality is viewed seriously for business in New Zealand. You should always be on time or a little early for appointments because (7)_____ is viewed as impolite.

Third, you shall also pay attention to the etiquette in negotiating. New Zealand is a country that is (8)_____ about equality. Also, honesty and (9)_____ in negotiations are highly valued, so you should always avoid (10)_____ ____ and ostentation in New Zealand.

5.3　True or False: New Zealand Customs and Etiquette

Directions: Put T for true or F for false for each of the following statements.

(　　) 1. In 1893, New Zealand became the first country to give women the right to vote.

(　　) 2. The word "Kiwi" could refer to a brand of shoe polish in New Zealand.

(　　) 3. New Zealand has a highly developed free market economy.

(　　) 4. When greeting, women in New Zealand seldom shake hands with men or other women in business settings.

(　　) 5. New Zealanders never address others by their first names, for they think it is impolite.

5.4　Multiple Choice: To Know More About New Zealand

Directions: Mark the correct answer to each question. Look up the following facts on the Internet or in some reference books and try to get more background information.

1. When is the national day in New Zealand?

　A. February 6.　　B. May 10.　　　　C. August 5.　　　　D. October 1.

2. New Zealand became an independent dominion within the British Commonwealth in _____.

　A. 1852　　　　B. 1907　　　　　C. 1910　　　　　D. 1949

3. Most of New Zealand's population lives in the _____.

   A. North Island　　　　　　　　　B. South Island

   C. Stewart Island　　　　　　　　D. White Island

4. In New Zealand, _____ in public is considered rude.

   A. speaking quietly　　　　　　　B. chewing gum

   C. listening to music　　　　　　D. jogging

5. When you are invited to a New Zealander's home for dinner, it is not appropriate
   to bring _____ as a gift.

   A. a bunch of flowers　　　　　　　B. a bottle of whiskey

   C. an expensive handbag　　　　　　D. a box of chocolates

5·5　Case Study

Directions: Read the following case and answer the questions.

> Mr. Stephens, an American businessman, was on a business trip in New Zealand. Mr. Smith, his New Zealand business partner, met Mr. Stephens for the first time at his office. After the meeting, Mr. Smith invited him to a restaurant for lunch. When paying the bill, Mr. Stephens was a bit puzzled that Mr. Smith didn't tip the waiter.

1. Why did Mr. Stephens feel confused in this case?

2. Conduct further research and find out the cultural differences of tipping in different cultures.

A Mini Business Project

Directions: Suppose that you are a training manager in a multinational company and you are invited to give a talk on body language and gestures in different cultures. Please prepare your talk based on the following outline.

- doing research on the definition of body language and gestures in communication;
- discussing the importance of body language and gestures in communication;
- explaining the differences of body language and gestures in various cultures.

Note: You or your team is asked to prepare a presentation using PowerPoint slides, and write an executive summary using Microsoft Word. You may use appropriate visual aids (e.g., video clips) to support your presentation, and you may also refer to the sample project files online for reference.

Words and Expressions

archipelago	/ˌɑːkɪˈpeləgəʊ/	*n.*	群岛
arduous	/ˈɑːdʒuəs/	*adj.*	艰苦的；艰难的
clenched	/klentʃt/	*adj.*	（牙齿）紧咬的；紧握的
cricket	/ˈkrɪkɪt/	*n.*	板球（运动）
dominion	/dəˈmɪniən/	*n.*	领土；英联邦自治领
egalitarian	/iˌgælɪˈteəriən/	*n.*	平等主义者；平等主义
emphatic	/ɪmˈfætɪk/	*adj.*	强调的，坚决的；明显的
influx	/ˈɪnflʌks/	*n.*	（人或物的）大量涌入，大量流入
offshore	/ˌɒfˈʃɔː(r)/	*adj.*	海上的；近海的
ostentation	/ˌɒstenˈteɪʃn/	*n.*	卖弄；虚饰

rivalry	/'raɪvlrɪ/	*n.*	竞争；较量
rugby	/'rʌgbi/	*n.*	英式橄榄球
sovereignty	/'sɒvrənti/	*n.*	主权；最高统治权；最高权威
uncultured	/ˌʌn'kʌltʃəd/	*adj.*	未受教育的；无教养的
hail from			来自，出生于
hunch one's shoulders			耸肩
rain gear			雨具用品
self-identify			自我认同
self-reference			自指，自称
snap judgement			快速判断

Notes

Scan the QR code for more information about New Zealand culture.

Unit 14

Brazilian Culture, Customs, and Business Etiquette

Brazil: Overview

1.1 Geography and Demographics

Geography

Brazil, officially known as the Federative Republic of Brazil, and in Portuguese, República Federativa do Brasil, occupies half of the landmass of South America. It shares borders with, from south to north, Uruguay, Argentina, Paraguay, Bolivia, Peru, Colombia, Venezuela, Guyana, Suriname, and French Guiana. Stretching from north to south, Brazil's landscapes range from tropical to subtropical and include wetlands, savannas, plateaus, and low mountains. However, it has no desert, high-mountain, or arctic environments. Most of the Amazon River basin is also in Brazil.

Population and People

Brazil had a population of approximately 215.3 million in 2022 which is mainly concentrated along the eastern coastline. It is the seventh most populous country in 2022 and accounts for about one-third of Latin America's population. Over 90% of the people live on 10% of the land, with over 15 million in the cities of São Paulo and Rio de Janeiro. Brazilians' cultural heritage is rich and varied, with 55% of European descent (primarily Portuguese), 38% a mixture of cultures (combining African, German, Japanese, Amerindian, etc.), 6% African, and only 1% Amerindian. Brazil has a very young population, with nearly 50% under the age of 20.

Language

Although Portuguese is the first language of most Brazilians, the language has undergone many transformations since it was first introduced into Brazil in the 16th century. It has been supplemented by many foreign words and expressions introduced by Italians, Germans, Japanese, and Spanish-speaking immigrants, and foreign products and technologies have also introduced additional terms. There are dozens of languages spoken by the indigenous peoples of Brazil, and they have had a significant influence on Brazilian Portuguese.

1.2   History, Economy, and World Influence

History in Brief

Brazil was colonized by Portugal after the arrival of Pedro Alvares Cabral in 1500. It was one of Portugal's most important, and by far the largest colonies. When Napoleon Bonaparte occupied Portugal in 1807, members of the Portuguese royal family fled to Brazil, and Rio de Janeiro became the seat of the Portuguese Empire from 1808 to 1821. However, the Portuguese Emperor became increasingly unpopular, and after he returned to Lisbon in 1822, Brazil declared independence from the United Kingdom of Portugal, Brazil and the Algarves. The new Brazilian Empire experienced instability until its second emperor, Dom Pedro II, came of age. He ruled for over 58 years and was a dedicated, enlightened, and modest ruler nicknamed "the Magnanimous". He was overthrown by the military in 1889 and Brazil was proclaimed a republic. Subsequently, there was a succession of presidents and military coups until 1990 when Fernando Collor de Mello became the first directly elected president in 29 years.

Economy in Brief

Brazil is considered one of the global giants of the mining, agriculture, and manufacturing industries, as well as having a strong and rapidly growing service sector. It is a leading producer of many different minerals, including iron ore, tin, bauxite, manganese, gold, and quartz, as well as diamonds and other gems. It also exports vast quantities of steel, automobiles, electronics, and consumer goods. In terms of the agricultural sector, Brazil is the world's primary source of coffee, oranges, and cassava (manioc) and is a major producer of sugar, soy, and beef. However, the role of agriculture in the Brazilian economy has diminished since the mid-20th century with the rapid urbanization and exploitation of its mineral, industrial, and hydroelectric potential. The city of São Paulo has become a major industrial and commercial center as a result of this development. The nation's burgeoning cities, huge hydroelectric and industrial complexes, mines, and fertile farmlands make it one of the world's major economies.

World Influence

As the largest South American economy and the world's eighth largest, Brazil produced US$3.4 trillion in goods and services in 2018, as measured by purchasing power parity which is a method for comparing the GDPs of countries with different exchange rates. Brazil's growth rate slowed from 7.5% in 2010 to –3.6% in 2016, but recovered with 2.1% growth in 2018. It also suffers from stagflation, with an inflation rate of 8.7% in 2016, although it decreased to 3.6% in 2018.

Brazil is an important political force in Latin America, playing a leading role in the creation of Mercosur (the largest trading bloc in South America), the Banco del Sur (the Bank of the South), and the G20 coalition that represents the interest of developing countries.

1.3 Brazilian Holidays

Brazil is well known for being a lively, colorful country that knows how to celebrate. Its public holidays (feriados públicos) are each celebrated in a unique Brazilian way. The major national holidays in Brazil include New Year's Day and Carnival.

As in many other countries, the celebrations for New Year's Day on December 31 are more important than those on January 1. On New Year's Day, Brazilians traditionally eat lentils and rice to bring good fortune and prosperity for the coming year.

Carnival is a six-day festival starting on the Friday afternoon before Ash Wednesday, which marks the beginning of Lent. The dates are different each year but it always falls in February or March. It is Brazil's most famous and exuberant holiday. An important part of the celebrations is the samba school competitions. Millions of Brazilians spend much of the year preparing for the competitions, in which both children's and adults' groups make up the several thousand dancers and musicians, and many others help to make floats and elaborate costumes. Table 14–1 is a list of holidays in Brazil.

Table 14–1   A List of Public Holidays in Brazil in 2022

Day	Date	Holiday Name
Saturday	Jan. 1	New Year's Day
Monday	Feb. 28	Carnival
Friday	Apr. 15	Good Friday
Thursday	Apr. 21	Tiradentes Day
Sunday	May 1	Labour Day

Day	Date	Holiday Name
Thursday	June 16	Corpus Christi
Saturday	July 9	State Rebellion Day
Wednesday	Sep. 7	Independence Day
Wednesday	Oct. 12	Lady of Aparecida
Friday	Oct. 28	Civil Servants Day
Wednesday	Nov. 2	All Souls' Day
Tuesday	Nov. 15	Republic Day
Sunday	Nov. 20	Black Awareness Day
Sunday	Dec. 25	Christmas Day

Brazilian Cultural Orientations

Brazil's identity is marked by a profound love of music, dance, and festivities, as well as a strong sense of community and warmth toward others. The country's vibrant culture emphasizes the importance of socializing, having fun, and sharing experiences with others. The following section draws upon the 6-D Model framework to provide an overall analysis of the cultural orientations of Brazil.

• Power Distance

With a relatively high score on power distance, there is a belief in Brazilian society that hierarchy should be respected and that inequalities among people are acceptable. In Brazil, it is important to show respect to the elderly, and children are expected to take care of their elderly parents. In companies, there is one boss who takes complete responsibility for decisions. Status symbols of power are very important in order to indicate social position.

• Individualism vs. Collectivism

Brazil has a relatively low score on individualism, meaning that, from birth onwards, Brazilians are integrated into strong, cohesive groups, especially represented by the larger extended family of uncles, aunts, grandparents, and cousins, which continues to protect its members. This is an important aspect of the work environment too, where it is expected that an older and more powerful member of a family would "help" a younger nephew to be hired for a job in his own company. In business, it is important to build trustworthy and long-lasting relationships. For example, a meeting usually starts with general conversations in order to get to know each other before doing business. The preferred communication style is context-rich, so Brazilian people will often speak profusely and write in an elaborate fashion.

• Masculinity vs. Femininity

Brazil scores right in the middle on the masculinity dimension. It indicates that Brazilians place importance on both masculine and feminine aspects of life. Brazilian people want to exhibit the masculine dimension through being the best (emphasizing achievement, competition, and success) and also the feminine dimension through quality of life (happiness, teamwork, harmony, and empathy).

• Uncertainty Avoidance

Brazil scores rather highly on uncertainty avoidance, so do most of the Latin American countries. These societies show a strong need for rules and elaborate legal systems in order to structure life. In Brazil, as in all high uncertainty avoidance societies, bureaucracy, laws, and rules are very important in making the world a safer place to live in. Due to their high score on this dimension, Brazilians are very passionate and demonstrative people, and their emotions are expressed in their body language. Brazilians like to have good and relaxing moments in their everyday life, chatting with colleagues, enjoying a long meal, or dancing with guests and friends.

• Long-term vs. Short-term Orientation

Brazil scores intermediately on long-term orientation. In relation to its high uncertainty avoidance, Brazil can be suspicious of change and will use old methods to answer current predicaments. However, Brazilian society also understands that the world is constantly evolving with new issues. As a result, Brazil also tries to direct some of its resources to educating the population on these issues. This can be seen in Brazil's acceptance of the Internet and other emerging technologies. It had a total population of nearly 162 million users connected to the digital world in 2021. Globally, Brazil ranks the sixth in terms of Internet users in a country, and social media has quickly become popular, especially among the younger generation.

• Indulgence vs. Restraint

Brazil's slightly high score on the indulgence dimension makes it an indulgent society. People in societies that score high on indulgence generally exhibit a willingness to realize their impulses and desires with regard to enjoying life and having fun. Brazilian people possess a positive attitude and have a tendency to be optimistic. They also place a higher degree of importance on leisure time, acting as they please and spending money as they wish.

3 Brazilian Business Practice and Etiquette

3.1　Business Appointments

- As the lack of punctuality is a fact of life in Brazil, you should expect to wait for your Brazilian counterpart.

- Be sure to make appointments in advance, preferably at least two weeks, and never make impromptu calls at business or government offices. Don't try to engage in any business transactions around the time of Carnival.

- Official business hours are usually 8:30 a.m. to 5:30 p.m., but more senior business executives start work later in the morning and stay until late in the evening. The best times to make appointments to meet people are between 10:00 a.m. and noon, and between 3:00 p.m. and 5:00 p.m. If your business runs past midday, you can expect to spend at least two hours at lunch.

- As it takes a considerable amount of time to establish the strong relationships that are necessary for doing business in Brazil, you must be prepared to make long-term commitments, in terms of both money and time, if you want your business to succeed.

- Personal connections are the key to conducting business in Brazil, and your Brazilian business associates will expect to establish a long-term relationship with you. Hiring a Brazilian contact in your industry (called a "despechante" in Portuguese) before traveling to Brazil can be invaluable in helping you to meet the right people.

3.2 Business Negotiations

- Brazilians like to build personal relationships before advancing on work negotiations, as they feel much more comfortable doing business with people they know. Knowing how to use the local business culture to your advantage is key to the success of your business in the country.

- When negotiating with Brazilians, be patient. The process usually takes several trips to complete. In your discussions, do not expect to get right to the point. Try to avoid confrontations and hide any frustration you may feel.

- During negotiations, don't be surprised if your associates want to discuss all aspects of the contract simultaneously, rather than in sequential order. Seemingly extraneous data may need to be reviewed repeatedly. It's important to be as flexible as possible, and try not to make any definite commitments.

- As Brazilians tend to value who they do business with more than the name of the company, changing your negotiating team could undermine the entire contract, so avoid it if you can.

- It's best not to take an outside lawyer with you. You can use a local accountant and a notario (similar to a lawyer) or lawyer to deal with contracts. Expect highly animated conversations, with lots of interruptions, disagreements, and physical contact.

3.3 Business Entertaining

- If you would like to entertain your Brazilian business associates, ask locals to recommend a prestigious restaurant, or if you are staying at a first-class hotel with an excellent restaurant, you can eat there.

- Business is not usually discussed during meals. Any business discussion can start after the meal once coffee has been served.

- If you are invited to a party, it is most likely to be at a private club rather than at somebody's home. You don't need to arrive on time. It's best to be at least 15 minutes late.

- In the afternoon, between 4:00 p.m. and 5:00 p.m., a light snack is usually served, usually cookies, cakes, and beverages.

- Dinner in Brazil can take place any time from 7:00 p.m. to 10:00 p.m., and dinner parties can easily continue until 2:00 a.m. It is even possible for a dinner party to continue until 7:00 a.m. the following morning.

3.4 **Business Protocol**

Greetings

- Greetings are generally very warm, with extended handshakes when you first meet, and then embraces once you have established a friendship. It is common for women to kiss each other on alternating cheeks. They kiss twice if married, and three times if single, where the third time is supposed to be a sign of "good luck" for finding a spouse.

- When arriving or departing, you should shake hands with everyone in the group you are greeting.

- When talking to a Brazilian companion, inquire into the well-being of their family, spouse, children, etc. Family life is considerably important to Brazilians.

Titles/Forms of Address

- Use titles such as Doctor or Professor to address your Brazilian business acquaintances if they have such a title. Otherwise address them with Senhor (Mr.) or Senhora (Mrs.) followed by their last name. Note that some people may introduce themselves with their title followed by their first name. For example, a doctor may introduce herself as Doctor Maria.

Gestures

- Brazilians tend to have close physical contact, often touching arms, hands, or shoulders while conversing with each other. They are friendly and outgoing, and this kind of physical interaction is part of the culture, so try to accept it.

- Be careful if you use hand gestures toward a Brazilian. Some gestures have different and unexpectedly strong meanings compared to other countries. For example, the American "OK" sign of a circle made with your first finger and thumb is rude in Brazil, so be sure not to use it.

- To make a beckoning signal, extend your hand with the palm face down and wave your fingers toward your body.

- A good luck sign, known as the "Fig" is made by placing your thumb between your index and middle fingers while making a fist.

- Flicking your fingertips under your chin means that you don't know the answer to a question.

3.5 Business Gift-Giving

- When you first meet your Brazilian business associates, it is not required to offer them a gift. You can buy them a meal and later consider the individual's tastes when choosing gifts.

- Don't present gifts during a formal meeting. Wait until the meeting is over and present them in a relaxed social situation.

- Small electronic gadgets make appropriate gifts for your business associates, so do branded pens.

- If you are invited to a Brazilian associate's home, you can take candy, champagne, or scotch, and you can also take something for the children.

- Knives symbolize cutting off a relationship, and handkerchiefs connote grief, and therefore must be avoided as gifts. As black and purple are the colors of mourning, be sure not to give any gifts in these colors.

3.6 Business Outfit

- Brazil is a tropical country, so to keep cool in the hot weather, it's best to wear clothing made of natural fibers. Remember that mid-summer in Brazil is in January.

- Note that wearing a three-piece suit can give the impression of being an "executive", whereas two-piece suits are more often associated with office workers.

- When in Brazil on business, men should wear slacks and long-sleeved shirts when dressing casually. Only young people wear jeans (always clean and pressed).

- Conservative attire for women is very important when doing business in Brazil.

Be aware that inappropriate clothing choices and behavior could have a serious impact on your firm. You also need to ensure that your nails are well manicured.

- As the colors of the Brazilian flag are green and yellow, you should avoid wearing this combination of colors.

Tips: Giving Thanks and Making Apologies

About Giving Thanks

Expressing gratitude is of the utmost importance in both our personal and professional lives, and it can make others feel validated and respected, propelling them toward achieving their full potential. When you express appreciation for something nice someone has done for you, they're more likely to do it again.

In the workplace, appreciation produces higher levels of enthusiasm and satisfaction, resulting in a happier work environment, motivated staff members, and higher job satisfaction. Gratitude has a large role to play in business, too. It's not hard to say "thank you" in business, and it makes a big difference when you do (or don't) make that small effort. It improves collaboration, increases innovation, and creates a cycle of recognition and positive reinforcement.

- **Say "thank you" at right time.**
  You can express your gratitude in different situations. For instance, when you get new business, a customer gives you very positive feedback, an employee or coworker does a great job or helps you finish a project, or someone on your team makes a client or customer happy.

- **Get to know many ways of expressing gratitude.**
  There are many ways to express your gratitude. Pick up the phone, mail a handwritten card, send a short and intentional e-mail, reward repeat business

with a loyalty program, take your team out for a fun outing or give small gifts to employees for doing a great job.

About Making Apologies

Apologizing is a human behavior that acknowledges and resolves an issue. In business, it's an essential part of a growth strategy. Apologizing to disappointed customers can reduce returns, improve brand reputation, retain loyal clients, and increase recurring revenue. Scientific research has identified the key components of any apology: expression of regret, explanation of what went wrong, acknowledgment of responsibility, declaration of repentance, and the offer of repair and request for forgiveness.

- **Pay attention to the attitude of apology.**

  It's not just what you say, but how you say it. Sincerity forms the foundation of a corporate apology. The more sincere your apology seems, the more likely it is to be accepted. Small shifts with body language, such as eye contact, hand gestures, facial expressions, and other body movements, play a huge role in the acceptance of your apology.

- **Apologize even if it's not your fault.**

  Apologizing does not always mean that you're wrong and the other person is right. It just means that you value your relationship more than your ego. Yet swallowing your pride and apologizing—even if you don't feel responsible—still makes sense. Don't cover up mistakes and hope nobody notices.

- **Explain what went wrong.**

  The simplest way to get those components into your business apology is to explain what went wrong and what you've done (or will do) to prevent it from happening again.

- **Offer an incentive.**

  Patience declines further when your customers need a response from you. Respond or apologize in a timely fashion. You shall know that repeat customers generate up to 40% of a store's overall revenue, and retaining them can be up to 20 times cheaper than acquiring new customers. An apology can turn an unhappy customer into a repeat one, or keep a current subscriber from becoming a past one.

The simple things matter. The power of a simple "thank you" cannot be underestimated. Saying "thank you" in business is powerful, thoughtful, memorable, inexpensive, and easy. Plus, the opportunities to say thanks in business are endless. On the other hand, apologies display empathy and they are what experts credit as a force for driving business forward. That could help secure higher business deals and promote company growth.

Exercises

5.1 Fact Files

Directions: Complete the following table and find the key facts about Brazil.

Official Name	
Capital City	
Official Language(s)	
Currency	
Population (Year 2022)	
The National Flower	
Current President	

5.2 Compound Dictation

Directions: Listen to the passage and fill in the blanks with the words or expressions that you hear.

Brazil is the largest country in South America and shares borders with every South American country except Ecuador and Chile. Brasília is its capital, but the two largest cities are Rio de Janeiro and São Paulo.

People in Brazil are (1)_____.
Most are (2)_____ of Europeans, Africans, or Native Americans, or a mix of these groups. Whatever their background, once a year, people in Brazil celebrate Carnival, the most (3)_____ festival across South America. When the Portuguese explored and colonized Brazil in the 1500s, they brought thousands of Africans as slaves to work on (4)_____.

Carnival is celebrated in many parts of the world. Dancing is a major part of the (5)_____. The most popular dance here is the Samba, a Brazilian folk dance of (6)_____. In Rio de Janeiro, Carnival is a time to display spectacular parade floats, Samba dancing and elaborate costumes. Here, Carnival is also (7)_____. Each parade group is judged according to ten (8)_____, including costumes, music, choreography, and floats. Brazilians spend all year preparing for this annual celebration. It attracts spectators from all over the world. And the festival doesn't end until Lent begins.

The Brazilian culture is influenced by African culture, from dancing to music, from food to the way Carnival has evolved. The African (9)_____ in Brazil remains strong too. Carnival brings people and their cultures together. It's clear that Brazil celebrates its (10)_____.

5.3 True or False: Brazilian Customs and Etiquette

Directions: Put T for true or F for false for each of the following statements.

(   ) 1. Brazilians tend to keep a large distance apart when speaking to each other.

(   ) 2. Handshaking is a common form of greeting between business colleagues in Brazil.

(   ) 3. Don't schedule extra time for business negotiations since they are seldom delayed or canceled without warning.

(   ) 4. Avoid using the American "OK" sign in Brazil, since it may offend your Brazilian associates.

(   ) 5. Do expect a dinner in Brazil to take longer, as it is always like a celebration.

5.4　Multiple Choice: To Know More About Brazil

Directions: Mark the correct answer to each question. Look up the following facts on the Internet or in some reference books and try to get more background information.

1. What is the capital city of Brazil?

    A. Rio de Janeiro.　　B. Brasília.　　　　C. São Paulo.　　　　D. Salvador.

2. When is the Brazilian Carnival?

    A. The first Friday before Christmas.

    B. The first Friday before Ash Wednesday.

    C. September 7.

    D. The fourth Thursday in November.

3. Which is Brazil's national sport?

    A. Basketball.　　　　B. Baseball.　　　　C. Volleyball.　　　　D. Football.

4. The _____ is the second longest river in the world, and runs through Brazil, Peru, and Colombia.

    A. Amazon River　　B. Congo River　　　C. Nile River　　　　D. Seine River

5. What is the most popular dance in Brazil?

    A. Belly Dancing.　　　　　　　　　　B. Tap dance.

    C. Samba.　　　　　　　　　　　　　D. Popping.

5.5　Case Study

Directions: Read the following case and answer the questions.

> Enzo and Chen are colleagues and good friends in a joint venture. Enzo is Brazilian and Chen is Chinese. One day, Enzo got promoted and would transfer to another department. To celebrate Enzo's promotion, Chen sent Enzo a gift wrapped in dark purple paper. However, when Enzo received the present, he seemed a bit embarrassed. Chen was also confused about Enzo's response.

1. What went wrong in this case and why?

2. Conduct further research and find out different strategies for sending flowers in different cultures.

6 A Mini Business Project

Directions: Suppose that you are the service supervisor of an established technology company that designs, develops, and sells consumer electronics and computer software in South America. Recently, customers are not satisfied with the software update that further slows the processing speed of their mobile devices. You are asked to apologize to the customers. Please explain how you will make an apology based on the following outline.

- doing research on the customer's complaints;
- acknowledging the problem and apologizing for the inconvenience caused;
- explaining the possible reasons;
- offering preferable solutions to the customer;
- ending with a promise;
- keeping the goodwill between your company and your customers intact.

Note: You or your team is asked to prepare a presentation using PowerPoint slides, and write an executive summary using Microsoft Word. You may use appropriate visual aids (e.g., video clips) to support your presentation, and you may also refer to the sample project files online for reference.

Words and Expressions

Amerindian	/ˌæməˈrɪndiən/	*n.*	美洲印第安人
arctic	/ˈɑːktɪk/	*adj.*	北极的；严寒的，极冷的
bauxite	/ˈbɔːksaɪt/	*n.*	铝土矿
burgeoning	/ˈbɜːdʒənɪŋ/	*adj.*	繁荣的
cassava (manioc)	/kəˈsɑːvə/(/ˈmæniɒk/)	*n.*	木薯
coalition	/ˌkəʊəˈlɪʃn/	*n.*	联合体；联盟

extraneous	/ɪkˈstreɪnɪəs/	adj.	无关的；没有直接联系的
exuberant	/ɪgˈzjuːbərənt/	adj.	热情洋溢的；兴高采烈的
impromptu	/ɪmˈprɒmptjuː/	adj.	即兴的；即席的
invaluable	/ɪnˈvæljuəbl/	adj.	极有用的，极宝贵的
magnanimous	/mægˈnænɪməs/	adj.	宽宏大量的；有雅量的
manganese	/ˈmæŋgəniːz/	n.	锰
manicured	/ˈmænɪkjʊəd/	adj.	精心护理的；修剪整齐的
overthrow	/ˌəʊvəˈθrəʊ/	v.	推翻；打倒
Portuguese	/ˌpɔːtʃʊˈgiːz/	n.	葡萄牙语；葡萄牙人
predicament	/prɪˈdɪkəmənt/	n.	窘况，困境；状态
prestigious	/preˈstɪdʒəs/	adj.	有威望的；有声望的
proclaim	/prəˈkleɪm/	v.	宣布；宣告；声明
profusely	/prəˈfjuːsli/	adv.	丰富地
propel	/prəˈpel/	v.	推进；驱动
quartz	/kwɔːts/	n.	石英
repentance	/rɪˈpentəns/	n.	悔改；后悔
savanna	/səˈvænə/	n.	热带草原；热带的稀树大草原
stagflation	/stægˈfleɪʃn/	n.	滞胀
subtropical	/ˌsʌbˈtrɒpɪkl/	adj.	亚热带的
succession	/səkˈseʃn/	n.	连续不断的人（物）；更迭
validated	/ˈvælɪˌdeɪtɪd/	adj.	被认可的；经过验证的
beckoning signal			手势信号
cultural heritage			文化遗产
industrial complex			大工业中心；产业综合体
military coup			军事政变

Notes

Scan the QR code for more information about Brazilian culture.

Unit 15

South African Culture, Customs, and Business Etiquette

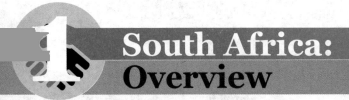

1 South Africa: Overview

1.1 Geography and Demographics

Geography

South Africa is situated in the very southern part of the African continent. Its coastline stretches more than 3,000 km, starting on the western Atlantic coast at the desert border with Namibia, around the southern tip of Africa and up the eastern Indian Ocean coast to the border of subtropical Mozambique. South Africa has a wide range of landscapes from bushveld, grasslands, forests, deserts, mountains, wide unspoiled beaches to coastal wetlands. Different currents flow along the coasts of South Africa, and the contrast in the temperature of the water brought by these currents is one reason for the significant differences in climate and vegetation, as well as differences in marine life on the two coasts. The Orange River, which forms the border with Namibia, is South Africa's longest river. The land of South Africa can be divided into two major categories: the interior plateau, and the land between the plateau and the coast. South Africa has three capital cities, with the executive, judicial, and legislative branches of government based in Pretoria, Bloemfontein, and Cape Town respectively. The largest city is Johannesburg.

Population and People

South Africa had a population of 58.9 million in 2022. Gauteng comprises the largest share of the South African population, with approximately 15.2 million people. The province of KwaZulu-Natal has the second largest population, with an estimated 11.3 million people, while Northern Cape, with a population of approximately 1.26 million people, is the province with the smallest share of the population. South Africa is referred to as a rainbow nation to describe the unity of various cultural, racial, or ethnic groups in the country.

Language

South Africa is a multicultural society characterized by its rich linguistic diversity. Language is an indispensable tool that can be used to deepen democracy and also contribute to the social, cultural, intellectual, economic, and political life of South African society. South Africa has eleven official languages. These are Afrikaans, English, Ndebele, Pedi, Sotho, Swati, Tsonga, Tswana, Venda, Xhosa, and Zulu. There are over 30 languages in South Africa, of which 25 are reported to be in current use. Almost 25% of the population speak Zulu as their first language, while over 57% speak a certain amount of English. South African English follows the conventions of British English. While most South Africans can communicate in more than one language, English is the most widely spoken and also the official language in business and commerce.

1.2 History, Economy, and World Influence

History in Brief

Humans are known to have lived in the region that is now South Africa for at least 100,000 years. The first Europeans to encounter South Africa were Portuguese sailors who were searching for a new route to Asia. Bartholomeu Dias rounded the Cape of Good Hope in 1487. However, it was the Dutch who were the first to establish a permanent outpost, when the Dutch East India Company expedition arrived on April 6, 1652. This is the date that is celebrated in South Africa as Founders' Day.

Some farmers moved to areas beyond the rule of the Dutch East India Company, creating homesteads in lands that were already occupied by Africans. This is the origin of the Boers who were extremely self-sufficient. The offspring of Boers, Khoekhoen, and Asians (mainly Malays) who were brought to South Africa by the Dutch, formed the racial group known in South Africa as "colored".

South Africa was greatly affected by the Napoleonic Wars. After the French captured the Netherlands, the British took control of the South African colony in 1795, but it was not until 1914 that South Africa was formally ceded to Great Britain.

South Africa may have continued to be a predominantly agricultural country had it not been for the discovery of diamonds in 1869 and then two decades later, gold in 1886. Gold was discovered in the Transvaal where the Boers had settled, which doomed their independence. Thousands of miners from all over the world came to work in the Witwatersrand gold fields. Britain then decided to annex the Transvaal, and after a number of minor incidents over a period of decades, a full-fledged war broke out between the British and the Boers in 1899.

After the war, South Africa was ruled by the British, but accommodation had to be made with the Boers. The Union of South Africa was formally established on May 31, 1910. Even though the Boers had been defeated in battle, they became politically powerful in the new parliament and insisted that only whites could serve in parliament. This was the beginning of the process of disenfranchising the non-white population which became increasingly serious, with blacks prohibited from owning land in 1913, from intermarrying with other races in 1949, and from living in areas designated for whites in 1950. The era of apartheid, or the separation of the races, had begun.

As internal opposition to apartheid grew, the restrictions became ever more severe. In 1960, the African National Congress (ANC) was outlawed after 50 years of nonviolent struggle. In 1961, the ANC signaled official adoption of violence. Subsequent acts of violence and sabotage led to arrests of key ANC leaders including Nelson Mandela. After a lengthy trial in 1964, they were sentenced to life imprisonment. The international community also began to impose sanctions on South Africa, in an effort to put pressure on the government to end apartheid.

Finally, under the pressure of international condemnation and constant rioting in the black townships, South Africa's leaders were forced to implement changes. President F.W. de Klerk finally made some real reforms in 1990. He freed ANC President Nelson Mandela from decades of imprisonment, and began the process of dismantling apartheid. Eventually, on April 27, 1994, South Africa held its first one-person, one-vote election, and the black majority was finally allowed to vote. The transitional government, with Nelson Mandela as president, took office on December 7, 1994.

Economy in Brief

The South African government's main economic policy goal is to accelerate inclusive growth and create jobs, while its main fiscal objective is to ensure sustainable finances by containing the budget deficit and stabilizing public debt. Economic growth is expected to improve moderately from 1.5% in 2019 to 2.1% in 2021. From a long-term perspective, South Africa requires higher and more inclusive growth in order to address the economic problems of unemployment and poverty. The government is therefore implementing growth-enhancing reforms in line with President Cyril Ramaphosa's Economic Stimulus and Recovery Plan, which has a number of aims including igniting economic activity, restoring investor confidence, preventing further job losses and creating jobs.

World Influence

South Africa has been classified by the World Bank as a newly industrialized country, as the second largest economy in Africa. It is the most developed of the sub-Saharan economies, with the deepest capital markets and understanding of the continent.

As Chair of the Indian Ocean Rim Association since 2018, South Africa advocates for the restructuring of the global political, economic, and financial architecture to be more balanced, representative, inclusive, and equitable. It also aims to ensure that the international system rests on the important pillars of multilateralism and international law.

In 2019, South Africa assumed tenure as a non-permanent member of the UN Security Council, and was expected to use this membership to promote international peace and security through advocating for peaceful dispute resolution and inclusive dialogue. South Africa also works very hard to enhance cooperation and improve efficiency between the UN, the African Union, and other regional and sub-regional organizations.

1.3 South Africa's Holidays

There are a number of national holidays in South Africa. On April 27, it's the Freedom Day. It commemorates the first post-apartheid election held in South Africa on April 27, 1994. Prior to this election, Black South Africans had no voting rights at all, and non-white citizens had limited right to vote. This made it the first non-racial national election in South Africa. The Freedom Day which marks the end of the period of colonialism and apartheid, is the National Day of South Africa, a day of glory and remembrance for all South Africans. Table 15–1 shows a list of main holidays in South Africa.

Table 15–1　A List of Main Holidays in South Africa in 2022

Day	Date	Holiday Name
Saturday	Jan. 1	New Year's Day
Monday	Mar. 21	Human Rights Day
Friday	Apr. 15	Good Friday
Monday	Apr. 18	Easter Monday
Wednesday	Apr. 27	Freedom Day
Sunday	May 1	Workers' Day
Thursday	June 16	Youth Day
Tuesday	Aug. 9	National Women's Day
Saturday	Sep. 24	Heritage Day
Friday	Dec. 16	Day of Reconciliation
Sunday	Dec. 25	Christmas Day
Monday	Dec. 26	Day of Goodwill

2. South African Cultural Orientations

　　South Africa's cultural identity is deeply rooted in its profound respect for diversity, a strong sense of community, and its commitment to social justice and equality. The country's cultural landscape reflects this ethos, showcasing a rich and vibrant blend of indigenous, African, European, and immigrant traditions that celebrate the country's diversified heritage. The next section examines the cultural orientations of South Africa utilizing the 6-D Model framework as a lens for examination.

- ## Power Distance

    South Africa achieves a very intermediate score on power distance, meaning that people tend to accept a hierarchical order in which everybody has a place and which needs no further justification. Hierarchy in an organization is seen as a reflection of inherent inequalities. Therefore, centralization is popular. Subordinates expect to be told what to do, and the ideal boss is a benevolent "autocrat".

- ## Individualism vs. Collectivism

    South Africa, with a slightly high score on individualism, is an individualistic society. This means that there is a high preference for a loosely-knit social framework in which individuals are expected to take care of themselves and their immediate families only. In individualistic societies, the relationship between employer and employee is a contract based on mutual advantage. Moreover, hiring and promotion decisions are supposed to be based on merit only, and management is about the management of individuals.

- ## Masculinity vs. Femininity

    South Africa scores above the intermediate level on masculinity and can thus be considered a masculine society. In masculine countries, people "live in order to work". Managers are expected to be decisive and assertive. The emphasis is on equity, competition, and performance, and conflicts are resolved by fighting them out.

- ## Uncertainty Avoidance

    South Africa scores around the intermediate level on this dimension and thus has a low preference for avoiding uncertainty. In societies exhibiting low uncertainty avoidance, people believe there should be no more rules than are necessary and if they are ambiguous or do not work, they should be abandoned or changed. Schedules are flexible, hard work is undertaken when necessary but not for its own sake, precision and punctuality do not come naturally, and innovation is not seen as threatening.

- ## Long-term vs. Short-term Orientation

    South Africa has a low score on long-term orientation. This suggests that the culture in South Africa is more normative than pragmatic. People in South Africa are normative in their thinking. They exhibit great respect for traditions, a relatively small propensity to save for the future, and a focus on achieving quick results.

- ## Indulgence vs. Restraint

    South Africa scores relatively high on indulgence and has a culture of indulgence.

People generally exhibit a willingness to realize their impulses and desires with regard to enjoying life and having fun. They possess a positive attitude and have a tendency toward optimism. In addition, they place a higher degree of importance on leisure time, act as they please and spend money as they wish.

3 South African Business Practices and Etiquette

3.1 Business Appointments

- In South Africa, you should always make appointments for business meetings in advance. It is always best to phone ahead first if you plan to visit.

- Punctuality is important in business, so be sure to be on time for all of your business engagements. However, it is not so important for social events, but don't be more than 30 minutes late.

3.2 Business Negotiations

- Negotiation approaches in South Africa may depend on your counterparts' cultural background. White South Africans usually have a very brief social exchange before starting to talk business, whereas South Africans of other races are more likely to spend more time on small talk, as it is important for them to spend time getting to know you.

- The most important aspect of South African business culture is to build stable personal relationships because the majority of South Africans prefer to do business with the person who they trust.

- Be sure to avoid high pressure and the expression of strong emotions in your business dealings with white South Africans, as most would rather let a deal fall through than be rushed.

- Direct confrontation is rare. Most South Africans do not appreciate haggling over profits and expenses. Instead, they aim at creating a win-win situation for the mutual benefit of all parties involved. Expect negotiations to move slowly.

3.3   Business Entertaining

- Business breakfasts tend to be relatively uncommon in South Africa, but business executives might discuss business during an early-morning round of golf. Business meetings are, however, held over lunch or dinner in a restaurant, but note that business is not usually discussed over a meal in someone's home.

- You are quite likely to be invited to a white South African's home, especially in good weather, for a pool-side barbecue, known as a braai. If invited, ask your host what you can bring. Even if your host says you don't need to bring anything, you should at least bring a bottle of wine, or you can take a dessert, but note that alcohol can only be purchased at very limited times.

- On weekends, a lunchtime braai can last all afternoon and into the evening. While business is rarely discussed at braais, braais are important events for establishing business relationships with your South African business associates who must like and trust you first before working with you.

- It is not so common to receive an invitation to the home of non-white business associates who prefer to do their business entertaining in restaurants.

3.4   Business Protocol

Greetings

- A handshake is common when meeting, although the African greetings might vary according to the respective cultural belonging. And there is a special African handshake common to black Africans, which you should learn from the locals.

- Suitable topics of conversation with your South African business associates include sport, outdoor recreation, travel, food, and music. Avoid discussing South African politics, and if pressed for your opinion, be sure you can offer a knowledgeable evaluation, so do some homework before you go.

- While South Africa has many different subcultures within its country, most of these cultures have a strong sense of respect for their elders. To avoid coming across as offensive, always behave respectfully around elder individuals, even if they play a less important role in the business meeting than someone else.

Titles/Forms of Address

- The names of English and Afrikaans-speaking South Africans are in the usual order of first name then surname.
- In South Africa, only family members and close friends use first names to address each other, so be sure to address people with a title such as Mr. or Ms., or use their professional title if they have one.

Gestures

- South Africa is a conservative country where showing affection in public is usually frowned upon, although a brief hug or kiss on the cheek is acceptable between friends.
- For many South Africans, the feet are considered unclean, so be careful not to move anything or touch anything with your feet. Also, do not show the soles of your feet (or shoes). This means that you have to be careful how you sit.

3.5 Business Gift-Giving

- Since gifts are only given by friends, don't give gifts until you have established a personal relationship. Otherwise, your gift may be seen as a bribe.
- If you are invited to someone's house, be sure to take something with you. Wine, candy, or flowers are the most common gifts, although small electronic devices are becoming more common.
- Some South African ethnic groups will decline a gift three times before accepting it to show that they are not greedy. If this happens, keep insisting until they accept it.

3.6 Business Outfit

- Dress standards in South Africa vary from city to city, with Johannesburg being the most formal, Cape Town only formal in the business district, and seaside resorts such as Durban the most informal.
- Businessmen in South Africa are expected to dress formally in a jacket and tie, while businesswomen may wear anything from a business suit to a light-colored long-sleeved blouse and skirt, depending on the dress standards of the business. Dress to match your South African business associates.

- South Africans love the outdoors, and so there are a lot of outdoor entertainments. For these events, jeans or shorts are acceptable for both genders. Women may wear short-sleeved shirts or even halter tops. Many people wear sandals throughout the summer.

- You should be aware that the sun in South Africa is very intense, so be sure to protect your skin, either with clothing or by putting on sunblock.

4 Tips: Exchanging Business Cards

Business cards are a staple of business success. Understanding business card etiquette is one way to ensure that you make a positive impression and grow your business when introduced. Here are the basic rules to follow for a profitable and productive exchange of business cards.

- **Be prepared.**
  Always have a handful of business cards with you to present to potential clients or other business associates. There is nothing more unprofessional than the business person who has to say, "Oh, I'm sorry. I just gave out my last card." or "I'm sorry. I didn't bring any."

- **Keep your business cards clean and tidy.**
  Keep your cards in a business card case or in a holder that protects them from wear and tear. A crumpled business card makes a poor first impression.

- **Hand out your business cards with discretion.**
  Give and receive cards with your right hand or with both of your hands. Don't cover any of the information printed on the surface with your thumbs. Make sure your cards are facing toward the receiver so that they can read the text without having to turn it around. If you have a bilingual card, ensure the correct language of the receiver is facing up.

- **Receive cards properly.**
  When accepting a business card, have a good look at it for a few seconds. Note the logo, the business name, or some other pieces of information. Always make

a comment about a card when you receive it, offering a compliment about the logo, design, or any good reputation about the card giver.

- **Keep your business cards up to date.**

  Make sure that the details of the card are correct. When any of your contact information changes, update it immediately. Also, keep the business card design updated and relevant. Please do not cross out the wrong information and edit with a pen.

- **Exchange business cards smoothly.**

  When you first meet someone, it's okay to ask for a business card from them. Don't force a card on anyone. Wait until someone asks for your card. If the person is of a higher position than yourself, you should wait for them to offer their card to you first.

The business card is a representation of you and your business. Exchanging business cards professionally represents your respect for your customer and it is your opportunity to demonstrate that you value their business and relationship.

5 Exercises

5.1 Fact Files

Directions: Complete the following table and find the key facts about South Africa.

Official Name	
Capital City/Cities	
Official Language(s)	
Currency	
Population (Year 2022)	
The National Flower	
Current President	

5.2   **Compound Dictation**

Directions: Listen to the passage and fill in the blanks with the words or expressions that you hear.

The Republic of South Africa is a country in the southern region of Africa. In 2022, about 59.89 million people live in South Africa. The biggest city is Johannesburg. South Africa has three capital cities, with the (1)_____ _____ branches of government based in Pretoria, Bloemfontein, and Cape Town respectively. The government is based in Pretoria, the (2)_____ in Cape Town and the Supreme Court in Bloemfontein. This makes South Africa a unique country with three capitals for different purposes.

It is a multiparty parliamentary (3)_____. The president is both chief of state and (4)_____. There are two (5)_____, the National Assembly, and the National Council. The National Council has special powers to protect cultural and (6)_____ of ethnic minorities.

About 81% of the population are Black South Africans. The remaining population consists of Africa's largest (7)_____ of European (White South Africans), Asian (Indian South Africans and Chinese South Africans), and multiracial (Colored South Africans) ancestry. South Africa is a (8)_____ encompassing a wide variety of cultures, languages, and religions. Its pluralistic makeup is reflected in the Constitution's recognition of 11 official languages.

South Africa joined the BRICS in 2010 and is by far the smallest BRICS country in both economic and demographic terms. Inviting South Africa to join the BRICS was a signal by the most important (9)_____ that South Africa is an (10)_____ and gateway to Africa, which could also defend the interests of the entire continent.

5.3   **True or False: South African Customs and Etiquette**

Directions: Put T for true or F for false for each of the following statements.

(   ) 1. A long period of silence during a conversation is appreciated in South Africa since it symbolizes a time of thought and reflection.

(   ) 2. An impressive rank and title will not automatically win respect for businesswomen as they often work for men in South Africa.

(   ) 3. South Africans do not generally appreciate any form of physical contact when talking but prefer to keep a small distance between themselves and others.

(   ) 4. The conception of deadlines in South Africa is particularly casual and people there do not make firm commitments to deadlines.

(   ) 5. It is highly offensive if you do not show respect to an elder business partner, especially in some rural areas where Black South Africans are dominant.

5.4   Multiple Choice: To Know More About South Africa

Directions: Mark the correct answer to each question. Look up the following facts on the Internet or in some reference books and try to get more background information.

1. South Africa is also called a _____.

     A. rainbow nation   B. petrol nation

     C. diamond nation   D. rainfall nation

2. Which of the following countries does not share a border with South Africa?

     A. Namibia.   B. Zimbabwe.   C. Botswana.   D. Nigeria.

3. South Africa was the _____ economically affluent country in Africa according to its GDP in 2022.

     A. first   B. second   C. third   D. fourth

4. Which is South Africa's pillar industry?

     A. Chip manufacturing.   B. Mining.

     C. Aviation industry.   D. Agriculture.

5. Which of the followings is NOT one of South Africa's official languages?

     A. Hebrew.   B. Zulu.   C. English.   D. Afrikaans.

5.5   Case Study

Directions: Read the following case and answer the questions.

> Bill worked as the corporate counsel for a British company, and he was dispatched to South Africa to conduct business with a local company last year. In the first weeks in South Africa, he took care to wear very formal suits when doing business with local people. However, to his surprise, he found that his local business associates were rather casual with their attire even when they met him on formal occasions: They could wear chinos and open-neck and short-sleeved shirts!

1. Is it appropriate to dress casually in business settings in South Africa?
2. Conduct further research and find out similarities and differences about the business attire in Britain and in South Africa.

6   A Mini Business Project

Directions: Suppose that you are invited to a business buffet in South Africa, and you want to exchange business cards with the local participants. Please do some preparation and conduct business networking smoothly based on the following aspects.

- preparing your business cards (layout and content) in advance;
- presenting your business cards in an appropriate way;
- receiving others' business cards in an appropriate way;
- exchanging business cards in different cultural settings (Dos and Don'ts).

Note: You or your team is asked to prepare a presentation using PowerPoint slides, and write an executive summary using Microsoft Word. You may use appropriate visual aids (e.g., video clips) to support your presentation, and you may also refer to the sample project files online for reference.

Words and Expressions

accommodation	/əˌkɒməˈdeɪʃn/	*n.*	和解；调和
apartheid	/əˈpɑːtaɪt/	*n.*	种族隔离（前南非政府推行的政策）
braai	/braɪ/	*n.*	（南非）露天烧烤餐会
bushveld	/ˈbʊʃˌvelt/	*n.*	（南非）灌木丛生地区
cede	/siːd/	*v.*	放弃；割让（领土）
condemnation	/ˌkɒndemˈneɪʃn/	*n.*	谴责
crumpled	/ˈkrʌmpld/	*adj.*	褶皱的；弄皱的
discretion	/dɪˈskreʃn/	*n.*	谨慎，慎重
disenfranchise	/ˌdɪsɪnˈfræntʃaɪz/	*v.*	剥夺某人的权利（尤指选举权）
dismantle	/dɪsˈmæntl/	*v.*	（逐渐）废除；取消
full-fledged		*adj.*	成熟的；完全合格的
haggle	/ˈhægl/	*v.*	争论；（尤指）讲价
homestead	/ˈhəʊmsted/	*n.*	宅地；家园；田产
ignite	/ɪɡˈnaɪt/	*v.*	引发，激起
intermarry	/ˌɪntəˈmæri/	*v.*	不同种族（或国家、教派）间通婚
outpost	/ˈaʊtpəʊst/	*n.*	前哨（基地）
sabotage	/ˈsæbətɑːʒ/	*n.*	蓄意毁坏；刻意阻碍
sanction	/ˈsæŋkʃn/	*n.*	制裁；处罚，惩罚
sunblock	/ˈsʌnblɒk/	*n.*	防晒霜；防晒油
vegetation	/ˌvedʒəˈteɪʃn/	*n.*	（统称）植物；（尤指某地或环境的）植被
budget deficit			预算赤字
halter top			露背吊带上衣

Notes

Scan the QR code for more information about South African culture.